Cara Tompkin 1985

The Golden Game

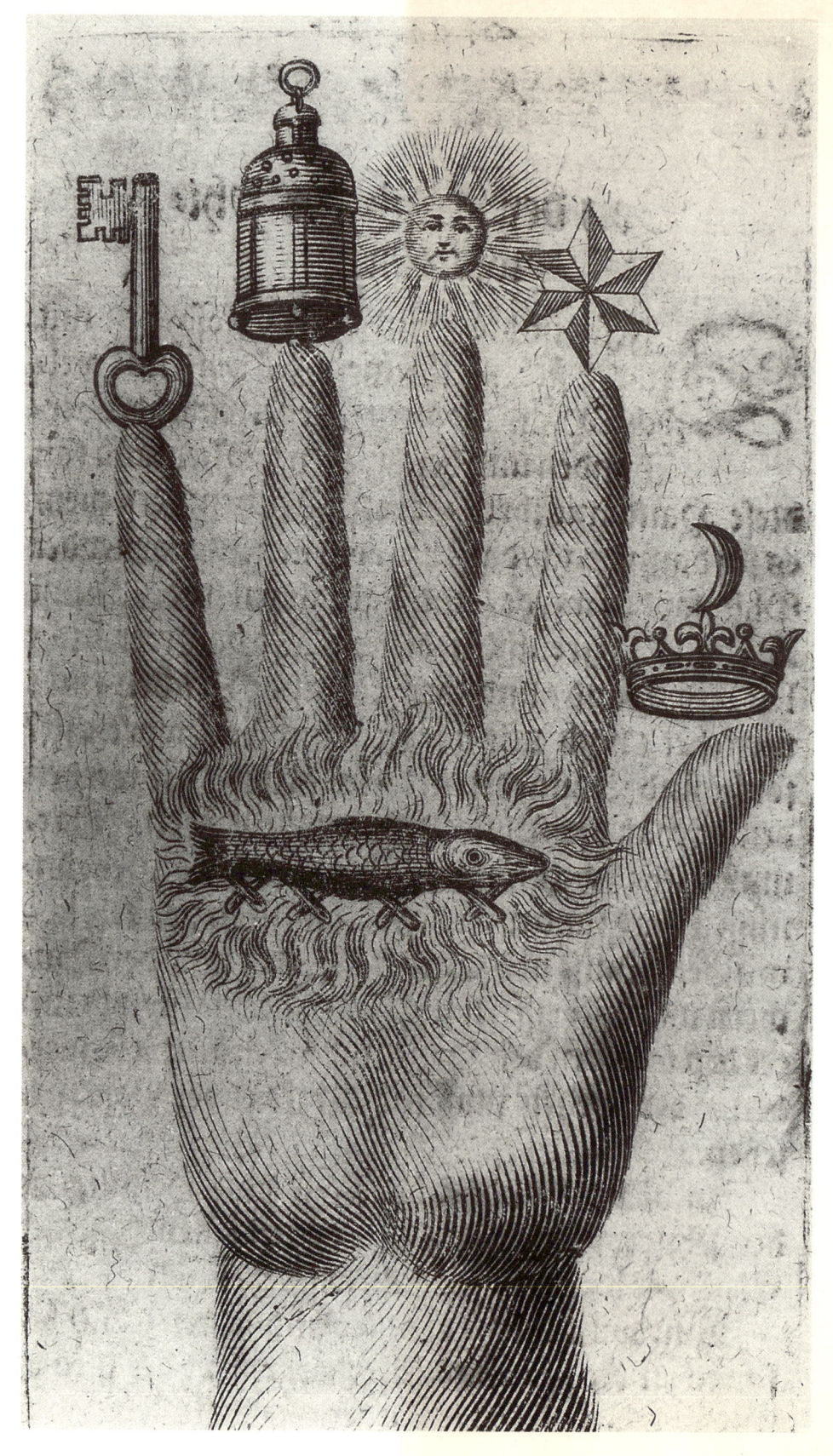

The Golden Game

Alchemical Engravings of the Seventeenth Century

BY STANISLAS KLOSSOWSKI DE ROLA

GEORGE BRAZILLER, INC., NEW YORK

*This book is dedicated
with Love
to the Living Memory
of Eugène Canseliet
F.C.H.*

Published in the United States in 1988 by George Braziller, Inc., New York.
First published in Great Britain by Thames and Hudson Ltd., London.
Copyright © Thames and Hudson Ltd. London 1988.

All rights reserved.

For information address the publisher:

George Braziller, Inc.
60 Madison Avenue
New York, New York 10010

Library of Congress Cataloguing in Publication Data:

Klossowski de Rola, Stanislas.
    The golden game: alchemical engravings of the seventeenth century
    by Stanislas Klossowski de Rola.—1st ed.
       p. cm.
    Bibliography: p.
    Includes index.
    ISBN 0-8076-1200-6
     1. Alchemy in art. 2. Engraving—17th century. I. Title.
NE962.A46K56 1988
769'.4954112—dc19   88-9500
                                                                               CIP

Printed in the German Democratic Republic
First edition.

CONTENTS

Preface	7
Introduction	8
Author's note	24
François Beroalde de Verville, *Le Tableau des riches inventions*, 1600	25
François Beroalde de Verville, *Le Voyage des princes fortunez*, 1610	25
Heinrich Khunrath, *Amphitheatrum sapientiae aeternae*, 1602	29
Andreas Libavius, *Alchymia*, 1606	45
Steffan Michelspacher, *Cabala*, 1616	52
Michael Maier, *Arcana arcanissima*, 1614	59
Michael Maier, *Lusus serius*, 1616	60
Michael Maier, *Examen fucorum*, 1617	61
Michael Maier, *Jocus severus*, 1617	61
Michael Maier, *Atalanta fugiens*, 1618	68
Michael Maier, *Symbola aureae mensae*, 1617	105
Michael Maier, *Tripus aureus*, 1618	117
Michael Maier, *Viatorium*, 1618	127
Johann Daniel Mylius, *Opus medico-chymicum*, 1618	133
Johann Daniel Mylius, *Antidotarium*, 1620	156
Oswald Croll, *Basilica chymica*, 1622	157
Michael Maier, *Septimana philosophica*, 1620	161
Johann Daniel Mylius, *Philosophia reformata*, 1622	167
Musaeum hermeticum, 1625	183

Lambsprinck, *De lapide philosophico*, 1625	187
Johann Daniel Mylius, *Anatomia auri*, 1628	198
David de Planis Campy, *L'Hydre morbifique exterminée*, 1628	208
David de Planis Campy, *L'Ouverture de l'escolle*, 1633	209
Elias Ashmole, *Theatrum chemicum britannicum*, 1652	214
Johann Joachim Becher, *Oedipus chimicus*, 1644	222
Joannes de Monte-Snyders, *Metamorphosis planetarum*, 1684	224
Theodorus Kerckring, *Commentarius in Currum triumphalem Antimonii*, 1671	226
Joannes de Monte-Snyders(?), *Chymica vannus*, 1666	228
Goossen van Vreeswijk, *De Roode Leeuw*, 1672	240
Goossen van Vreeswijk, *De Groene Leeuw*, 1674	246
Goossen van Vreeswijk, *De Goude Leeuw*, 1675	253
Goossen van Vreeswijk, *De Goude Son*, 1675	260
Altus, *Mutus liber*, 1677	266
Barent Coenders van Helpen, *Escalier des sages*, 1689	285
Alexandre Toussaint de Limojon de Saint-Didier, *Le Triomphe hermétique*, 1689	301
Baro Urbigerus, *Aphorismi Urbigerani*, 1690	302
Christopher Love Morley and Theodorus Muykens, *Collectanea chymica*, 1693	303
Jacob Böhme, *Theosophische Wercken*, 1682	308
Bibliography	318
Formats and dimensions	318
Index	319

PREFACE

This book presents a comprehensive selection of the finest engraved alchemical emblems of the seventeenth century, brought together for the first time.

All of the material reproduced is drawn from works preserved in research libraries which, therefore, lies beyond the reach of the interested layman, while the rare reprints of one or the other better-known title almost invariably seem to be either out of print or else of unsatisfactory quality. There are also times when even the specialist fares no better: for instance, there is not one single title by Goossen van Vreeswijk to be found at the Bibliothèque Nationale in Paris. In consequence, while filling an obvious gap, the present volume has the ambitious aim to be both pleasurable and useful.

Over the years invested in this work I have become indebted to many people for their help and support. Some of them have asked not to be named; nevertheless I must assure them all of my everlasting gratitude.

I would like to thank first and foremost my editor, Mr David Britt, for years of collaboration, patience and comprehension beyond the call of duty, during which he waded fearlessly through a maze of material all too often 'prolix and recondite'. I would like to thank the staff of the British Library; Mr C.D. Blockhuis, Head of the Department of Bibliographical Information and Loans at the Leiden University Library, for sending me valuable information on Goossen van Vreeswijk, Mr Marc Sursock for the loan of his pristine copy of Heinrich Khunrath's *Amphitheatrum sapientiae*, which he very kindly allowed us to photograph. I am grateful to Mr Bernard Renaud de la Faverie for showing me an article describing the treasures of the Bibliotheca Philosophica Hermetica in Amsterdam, where I was received with extraordinary kindness by the staff headed by Dr F.A. Janssen, its erudite curator, and by its owner Mr J.R. Ritman who is an enlightened modern Maecenas. Many thanks are due to Miss Patricia Tahil for kindly making available to me her translation of the 160 mottoes surrounding the 'Seals of the Philosophers' in Johann Daniel Mylius' *Opus medico-chymicum*.

In addition I must thank Miss Venetia Spicer, Miss Anna André, Miss Patrizia Brouwer and Miss Shireen Al-Hayderi for their invaluable help, encouragement and tactical support, without which I could never have completed the task at hand.

INTRODUCTION

During the tumultuous course of the seventeenth century an unprecedented quantity of alchemical works were printed; and a significant number of them contain copperplate engravings whose function transcends both illustration and decoration.[1] These so-called 'Hieroglyphicall Figures'[2] and 'Hermetick Emblems'[3] constitute an independent pictorial language which, in silence but not without eloquence, conveys the secrets of alchemy to those aspiring 'Sons of the Art' — as the alchemists called their disciples — who alone can discover them. And as this idiom plays with consummate skill upon double meanings, natural analogies and hermetick interpretations of classical mythology, I have called it the Golden Game.[4]

To trace its origins we must turn to Egypt, which was for every alchemist the mystical homeland of his art, the birthplace of its legendary father Hermes Trismegistus. There, it was believed, the gods revealed their wisdom in visions to the ancient sages, who consigned it to the mysterious pictures which they called hieroglyphs — sacred signs.

To the Greeks, Egypt and its immemorial civilization were always a source of wonder and fascination. Yet the fundamental differences in their ways of thinking, which prompted Herodotus to remark that the Egyptians had made themselves customs and laws of a kind contrary to those of other men, prevented the Greeks from ever being able to understand them. And that is why, as the modern scholar Iversen puts it,

> in order to conceive and express in their own tongue the Egyptian conceptions of religious and philosophic problems, they had to translate them into the terms of their own logic, and this process invariably involved an interpretation based on utterly un-Egyptian premises. This procedure, which is of fundamental importance for the proper understanding of the Greek traditions of Egypt, is very clearly illustrated by the Greek attitude towards the Egyptian mythical material. In Platonic and post-Socratic philosophy the Egyptian myths were always considered in the way in which the Greeks had become accustomed to consider their own, which means that the relationship between myth and reality was considered as being of a symbolic and allegorical nature. But the establishment of this symbolic relationship was a fundamental misinterpretation of the very basis of Egyptian thought, and substituted the mythical truth of the Egyptians, with its indissoluble magical identification of myth and matter, by an utterly un-Egyptian interpretation created by Greek philosophy and poetry. . . .
>
> But in no field is the strange cultural relationship between Egypt and Greece better illustrated, and nowhere else are the fatal consequences of the Greek symbolic interpretation of Egyptian facts made more apparent,

than in the Greek conception of hieroglyphic writing and the subsequent development of the so-called hieroglyphic tradition.[5]

The Greeks' sustained interest in Egyptian hieroglyphs was in fact the consequence of a misconception. Misreading their cryptic and fragmentary sources, they came to believe that hieroglyphs bore no relation to ordinary language but were the pictorial and allegorical expression of sacred knowledge. Plotinus (AD 204–270) has left a definitive formulation of this idea:

> As it seems to me, the wise of Egypt – whether in precise knowledge or by native intuition – indicated the truth where, in their effort towards philosophical statement, they left aside the writing-forms that take in the detail of words and sentences – those characters that represent sounds and convey the propositions of reasoning – and drew pictures instead, engraving in the temple-inscriptions a separate image for every separate item: they exhibited the absence of discursiveness in the Intellectual Realm.
>
> For each manifestation of knowledge and wisdom is a distinct image, an object in itself, an immediate unity, not an aggregate, of discursive reasoning and detailed willing.[6]

In a commentary appended to his Latin translation of Plotinus, published in 1492, Marsilio Ficino (1433–99) observed:

> Our way of thinking about 'time' is complex and shifting. For example, 'time goes quickly', 'time revolves and ends up where it began', 'time teaches prudence', 'time gives and takes away'. This whole range of thought was comprehended in a single firm figure by the Egyptians when they drew a winged serpent with its tail in its mouth. And there are many other such figures described by Horus.[7]

By Horus, Ficino meant Horus Apollo or Horapollo, the author of the *Hieroglyphica*, alleged to be the Greek translation of an Egyptian work, which was discovered in 1419 by a Florentine monk, Cristoforo Buondelmonti,[8] on the Greek island of Andros. Purchased by Buondelmonti on behalf of Cosimo de' Medici, the manuscript of the *Hieroglyphica* eventually reached Florence in 1422, where it caused a sensation. For there, at last, was a work explaining the hidden meaning of the mysterious Egyptian hieroglyphs. Its text was widely circulated and eagerly commented upon, despite its many shortcomings; and it is responsible for the Renaissance view of hieroglyphs.

The manuscript begins with an introduction stating that the work was originally written in Egyptian by Horapollo of Nilopolis and afterwards translated into Greek by Philippos. Although neither author nor translator can be identified with certainty,[9] there are, it appears, indications that the putative original was written in the fourth or fifth century AD; the Greek text is not much later.[10]

Hieroglyphs drawn by Albrecht Dürer for Willibald Pirckheimer's ms. translation of Horapollo, c.1514.

The *Hieroglyphica* consists of two books: the first is divided into 70 chapters and the second into 119 chapters, each devoted to a single hieroglyph. The commentaries which expound the allegorical relationship between hieroglyph and meaning are a strange cocktail of fantasy mixed with a surprising dash of fact. This makes it all the more regrettable that nothing has transpired concerning the author's sources of information. For it does appear that Horapollo was in contact with the true hieroglyphical tradition, and that at the time a first-hand knowledge of the system was still alive,[11] even though his access to it was imperfect. Iversen concludes:

> if somebody entirely ignorant of the principles of hieroglyphic writing asked a modern Egyptologist about the meanings of various signs of a hieroglyphic inscription merely by pointing at the most characteristic and conspicuous of them, his general impression about their nature would probably come very close to those entertained by Horapollo.[12]

Copied many times during the fifteenth century,[13] the *Hieroglyphica* was printed for the first time by Aldus in 1505.[14] Translated into Latin, French, Italian and German, it was in one or the other language published more than twenty times during the sixteenth century alone.

Perhaps the most interesting of the manuscript copies of the *Hieroglyphica* is a Latin translation undertaken by the Nuremberg humanist Willibald Pirckheimer at the request of Emperor Maximilian I and presented to him at Linz in 1515. This manuscript, illustrated with drawings by Pirckheimer's friend Albrecht Dürer, was rediscovered by the Austrian art historian Karl Giehlow in the Vienna library at the end of the last century. Giehlow was thus able to solve, once and for all, the 'hieroglyphic mystery' of Dürer's *Ehrenpforte* (1515), the gigantic *Triumphal Arch of Maximilian* which is the largest woodcut ever created, an assemblage of prints measuring $11\frac{1}{2}$ by $9\frac{3}{4}$ feet.[15] At the very top of this monument there is a panel – described by Stabius, Maximilian's historiographer, as 'a mystery in sacred Egyptian letters' – showing the Emperor enthroned and surrounded by symbols gleaned from Dürer's illustrations of Horapollo. Following E.H. Wittkower's lead, I now turn to Erwin Panofsky's translation from Stabius' German and Pirckheimer's Latin texts, which allows us to decipher the image (the interpolations are Panofsky's):

> Maximilian [the Emperor himself] – a prince [dog draped with stole] of great piety [star above the Emperor's crown], most magnanimous, powerful and courageous [lion], ennobled by imperishable and eternal fame [basilisk on the Emperor's crown], descending from ancient lineage [the sheaf of papyrus on which he is seated], Roman Emperor [eagles embroidered in the cloth of honor], endowed with all the gifts of nature and possessed of art and learning [dew descending from the sky] and master of a great part of the terrestrial globe [snake encircling the sceptre] – has with warlike virtue and great discretion [bull] won a shining victory [falcon on the orb] over the mighty King here indicated [cock on a serpent, meaning the King of France], and thereby watchfully

The Emperor Maximilian, detail from a component woodcut of the *Triumphal Arch of Maximilian*, by Albrecht Dürer, 1515.

protected himself [crane raising its foot] from the stratagems of said enemy, which has been deemed impossible [feet walking through water by themselves] by all mankind.[16]

Horapollo's method was greeted with enthusiasm by the humanists because it provided them with the means to imitate the Egyptians, by expressing secret subtleties in symbolic pictures which could be understood only by the learned. It held sway for four hundred years and, although it may have impeded a genuine understanding of Egyptian hieroglyphs, it had the merit of inspiring many creative minds to invent 'hieroglyphs' of their own.

Emblems and their publishers

The first literary work whose iconography undeniably showed Horapollo's influence was the *Hypnerotomachia Poliphili*, an erudite allegorical tale written in Italian, in 1467, by a Dominican monk, Fra Francesco Colonna.[17] The first printed edition, published at Venice by Aldus in 1499, is a typographical masterpiece, adorned with 192 woodcuts which greatly contributed to its success. Following its reprint by the Aldine Press in 1545,

Introduction · 11

the book was freely translated into French. Now called *Le Songe de Poliphile*, it was well received in France, where Jacques Kerver published it three times (1546, 1553 and 1561); and in 1600 François Beroalde de Verville produced an improved translation with the following title: *Le Tableau des riches inventions couvertes du voile des feintes amoureuses, qui sont représentées dans le Songe de Poliphile desvoilées des ombres du songe et subtilement exposées par Beroalde.*[18]

In his introduction, dedicated 'To the Beautiful Spirits who shall arrest their gaze upon those projects of serious pleasure', Beroalde praises

> this Author who follows the manner of the Ancients who veiled any kind of philosophical truth with certain agreeable figures which attracted men's hearts, either to detain them upon the husk of what offered itself, or to strive to open that which hid the inner beauty in order to enjoy it, thus both pleasing the vulgar and satisfying those desirous of perfection. And since perfect love is the good, just and vehement desire that one has towards that which is excellent, Poliphilus has based his subject upon the difficulties of love, since there is nothing that so uplifts the spirit as amorous thoughts towards a meritorious object.[19]

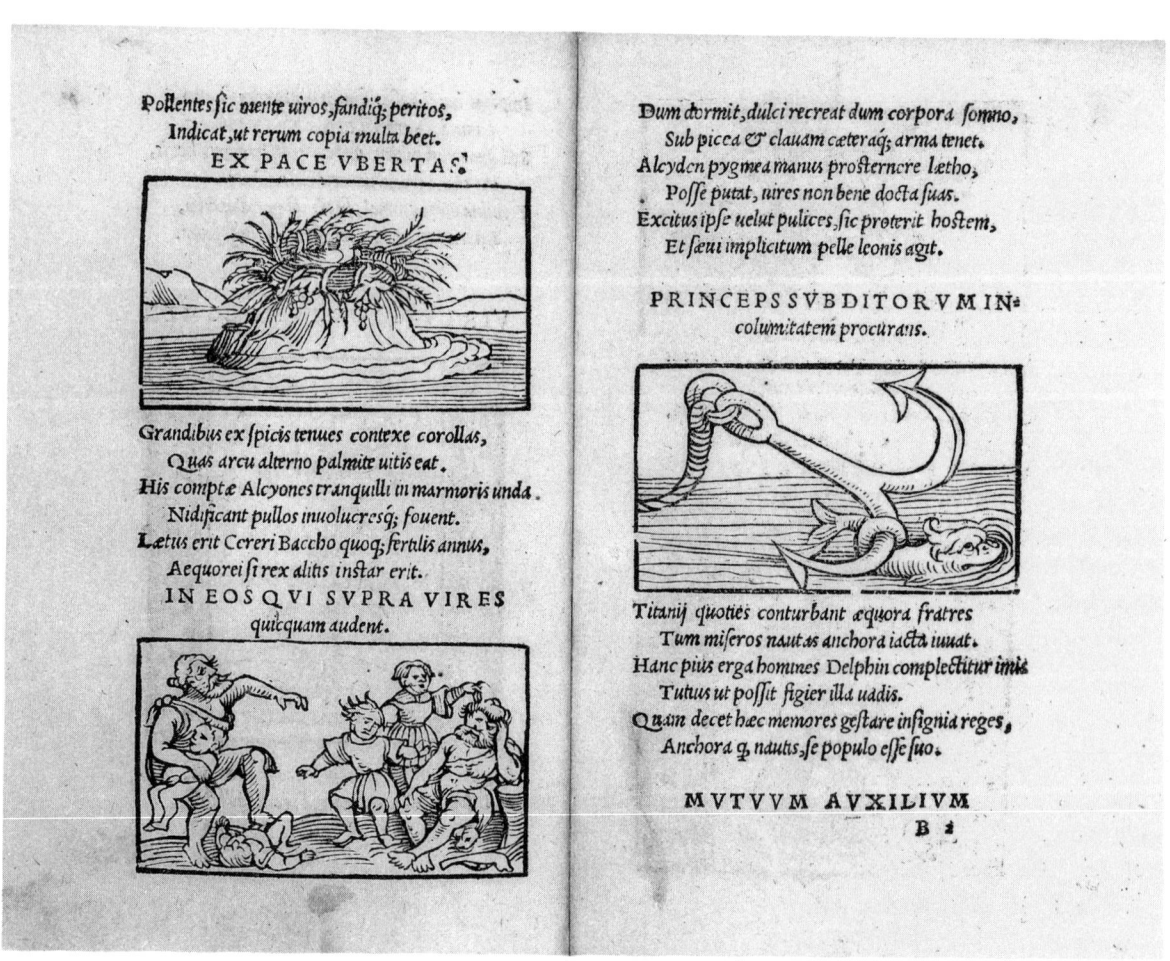

'Riches from peace'; 'Against those who dare aught beyond their strength'; 'The prince ensuring his subjects' safety'. Emblems from Andrea Alciati, *Emblematum liber*, Augsburg 1531.

Hieroglyphic inscription from Francesco Colonna, *Hypnerotomachia Poliphili*, Venice 1499.

Lequale uetustissime & sacre scripture pensiculante, cusi io le interpretai.

EX LABORE DEO NATVRAE SACRIFICA LIBERALITER, PAVLATIM REDVCES ANIMVM DEO SVBIECTVM. FIRMAM CVSTODIAM VITAE TVAE MISERICORDITER GVBERNANDO TENEBIT, INCOLVMEM QVESERVABIT.

The fashionable *Emblemata* of the sixteenth century were in fact 'hieroglyphs' directly inspired by Horapollo. Allegorical images accompanied by a few cryptic lines of prose or verse, emblems presented to the learned a kind of pictorial riddle containing a solution of a moral nature.[20] But emblems which could easily conceal more than one meaning constituted ideal vehicles for the secret transmission of esoteric information, and as such, were, as we shall see below, adopted by the alchemists.

The first of countless emblem books was Andrea Alciati's *Emblematum liber*, completed in 1521 but published at Augsburg by Heinrich Steyner in 1531.[21] This work was reprinted no less than 130 times between 1532 and 1781. The vogue took hold in France with the publication of *Le Theatre des bons engins* by Guillaume de la Perrière (Paris 1539) and of the *Hecatomgraphie* by Gilles Gorrozel (1540). At Basle in 1556 appeared Pierio Valeriano's *Hieroglyphica*,[22] a capital work from which Cesare Ripa derived his famous *Iconologia* published in 1593. The *Iconologia*, a manual written in Italian providing the means of embodying abstractions in sensible forms, became the 'bible' of engraving workshops. Meanwhile Geoffrey Whitney's *A Choice of Emblems*, the first English emblem book, had appeared at Leyden in 1586.

Hieroglyph of Justice from Pierio Valeriano, *Hieroglyphica*, Basle 1556.

'Where pleasure holds sway, virtue is banished.'
Emblem from J.J. Boissard, *Emblematum liber*, Frankfurt 1593.

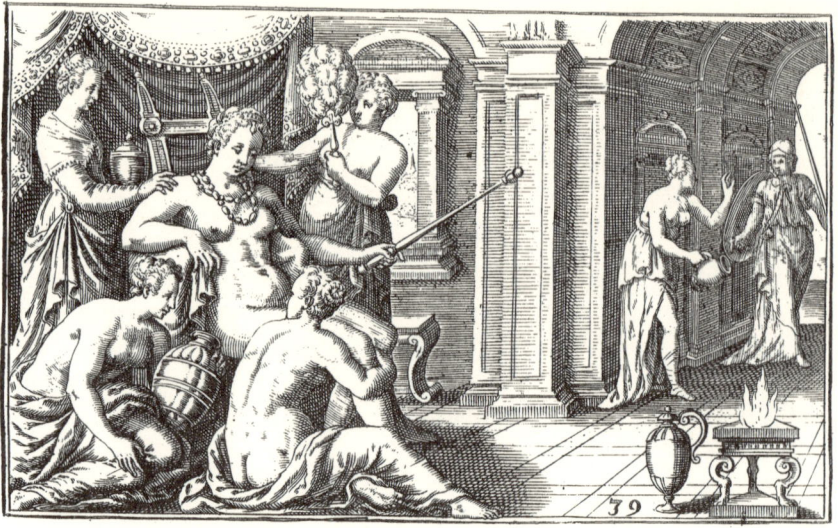

Title page of Robert Fludd, *Utriusque cosmi . . . historia*, Oppenheim 1617.

The hieroglyphic and graphic tradition of the emblem developed, in the hands of a few dedicated publishers, into the seventeenth-century flowering of hermetick publishing which produced the engravings featured in this book. The connection can be traced in the work of one remarkable family, that of de Bry. Theodor de Bry engraved and published at Frankfurt in 1593 the *Emblemata* of Jean-Jacques Boissard,[23] which the alchemist Michael Maier was to study carefully.[24] In collaboration with his sons Johann Theodor and Johann Israel, Theodor de Bry compiled and engraved two more emblem books, *Emblemata nobilitati* . . . (Frankfurt 1593) and *Emblemata secularia* (Frankfurt 1596), and the family went on to publish most of the important alchemical books of the first quarter of the seventeenth century.

The de Bry family were Protestants from Liège who moved to Frankfurt some time after 1581, when Liège came under oppressive Catholic domination. Theodor de Bry,[25] famous for his engraved work on America, ran a prosperous engraving and publishing firm and travelled often to England where he engraved the remarkable *Funeral Procession of Sir Philip Sidney*.[26]

When he died in 1598, his sons succeeded him. In 1610 Johann Theodor de Bry[27] opened another branch of the family business at nearby Oppenheim in the Upper Palatinate, eventually helped by his son-in-law, the Swiss artist and engraver Matthäus Merian.[28] At Oppenheim were published, among other things, Maier's *Atalanta fugiens* and several major works by the English esoteric philosopher Robert Fludd. The latter provides a contemporary testimony to the superior efficiency and quality of the de Bry firm:

> Our home-borne Printers demanded of me five hundred pounds to print the first volume, and to find the cuts in copper; but, beyond the seas, it was printed at no cost of mine, and that as I would wish. And I had 16 copies sent me over, with 40 pounds in gold as an unexpected gratuitie for it.[29]

'Venus deceives and is deceived, lying in wait in the shadows'; 'I was, and am not; thou art, and shalt not be'. Emblems from Theodor de Bry, *Emblemata nobilitati et vulgo scitu*, Frankfurt 1593 (with spaces for the reader's literary contributions).

Johann Israel de Bry had married, in 1607, the widowed mother of Lucas Jennis. Thus Jennis, about whom far too little is known, and who in due course became the leading publisher of alchemical works of his time, was also a member of the de Bry family. He appears to have embarked on his prolific publishing career around 1616, and to have operated, like his step-uncle, for a few years in Oppenheim[30] as well as in Frankfurt. But both publishers evidently left Oppenheim for the safety of Frankfurt well before the invasion of the Palatinate by Spinola's armies in the summer of 1620 and the consequent surrender of the unprepared city on 6 September of that year.

In 1623 Johann Theodor de Bry died in Frankfurt. Since he had no sons, and since his younger brother Johann Israel had already died in 1611, his gifted son-in-law Matthäus Merian succeeded him at the head of the de Bry firm, which remained in his family for 103 years. Lucas Jennis was still able to obtain Merian's artistic collaboration on occasion, as we can see from the engraved title-page of the *Musaeum hermeticum* (1625). It seems that Jennis' publishing career came to an end about 1642, and although countless alchemical books were published after he had gone, no other seventeenth-century publisher stands out as prominently as he and Johann Theodor de Bry had done.

Hieroglyphs, mythology and alchemy

Horapollo's interpretation of hieroglyphs contributed to a perennial tradition which saw all religious myth and imagery as the cloak of a hidden allegory. One of the many lost Greek treatises on hieroglyphs, that of Nero's tutor, Chaeremon,[31] was cited by the twelfth-century grammarian John Tzetzes in his commentary on the *Iliad* in order to prove that Homer used the very same method, and that he had become acquainted with it through hieroglyphical studies.[32]

It appears, in turn, that Tzetzes' ideas were known to Petrus Bonus of Ferrara who, in 1330, completed a famous alchemical treatise known as the *Pretiosa margarita novella*, in which he stated that the true aim of Homer, Virgil and Ovid was none other than the transmission of alchemical secrets.

> And in those stories and fables they inserted this art in a mystical way, with linguistic ornaments as their principal and hidden subject, but in such way that their secret object could only reveal itself to those who have the intelligence of it. Because, as we have already stated, this science, with all the things [concerning it] that can be done or said, is mystical. But some people who came after them considered only the manifest principal subject with its painted, ornate and dissembling words, or else, reducing it to the metaphorical expression of human ethics but ignoring its principal, hidden and true subject matter, exposed their writings and told these same fables and other similar ones. And so successively and continually do the following ones. And they falsely begged for themselves the name of poets, since, although fictive, poems however always possess a certain kind of hidden truth, which is fundamental in the mind of the poet, and the wise alone may extract this hidden truth of poems. In fact, one could otherwise neither consider them poems nor fiction but rather vain trifles; and in truth every poem and every figure cover a plurality of significations. That is why it has pleased some to hide and to reveal this secret in stories and fables, others [to do so] in tales concerning the gods. . . .[33]

The publication of two Italian dialogues, *La espositione de Geber Philosopho* and *Il legno della vita*, by Giovanni Bracesco da Iorci Novi, at Venice in 1544,[34] met with considerable success and probably inspired the first printing, in a much paraphrased and abridged form, of the *Pretiosa margarita novella* itself, which had remained in manuscript for two centuries.[35]

Bracesco, through the voice of Geber conversing with one Demogorgon, completes a discourse by saying: '. . . the above-mentioned things have been hidden by the Ancients under the veil of poetic fables'. Demogorgon reacts in disbelief: according to the learned sources he has read, those fictions are imbued with a moral sense. Geber dismisses that notion, which he says is held by people who have no knowledge of alchemy and who in consequence cannot perceive the true purpose of the Ancients. Citing Albertus Magnus (*De mineralibus*, book 1, chapter 4), who in turn quotes Empedocles, Geber attempts to explain the story of Pyrrha and Deucalion in alchemical terms. Unconvinced, Demogorgon denies that Albertus meant his words to be taken in that connection. Geber ignores this and continues his explanation, but Demogorgon finds it 'more obscure than the text itself'.

Undaunted, Geber explains the story of Jupiter and Ganymede, and that of Daedalus and Icarus, then the mutual passion of Venus and Mars. Demogorgon at that stage tartly states: 'I believe that this is one of those things that you are alone in understanding.' Unruffled, Geber proceeds with a prolix and – to one versed in alchemical subtleties – fascinating exposition of one Greek myth after another. Demogorgon wavers; he declares his admiration for Geber's ingenious interpretations but doubts whether such was the original intention of the Ancients.

Geber then replies:

> When once you have seen the practice of this Art, and are thus one of our sons, then will you know this truth; and if you will not deny the opinion of the ancient sages, which as I have told you is that every metal is in every metal as I have already explained, you will no longer be able to deny that such is the true sense and the true intention of the antique poets concerning the poetical fables, since they have in every possible way concealed this science; and many sages say that in those poetical fables, the ancients have hidden the secrets of Nature....

He gives more examples until at length Demogorgon capitulates and resolves to find, with the help of Geber's explanations, the true sense of all poetical fictions. Towards the end of the work, Geber declares:

> The Ancients concealed the secrets of nature not only in writings but also with various pictures, characters, ciphers, monsters and animals diversely depicted and transformed; and within their palaces and temples they painted these poetical fables, the planets and the celestial signs, with many other signs, monsters and animals; and they were not understood by anyone except by those who had knowledge of those secrets....

Thus the alchemists came to include every classical myth, every ancient fable and every conceivable allegorical figure, emblem, symbol – or 'hieroglyph' – in a complex system of multiple correspondences constituting a formidable initiatory challenge for every aspiring Son of Hermes.

A global reading of this system was undertaken by Michael Maier in his *Arcana arcanissima hoc est Hieroglyphica aegyptio-graeca* of 1614,[36] the first treatise wholly devoted to the hermetick interpretation of Graeco-Egyptian mythology. In the eighteenth century its entire text was copied, enlarged upon and paraphrased by the Benedictine scholar Dom Antoine Joseph Pernety, whose work *Les Fables Egyptiennes et Grecques dévoilées et réduites au même principe avec une Explication des Hieroglyphes et de la Guerre de Troye* appeared at Paris in 1786. A very useful *Dictionnaire mytho-hermétique* appeared the following year. All the traditional hermetick views about hieroglyphs and mythology are upheld and expounded in these remarkable books. As Pernety says in the *Dictionnaire mytho-hermétique*:

> The Ancients commonly employed fables, and those of the Egyptians and of the Greeks have been invented solely with regard to the Great Work, if we are to believe the Philosophers who have often quoted them in their works. It is according to their views that I have explained them in the Treatise that I have given to the public under the title of *Les Fables Egyptiennes et Grecques dévoilées*. Some Philosophers have used a mute language to speak to the eyes of the mind. They have shown by means of symbols and hieroglyphs in the manner of the Egyptians the Matters required for the Work as well as their preparation and often even the significant signs, or colours which this Matter assumes during the course of the operations; because it is according to those signs that the Artist knows whether he has proceeded correctly or not.
>
> Several Philosophers have added a discourse to those hieroglyphs; but this apparent explanation is always as difficult to understand as the symbol itself, often more so. Such are those of Nicolas Flamel, of Senior, of Basil Valentine, of Michael Maier; although of the latter d'Espagnet says that they are akin to a type of glasses that uncover clearly enough the truth that the Philosophers have hidden.[37]

Maier himself, in the eleventh discourse of his *Atalanta fugiens* (1617), underlines those very difficulties:

> The diversity of authors in their writings is such that the seekers after the truth concerning the goal of the art almost despair of discovering it. In fact allegorical discourses are in themselves difficult to understand and therefore the cause of numerous errors; they become particularly so in the case of the same terms being applied to diverse realities and of different terms [being applied] to the same realities.

There are many fascinating and scholarly works dealing with the critical and historical problems of alchemy; but it is unfortunate that most of them betray their authors' incapacity to interpret correctly the veiled language of the Wise. That is because the strictly esoteric nature of the Art of Hermes precludes its successful approach by conventional means of investigation. Therefore alchemical research should be geared towards the recovery of that secret theory which lies concealed within deliberately recondite texts and in 'aenigmaticall hieroglyphicall figures'.

Several Hermetick Philosophers have provided a method for the diligent seeker which can be used as a kind of Ariadne's thread to find one's way through the labyrinthine obscurity of alchemical literature: select the best books, read and re-read them, carefully compare the places where they agree and how they agree, for there the truth is to be found. Also compare where they differ and how they differ, for further discoveries will still be made. Be suspicious when they appear to speak most clearly and candidly; and meditate upon the places where they are most obscure. Thus little by little the pattern of truth will emerge, like the watermark in paper held up to the light.

Each and every individual who is seriously interested in alchemy must patiently submit to this ordeal, which is in fact an initiation. There are no short cuts, and over the years I have learnt through bitter experience that nothing in this field can be made 'easy' without damage. For the lesson of the Ancient Way can truly be learnt only by travelling upon it. All else is pure speculation, futility and vanity. Theory must indeed precede practice, but practice must in turn test theory; for there cannot be alchemy without laboratory operations, despite various claims to the contrary, just as there can be no fish without water.

In this connection there is a noteworthy analogy with the philosophy of China. The profound influence of Taoism on Chinese alchemy, from which it is virtually inseparable, finds its roots in the merging of the thought of the Wu (whom Joseph Needham in *Science and Civilization in China* calls 'the primitive shamans of Chinese society') with the thought of

> those Chinese philosophers who, in ancient times, believed that the study of Nature was more important for man than the administration of human society upon which the Confucians so much prided themselves, and that his moral perfection depended much more on his integration with the natural cosmos than on his social relations with other men. At the heart of ancient Taoism there was an artisanal element, for both the wizards and the philosophers, the diviners and the cosmological thinkers, were convinced that important and useful results could be achieved by using one's hands.[38]

One should never lose sight of the fact that the Philosopher's Stone, elusive goal of the alchemical Quest, is both a material and a spiritual realization. The process of its elaboration, summed up by the hermetick axiom *Solve et coagula*, consists basically of repeated Dissolutions followed by Crystallizations, of the secret Subject of the Wise, the *Materia Prima* or Stone of the Philosophers. The purification and subsequent Exaltation of this chosen Subject endow it with a particular magnetic quality. It is then able to receive and retain a mysterious celestial influx, occurring briefly in the spring, which endows it with extraordinary qualities. A spiritualization of matter thus precedes a materialization of spirit, and the Stone of the Philosophers becomes the Philosopher's Stone, a highly evolved substance capable of the most extraordinary effects.

The Philosopher's Stone is the true Universal Quintessence, capable of transmuting all metals into gold; it is also called the Universal Medicine or Panacea, as it removes the very causes of diseases, and the Fountain of Youth, as it rejuvenates the organism and prolongs life beyond its normal span. 'It is', writes Philaletha, 'the Balsam of Nature, expelling all diseases, and cutting them off as it were with one Hook, all that are accidental to the Humane frail Body, which is wonderful'.[39]

'And certainly,' writes Elias Ashmole, 'he to whom the whole course of Natures lyes open rejoyceth not so much that he can make Gold or Silver or the Divells to become subject to him, as that hee sees the Heavens open, the Angells of God Ascending and Descending, and that his own name is fairely written in the Book of Life.'[40]

ORA ET LABORA ET INVENIES.

NOTES TO THE INTRODUCTION

1 The invention of printing did not contribute to the diffusion of alchemical literature until a comparatively late date. Hundreds of alchemical manuscripts were in circulation, but only two texts are known to have been printed during the period of *incunabula*. Their number remained modest until the last decades of the sixteenth century. By that time printing had improved, allowing the reproduction of even the finest line drawings, and copperplate engravings replaced for the most part the coarser woodcuts used previously.

2 'The Ancient Egyptians taught much by Hieroglyphicks, which way many Fathers of this science have followed.' *An Exposition upon Sir George Ripley's Vision written by Æyrenaeus Philalethes, Anglus, Cosmopolita*, London 1677, reprinted in my *Alchemy: the Secret Art*, London 1973, p. 24.

3 To avoid possible confusion, I have used the archaic spelling 'hermetick' (as opposed to hermetic), since written thus it refers unequivocally to alchemy, the Secret Art of Hermes, synonymously called the Hermetick Philosophy.

4 My choice of title was inspired by those of Michael Maier's treatises. In Latin it might have read thus: *Lusus aureus: hoc est tractatus in quo tamen tota Philosophia hermetica et Sapientia veterum Philosophorum figuris hieroglyphicis depingitur. Solis filiis artis dedicatus.*

5 Iversen, *The Myth of Egypt*, pp. 40–41.

6 Plotinus, *The Enneads*, tr. Stephen McKenna, 4th edn, London 1969, v.8.6, p. 427.

7 Pope, *Story of Decipherment*, p. 21. The serpent is Ouroboros; see Emblema XIV of *Atalanta fugiens* (43).

8 Buondelmonti (1380–1430) had settled in Rhodes in 1408 and was the first Western European scholar to make a thorough survey of the Greek Islands. He wrote in 1420 his *Liber insularum archipelagi*, which was never printed but is extant in various manuscript copies of the fifteenth and sixteenth centuries.

9 There was a Horapollo – or Horapollon – of Phaenebythis, in the nome of Panapolis in Upper Egypt, in the second half of the fifth century of our era. According to Suidas he wrote commentaries on Sophocles, Alcaeus and Homer, and *Temenica*, a work on consecrated places. Photius calls him a dramatist as well, and credits him with a history of Alexandria.

10 Parthey, 'Horapollo von den Hieroglyphen', *Monatsschrift der preuss. Akad. der Wissenschaften zu Berlin*, 1871, 10.

11 Hieroglyphic inscriptions were still common a century or two earlier, under the reign of Diocletian, AD 248–305, and the last recorded one is dated August AD 394. And still that does not mean that the knowledge of hieroglyphics wholly disappeared. It might well have remained in the custody of the priests of Isis, who were finally driven out of their venerable sanctuaries only under the rule of Justinian in AD 535.

12 Iversen, *The Myth of Egypt*, note 33, p. 151.

13 Of the dozen or so extant manuscripts of the *Hieroglyphica*, nine are fifteenth-century copies.

14 Aldo Manuzio the Elder (1450–1515), the Venetian printer-publisher, is better known under his Latin name Aldus Manutius or simply as Aldus. The books that his Aldine Press published constitute a unique example in the annals of printing. No one had ever previously used such beautiful Greek type, of which he had nine different kinds made, while he had as many as fourteen Latin types. It is to him and to the engraver Francesco da Bologna that we owe the type forms called by the Italians *corsivi* and known in English as 'italic', used for the first time in his octavo edition of ancient and modern classics, beginning with Virgil (1501). Aldus' impressions on parchment are superb; he was the first printer to introduce the custom of taking some impressions on finer or stronger paper than the rest of the edition. The first such example is to be found in the *Epistolae graecae* (1499). The Aldine Press was active for a hundred years, and during that time printed 908 different works. Its emblem is an anchor entwined by a dolphin, with the motto *Festina lente* ('Hasten slowly') or *Sudavit et alsit* ('He sweated and froze').

15 A mounted set is on display at the Department of Prints and Drawings of the British Museum, London.

16 Erwin Panofsky, *Albrecht Dürer*, Princeton, N.J., 1943, p. 177. Quoted by E.H. Wittkower, *Allegory and the Migration of Symbols*, London and New York 1977, pp. 123–5. The 'dog with stole' image should, I feel, have been translated 'a prince of great judgment'.

17 Fra Francesco Colonna (born Treviso 1433, died Venice 1527), humanist and Dominican monk, taught rhetoric at Treviso.

18 François Beroalde de Verville was born in Paris in 1556, the son of a Protestant theologian from Geneva. He forswore Calvinism around 1585 and in 1593 became Canon of Saint-Gatien at Tours. He studied every science known to man in his time and among other things wrote *Les Aventures de Floride* (1593–1601), *Les Amours d'Aesionne* (1597), *La Pucelle d'Orleans* (1599), *Le Voyage des princes fortunez* (1610). The only work for which he is remembered is *Le Moyen de parvenir* (1610). His style is pleasantly reminiscent of Rabelais.

19 Beroalde, *Le Tableau des riches inventions*.

20 'The word emblem – derived from the Greek *emblēma* – meant originally an ornament of inlaid work such as was used on shields and vessels. But Alciati used it as the terminological expression for his new literary invention, consisting of a combination of a short fable or allegory written in Latin verse – the stanza – an allegorical picture illustrating the fable – the device – and a short motto expressing in proverbial form the quintessence of the representation. Each of the three elements was considered of equal importance, and the ensemble – the emblem – was adjusted so as to form an indissoluble artistic unity.' (Iversen, *The Myth of Egypt*, pp. 73–74.)

21 Andrea Alciati (born Alzate near Como 1492, died Pavia 1550), Italian jurist and humanist. He taught law at universities in France and Italy and was one of the founders of the scientific method in jurisprudence. His *Emblemata* were dedicated to the Imperial Counsellor Konrad Peutinger, who had discovered in Greece another manuscript of Horapollo's *Hieroglyphica*. Trebatius had translated this into Latin in 1515 and dedicated it to Peutinger.

22 Pierio Valeriano's real name was Giovan Pietro delle Fosse. He was born at Belluno in 1477. His uncle Fra Urbano Valerio Bolzanio, a friend of Francesco Colonna and tutor to Giovanni de' Medici who later became Pope Leo X, introduced him to the study of hieroglyphs, which became the ruling passion of his life. One of his tutors, the scholar Marcantonio Sabellico, was so delighted by his intelligence that he changed his pupil's name from Pietro to Pierio, a reference to the Pierides (another name for the Muses). Pierio became tutor to Ippolito and Alessandro de' Medici and was appointed *cameriere secreto* to Leo X. In 1537 he took holy orders, but he refused two bishoprics for the sake of his studies.

23 Jean-Jacques Boissard (born Besançon 1528, died Metz 1602) was a French archaeologist and antiquarian who travelled extensively through Greece and Italy. He has left several other works: *Habitus variarum orbis gentium* (1580) and *Romanae urbis topographia et antiquitates* (1597–1602).

24 See the account of Maier on p. 60. He refers to Boissard in his own book of alchemical emblems, *Atalanta fugiens*, which was published by Johann Theodor de Bry in 1617.

25 Theodor de Bry (born Liège 1528, died Frankfurt, 27 March 1598) is best known as an engraver but he was also a goldsmith, engraved stamps and designed clocks, medals and emblems. When he visited London, about 1587, he engraved the *Procession of the Knights of the Garter under Queen Elizabeth* (12 plates after Marcus Gheeraerts) and *The Funeral of Sir Philip Sidney* (34 plates after Thomas Lant). In England, through the mediation of the geographer Richard Hakluyt, he acquired a series of drawings – now in the British Museum – made in Virginia by John White on an expedition promoted by Sir Walter Raleigh (1585–86). He also obtained the sketches of Florida made by Jacques Le Moyne during the Laudonnière expedition (1563–65). Together these works provided material and inspiration for the great record of discovery and travel, the *Collectiones peregrinationum in Indiam orientalem et occidentalem*, which Theodor de Bry – with the help of his sons – began at Frankfurt in 1590.

26 Thomas Lant, Portcullis Pursuivant, produced a pictorial record of the funeral, with engravings by de Bry, a huge and handsome roll which John Aubrey remembered seeing in an alderman's house in Gloucester: 'He had contrived it to be turned upon two pinnes, that turning one of them made the figures march all in order.' (John Buxton, *Sir Philip Sidney and the English Renaissance*, London 1964.)

27 Johann Theodor de Bry (born Liège 1561, died Frankfurt 1623), Theodor de Bry's eldest son, was trained by his father, and his talent soon equalled and even surpassed that of his master. He took charge of the de Bry firm in 1598 and ran it for twenty-five years. His masterly work has at times erroneously been attributed to his gifted son-in-law Matthäus Merian.

28 Matthäus Merian (born Basle 1593, died Frankfurt 1650). In 1609, at the age of sixteen, this talented young Swiss engraver and etcher was apprenticed to Dietrich Meyer, a painter and engraver in Zürich. In 1613 he went to Nancy, then continued his studies in Paris, Stuttgart (1616) and the Low Countries. In 1618 he was in Frankfurt, where he married Maria Magdalena de Bry, the eldest of Johann Theodor de Bry's three daughters. He assisted his father-in-law at Oppenheim but appears to have returned to Basle

after the outbreak of the Thirty Years War. He succeeded his father-in-law on the latter's death in 1623 and returned to Frankfurt, where he completed in 1624 the *Collectiones peregrinationum in Indiam* . . . begun by Theodor de Bry and his sons in 1590. Besides the many hermetick engravings reproduced in this book, Merian illustrated the Bible, began in 1635 the series *Theatrum Europaeum*, and in 1642 published Martin Zeiller's *Topographia* with plates by himself and his sons Matthäus the Younger and Caspar. Among his last works was a *Dance of Death* (1649). The de Bry firm remained in Merian's family until 1726, when a great fire unfortunately destroyed it.

29 *Doctor Fludd's Answer unto M. Foster Or, the Squeesing of Parson Foster's Sponge, ordained by him for the Wiping away of the Weapon Salve* . . . London 1631, p. 21. In the passage quoted, Fludd refers to the first volume of his famous *Utriusque . . . Cosmi . . . historia*, which J.T. de Bry published in Oppenheim in 1617. See illustration on p. 14.

30 Oppenheim, conveniently close to Frankfurt, was like the other Palatinate towns a Calvinist city, hence its attraction for J.T. de Bry and Lucas Jennis. The opening of the Oppenheim branch of the de Bry firm in 1610 coincides in date with the accession of the future 'Winter King', Frederick V, as Elector Palatine.

31 Chaeremon of Alexandria (1st century AD), Stoic philosopher and grammarian, was superintendent of the portion of the Alexandrian library that was kept in the temple of Serapis, and as custodian and expounder of the sacred books (*hierogrammateus* or sacred scribe) belonged to the higher ranks of the priesthood. In AD 49 he was summoned to Rome, along with Alexander of Aegae, to become tutor to the youthful Nero. He was the author of a history of Egypt, of works on comets, Egyptian astrology and hieroglyphics, and of a grammatical treatise. Chaeremon was the chief of the party which explained the Egyptian religious system as a mere allegory of the worship of nature. His books were not intended to represent the ideas of his Egyptian contemporaries; their chief object was to give a description of the sanctity and symbolical secrets of ancient Egypt.

32 John Tzetzes (c. 1110–80), Byzantine grammarian and poet. His works include a lengthy didactic poem, *The Book of Histories*, called *Chiliades* from the arbitrary division of the work into 13 books of 1000 lines each, a great compilation of literary, historical, religious and antiquarian knowledge subsequently republished by the author in prose and verse. Among his other works are allegories on the *Iliad* and the *Odyssey* and commentaries on Hesiod and Aristophanes. Much about his own life and the circumstances of his times may be gathered from his writings, for Tzetzes was always happy to write about himself.

33 *Pretiosa margarita novella*, in *Bibliotheca chemica curiosa* . . ., Geneva 1702, pp. 42–43. See further: C. Crisciani, 'The Conception of Alchemy as Expressed in the Pretiosa Margarita Novella of Petrus Bonus of Ferrara', *Ambix*, 20 (1973), pp. 165–181.

34 *La Espositione de Geber Philosopho di misser Giovanni bracescho da Iorci novi, nella quale si dichiarano molti nobilissimi secreti della natura. Con Privilegio del Sommo Pontefice Paulo III et dello illustriss. Senato Veneto per anni diece. In Vinetia Appresso Gabriel Giolito de Ferrarii. MDXLIIII.*

35 *The Pretiosa margarita novella*, edited by Janus Lacinius Therapus, was first published by Aldus in 1546.

36 *Arcana arcanissima* was, as I long suspected, published at London in 1614 and not, as most authorities believe, at Oppenheim. Confirmation is supplied by a contemporary Frankfurt Book Fair catalogue; see p. 60.

37 See the article *Langage* in Dom Antoine Joseph Pernety, *Dictionnaire Mytho-Hermétique dans lequel on trouve les allégories fabuleuses des poètes, les métaphores, les énigmes, et les termes barbares des philosophes hermétiques expliqués, Se trouve à Paris chez Deladain l'aîné libraire rue St. Jacques, no. 240, 1787.*

38 Joseph Needham, *Science and Civilization in China*, Cambridge 1974, Vol. 5, Part 2, Section 33, p. 9.

39 Philalethes, op. cit. (note 2 above), p. 30.

40 Elias Ashmole, *Prolegomena in Theatrum Chemicum Britannicum*, London 1652.

PLATES
AND COMMENTARIES

AUTHOR'S NOTE

The full title of each illustrated book contained in the present volume will be found here along with the relevant bibliographical information. Whenever possible a brief biographical note is provided, and when available the name of the engraver.

The plates themselves are, in each case, followed by an alchemical commentary, written in the hope that my imperfect words may help to shed light on the cleverly concealed meaning of these hermetick emblems. I make no attempt to provide an answer to every question. In view of the complexity of the subject, in a context that cannot readily be understood without preparation, this would be beyond the bounds of possibility.

These commentaries are framed within the spirit of the Hermetick Tradition, and in consequence I have resisted the temptation of a so-called 'psychological' interpretation. However, I do not deny that the very universality of this symbolism might permit such an interpretation, providing one does not confuse the latter with the original intentions of the ancient alchemists. 'The key to the understanding of alchemical symbolism is natural analogy, but it is the hardest science to an unknowing man,' exclaims the anonymous author of the *Practice of Lights*. My commentaries are mere indications, seeking to guide the reader and the aspiring Son of the Art toward his or her own discoveries and consequent interpretation. My brothers in Hermes are therefore fully licensed to amend them as they please, for no 'explanation' can be more than an allusion. Each symbol contains wordless truths which through sight are sown in receptive minds, to bloom in due course as the flowers of intelligence and to ripen as the fruits of wisdom. For the true knowledge of this Secret Science is a Gift of God, which suddenly springs into consciousness from the soul pregnant with ideal Beauty.

Illustration on p. 23: 'What use are torches, light or eyeglasses, if people will not see?' Vignette from Heinrich Khunrath, *Amphitheatrum sapientiae* (see p. 29).

FRANÇOIS BEROALDE DE VERVILLE
Le Tableau des riches inventions
1600

Le Tableau des riches inventions couvertes du voile des feintes amoureuses, qui sont representees dans le Songe de Poliphile. Desvoilees des ombres du Songe, & subtilement exposees par Beroalde. A Paris. Chez Matthieu Guillemot, au Palais, en la gallerie des prisonniers. Avec privilege du Roy. 1600.

The picture of the rich inventions covered with the veil of amorous deceits, which are represented in the Dream of Poliphilus. Stripped of the shadows of the Dream, and subtly expounded by Beroalde. Paris, published by Matthieu Guillemot, at the Palace, in the Prisoners' Gallery. With Royal Privilege. 1600.

For Beroalde, see note 18, p. 21. The title-page was engraved by Thomas Le Leu, son-in-law of the painter Antoine Caron, or by Léonard Gaulthier (see below).

FRANÇOIS BEROALDE DE VERVILLE
Le Voyage des princes fortunez
1610

L'Histoire veritable ou le Voyage des princes fortunez divisee en IIII entreprises. Par Beroalde de Verville. A Paris, chez Pierre Chevalier, au mont Saint Hilaire. M.D.C.X. Avec Privilege du Roy.

The True History or the Journey of the Fortunate Princes, divided into four undertakings. By Beroalde de Verville. Paris, published by Pierre Chevalier, at Mont Saint-Hilaire. 1610. With Royal Privilege.

The engraver Léonard Gaulthier, born in Mainz in 1561, came to Paris in his youth and rapidly attained fame, working exclusively in copper, a medium he mastered with success. He became engraver to three successive kings, Henri III, Henri IV and Louis XIII, of whom he engraved numerous portraits. He is also known for portraits of Marie de Médicis and of various great lords of the kingdom. He died in Paris in 1641.

1 *Le Tableau des riches inventions*. The Eagle is a symbol of the Philosophick Mercury, the Volatile Principle linking heaven and earth. The Lion is Sulphur, the Fixed Principle. His four paws are severed to indicate the repetition of a twin operation summarized by the basic alchemical axiom *Solve et Coagula* ('Dissolve the Fixed and Coagulate the Volatile'). The first violent encounter between the same complementary antagonists is symbolized by the fight between the two Dragons (one winged and one wingless). The harmonious final outcome of their fight to the death is shown by the twining of their tails. The burning tree, a symbolic equivalent of the Phoenix, suggests the self-perpetuating nature of the alchemical Work.

The central medallion shows the action of Fire upon the seed of metals, which determines their degree of perfection. At its very centre is that certain metallic Earth which the Philosophers call 'our Stone', containing both Sulphur and Mercury. From it Philosophick Mercury is extracted, from which sprouts the Tree of Life upon which perches the Eagle – now revealed in its secondary symbolic guise as the Phoenix – holding in its claws the horn of Amalthea (the cornucopia or horn of plenty, a characteristic attribute of the Philosopher's Stone).

Always depicted as an eagle with red and gold feathers, the fabulous Phoenix, according to the tale of Herodotus (II.13), visited Heliopolis in Egypt from his home in Arabia every 500 years. He made an egg of myrrh, as large as he could; this egg he hollowed out and put his father into it, sealing it hermetically. The egg then, miraculously, had the same weight as before. As his life drew to a close, he built for himself, in Arabia, a nest to which he imparted the power of generation so that after his death a new Phoenix arose. As soon as the latter had grown, he in turn proceeded to Heliopolis and burned and buried the body of his father in the temple of Helios (Tacitus, *Annals* VI.34). Another account describes how the Phoenix, having grown to a great age, committed himself to the pyre (Lucian, *De Mort. per.* 27; Philostr. *Apollon.* III.49). Others again, state that when he died, a worm crept from his body which the heat of the Sun developed into a new Phoenix (Pliny X.4.i). Another variant of the same story, used by Hermetick Philosophers, and drawn from the *Metamorphoses* of Ovid (XV.392–407), states that after five hundred years of existence the Phoenix builds himself a pyre consisting of spices, settles upon it and dies. Out of the decomposing body he arises and, having grown anew, wraps the remains of his old body in myrrh and carries them to Heliopolis.

The patriarch holding the Moon in his teeth, with an open book in his hands and the Sun at his feet, is another symbol of Dissolution and Fixation. The flaming Dragon, above him, is the raw Matter swimming upon the waters of transformation. The tree stump is a 'dead' metallic substance which can be revivified by the dissolving waters of the Fountain of Youth (living waters extracted from the primitive Subject). The hour-glass indicates the need for both time and patience in hermetick matters. The myrtle branches growing in all directions signify that the origin, cause and end of all things is Love, of which, as the author Beroalde tells us, the myrtle is the symbol.

2 *Le Voyage des princes fortunez* is an allegorical novel 800 pages long, full of alchemical allusions. 'Steganography', writes Beroalde (f. 2), 'is the art of representing plainly [*naivement*] that which is easily conceived but which under the coarsened features of its appearance hides subjects quite other than that which seems to be presented; this is practised in painting when some landscape or harbour scene or portrait is shown which conceals within itself some other figure which can be discerned by looking from a certain viewpoint determined by the artist. This is done also in writing, when an author discourses at large on plausible subjects which enfold some other excellencies which are known only when read from the secret angle which uncovers splendours concealed from common appearance.'

On the frontispiece, the conjunction of the opposing Principles is shown as a royal embrace, ultimately resulting in the Solar Perfection of the Philosopher's Stone. The volatilization of the Fixed, in Dissolution, is represented by a mortal combat between the King and the winged Dragon. (The nudity of the King indicates the preliminary purification of the Matter). The result of the fight is Death and ensuing Putrefaction, symbolized by the Raven in the coffin. The King holding the Eagle demonstrates the Fixation of the Volatile. The naked Eve is the *Albedo*, Whiteness or First Perfection, which eventually emerges from the Night of Death.

Below, in reconquered Eden, flows the Fountain of Life.

Heinrich Khunrath
Amphitheatrum sapientiae aeternae
1602

Ampitheatrum sapientiae aeternae solius verae christiano-kabalisticum divino-magicum nec non physico-chymicum, tertriunum catholicon: instructore Henrico Khunrath Lips: theosophiae amatore fideli, et medicinae utriusque doct: Hallelu-Iah! Hallelu-Iah! Hallelu-Iah Phy diabolo! E millibus vix uni. Anno M.D.C.II. Rumpantur et ilia Momo. Cum Privilegio Caesareae Maiest: Ad decennium: A prima impressionis die.

The Amphitheatre of the eternal and sole true Wisdom, a Christian-Kabbalist, Divine-Magical, Physico-Chemical, Thrice-three-in-one Compendium, drawn up by Heinrich Khunrath of Leipzig, a true lover of theosophy and a doctor of both medicines: Hallelu-Iah! Hallelu-Iah! Hallelu-Iah Fie to the devil! For barely one in a thousand. In the year 1602. May Momus' bones be broken. With a Privilege from His Imperial Majesty for ten years from the first day of printing.

Conflicting dates in this work have led to disagreements concerning the date of the original edition and the number of plates in the later one. A careful review of the data does however yield a plausible solution.

The Privilege given by Emperor Rudolph II is dated 1 June 1598, which indicates that the manuscript of the work in its original form had been completed at that time. It was not printed until 1602, which date appears on the engraved title-page, on Khunrath's portrait and on the five large rectangular folding plates which are captioned. The same date appears at the conclusion of the whole work (p. 222): *Ex Musae nostro anno aerae Christianae 1602*.

I am, therefore, inclined to believe that these seven plates, probably executed by Jan Diricks van Campen (who signed Khunrath's portrait), are in fact the original ones, and that the four undated circular plates, designed by Khunrath and executed by Paullus van der Doort, were added in 1604. These circular plates are uncaptioned, and thus are the only ones which Khunrath mentions in his text, which is why a number of authors claim that they are the original plates. Be that as it may, Henrich Khunrath left the mortal plane behind at Dresden in 1605, and his friend Erasmus Wolfart S., 'who shared his secrets', published the first complete edition of the *Amphitheatrum sapientiae*, printed by Wilhelm Anton, at Hanover in 1609. On its last leaf appears the line *Excudebat Guilielmus Antonius MDCIX*.

Although there are numerous alleged re-editions of the book, the only one I have seen is that published at Hamburg in 1653.

Heinrich Khunrath seems to have always evoked much unfair censure: Langlet Dufresnoy in his *Histoire de la philosophie hermétique* says of him: 'by means of an affected obscurity, he aspired to present himself as a great man. It is true that too much clarity ill becomes the authors of this Science, which contrasts with all the others where one is esteemed by works which present to the mind a cloudless light.' Lynn Thorndike in his *History of Magic and Experimental Science* (vol. 7, ch. 10) deals scornfully with Khunrath and the *Amphitheatrum*, referring to its 'ranting tone' and 'religious patter'.

It is undeniably true that the text is protected from the profane by a mass of verbiage; but, once that is discounted, what remains makes sound alchemical sense. I am particularly impressed with Khunrath's pursuit of the Philosopher's Stone for the avowed end of merging with Divine Wisdom, his combined use of Kabbalah, music and alchemy and his bold interpretation of the holy scriptures. His emblems are a veritable treasure-house, and a prolonged study will constantly yield subtler levels of meaning. Their perusal with a good magnifying glass is recommended.

Nothing appears to be known of the engraver Jan Diricks van Campen. However, Hans Vredeman de Vries, who drew the circular plate of the Laboratory (subsequently engraved by Paullus van de Doort in Antwerp), was an architect and architectural painter of note. Born in Leeuwarden (1527), he studied in Amsterdam, then moved to Antwerp, Hamburg (1591), Prague and Leipzig. His ideas on perspective and architecture gained currency through his books, including *Theatrum vitae humanae* (1577). He died at Antwerp in 1604.

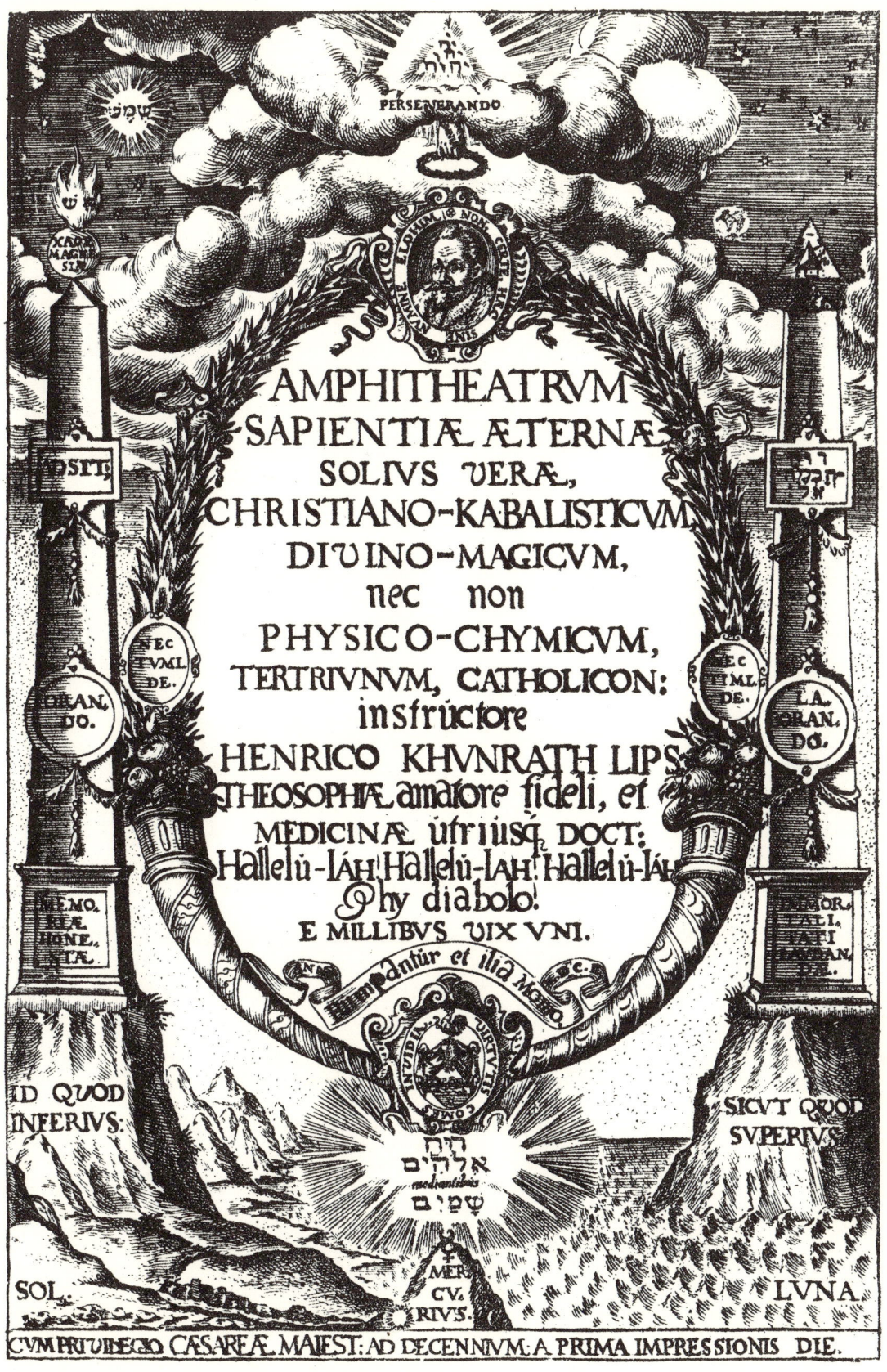

Amphitheatrum sapientiae · 33

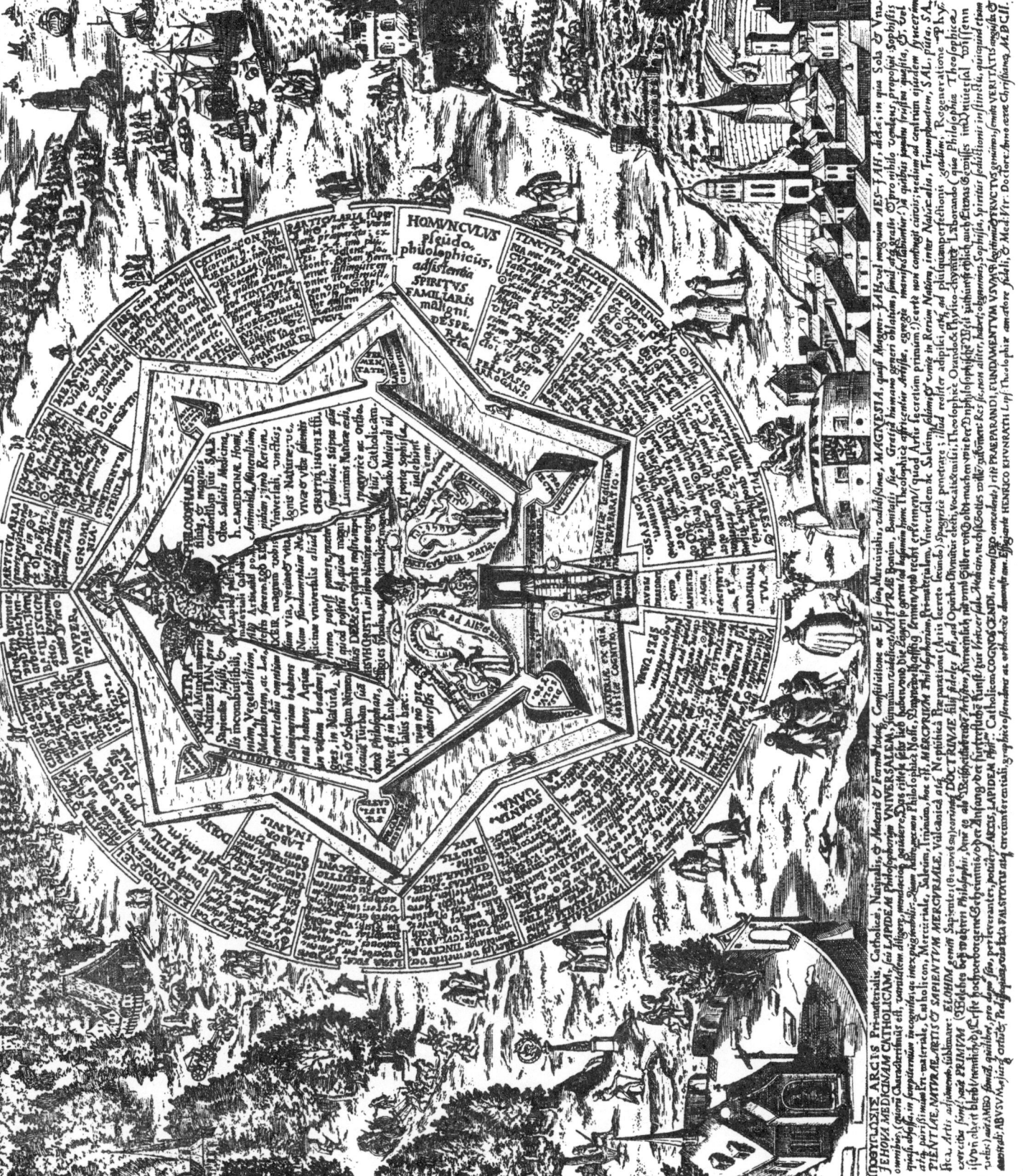

Amphitheatrum sapientiae · 35

Amphitheatrum sapientiae · 37

40 · HEINRICH KHUNRATH

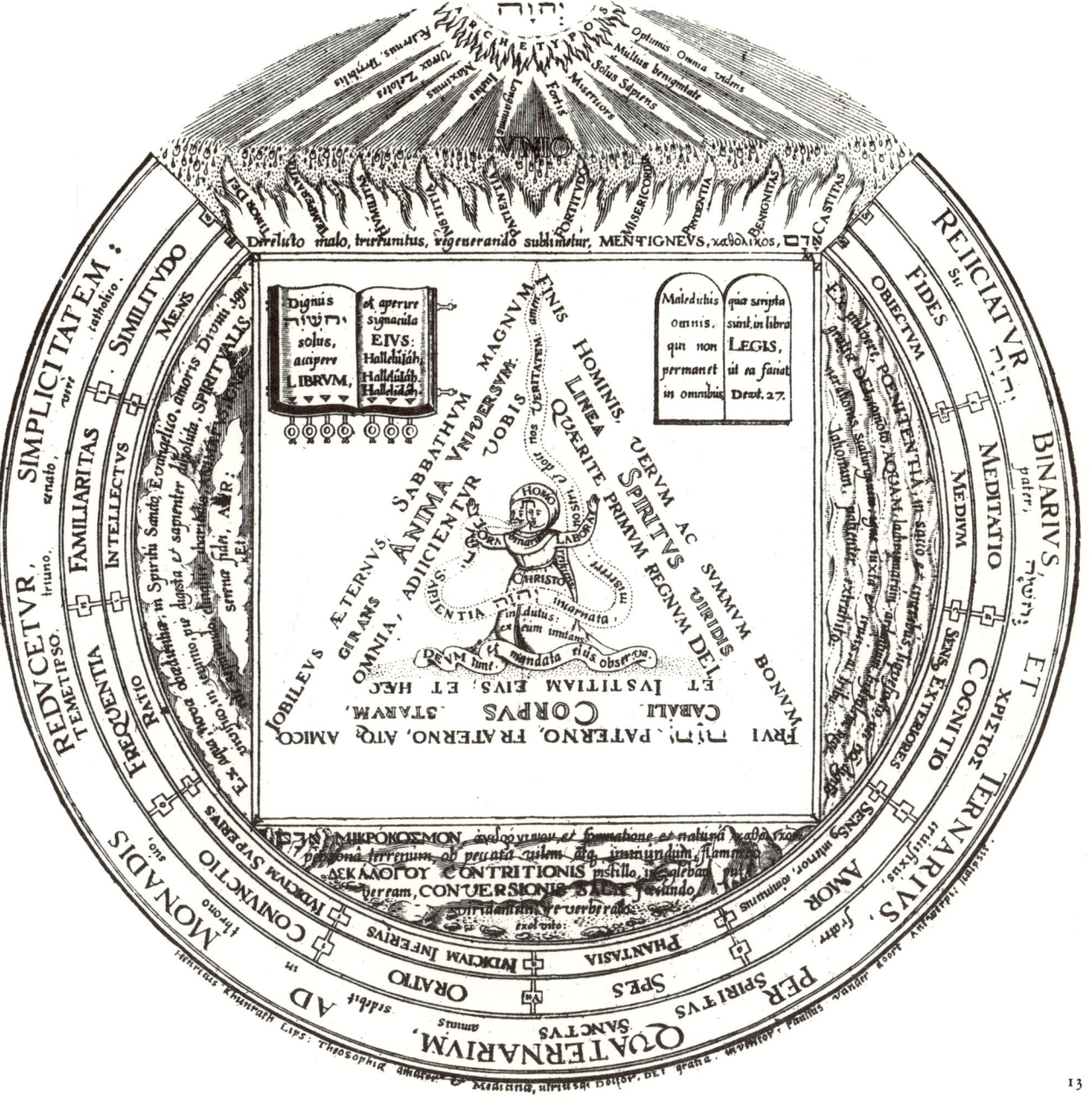

Amphitheatrum sapientiae · 41

3 The engraved title-page, with its twin pillars, alludes to many of the complementarities inherent in the Work (macrocosm and microcosm, prayer and work, Sun and Moon, Earth and Sea), and also, perhaps, to the Kabbalistic glyph known as the Tree of Life. Khunrath, crowned from on high, gives the moral: 'These things cannot be without God the Elohim.'

4 Portrait of Heinrich Khunrath in 1602 at the age of forty-two, by Jan Diricks van Campen of Magdeburg. Little is known about Khunrath's life: he was born at Leipzig in 1560 and graduated in medicine at Basle in 1588, where he defended a brilliant thesis on the theme *De Signatura Rerum*. According to Elias Ashmole, who cites Dr John Dee's diary, Khunrath was already a celebrity in 1589: 'Here that famous Hermetique Philosopher (Doctor Henric Kunrath of Hamburgh) came to visit him.' He was at the court of Emperor Rudolph II in 1598 and died at Dresden in 1605. The laurel leaf above his head encircles the inscription 'faithful son of the Doctrine'. The divine influx bears the message: 'My Grace is sufficient for thee.' The compass indicates the inscription *Deo Duce*, 'With God as Guide', and the acrostic by the unidentified M. Andr. Ruccius yields *Consilium Dei*, God's Counsel. The open book shows Psalm 71.17, 'O God, thou hast taught me from my youth: and hitherto have I declared thy wondrous works.'

5 The Art of Alchemy is divided into two equal and essential parts: manual labour, on one hand, and prayer, meditation and study on the other. Thus the word *Laboratorium* (inscribed above the mantelpiece) is composed of *labor* and *oratorium*, for the alchemist's laboratory is a place devoted both to labour and to prayer. The bases of the pillars supporting the mantelpiece bear the words *Ratio* and *Experientia*, for reason and experience precede and follow alchemical practice respectively. One may note the motto (used by Aldus) on the Distillation Furnace: *Festina lente*: Hasten slowly. Precipitateness is the devil's work, say the Wise. On the first crossbeam we read: 'Without Divine inspiration nobody is great.' Thus the Hermetick Philosopher prays before a tabernacle reminiscent of the tent of the Hebrews in the desert. Hanging in it is a framed inscription reading: 'Do not speak of God without Light.' Above is written: 'Happy is he who follows God's counsel.' Upon the table a magic book with pentacles (perhaps meant to be Senior's Tables) and a Bible. In the smoke of the incense burner are the words: 'Prayer rises like smoke, a sacrifice agreeable to God.'

At the centre of this beautifully balanced composition three musical instruments are laid on the writing-table with a hard-to-decipher inscription reading: 'Sacred music puts sadness and malevolent spirits to flight, because the spirit of Jehovah sings happily in a heart filled with holy joy.' But the entwined instruments are also the three Principles of the Great Work, the Salt, Sulphur and Mercury (of the Wise) whose harmonious combination is the reason why alchemy is often called the Art of Music. As a last reminder of the need for spiritual vigilance at all times, the inscription on the pediment, *Dormiens vigila*, enjoins the aspirant to be watchful even while sleeping.

6 The Way of the Wise, leading to the door of the Amphitheatre of Eternal Wisdom, passes through the study and contemplation of Nature in all her works. Meditation, study, prayer, and right association with friends who are able to guide one, are necessities upon this arduous journey and one must walk in accordance with the maxim: *cum Numine Lumen et in Lumine Numen*, 'the Light with God and God in the Light'.

7 Twenty-one gates seem to promise access into the heart of the hermetick citadel, wherein the principles and secrets of the true and sacred art of alchemy are kept shielded and hidden from ignorance, evil, malice, greed and stupidity.

Yet twenty of them lead only through tortuous paths to error, ruin, sorrow and despair. The only road leading toward the drawbridge is reached by elevation of the spirit toward the love of God and of Wisdom. Good works and moral rectitude are prerequisites, and the knowledge of the Subject of the Wise, of the Principles of the Art, and of the first Mercury, leads one across the drawbridge towards the final attainment.

8 The text of the Emerald Table of Hermes Trismegistus, as found in the *Poimandres*, summarizes the quintessence of alchemical thought. Quoted through the ages, the Table is here shown in Latin and German. It reads thus:

'The Words of the Secrets of Hermes.

'It is true without lie, certain and most veritable, that what is below is like what is above and what is above is like what is below, to perpetrate the miracles of one thing.

'And as all things have been and come from One by the mediation of One; thus all things have been born from this single thing by adaptation.

'The Sun is its father and the Moon its mother.

'The Wind has carried it in his belly and the Earth is its nurse. The father of all the perfection [*telesmus*] of all the world is here.

'Its force or power is entire if it is turned into earth.

'Thou shalt separate the Earth from the Fire, the subtle from the gross, softly, with great ingenuity.

'It rises from the Earth to the sky and again descends into the Earth, and receives the force of things superior and inferior.

'Thou shalt have by this means the glory of all the world. And therefore all obscurity shall flee from thee.

'And this is the strength strong of all strength. For it shall vanquish any thing subtle and anything solid penetrate.

'Thus the world was created.

'From this shall proceed admirable adaptations, of which the means is here.

'And in this connection I am called Hermes Trismegistus, having the three parts of the philosophy of all the world.

'It is finished, what I have said of the operation of the Sun.'

According to legend, the Emerald Table was discovered 'after the Flood . . . in a rocky cave' in the valley of Hebron. Fulcanelli demonstrates that the details of the alleged discovery lead to the realization that this so-called Table 'might well never have existed elsewhere than in the subtle and clever imagination of the old Masters'.

'We are told', writes Fulcanelli of the Table, 'that it is green – like spring dew, called for this reason Emerald of the Philosophers: first analogy with the saline Matter of the Wise. We are told also that it was drafted by Hermes: second analogy, since this Matter bears the name of Mercury, the Roman divinity corresponding to the Greek Hermes. Lastly, the third analogy is that, as this "green Mercury" is used for the three Works, it is called triple, whence the epithet Trismegistus (thrice greatest, great or sublime) added to the name of Hermes. The Emerald Table thus takes on the character of a discourse spoken by the Mercury of the Wise on the manner in which the Philosophick Work is elaborated. Thus it is not Hermes, the Egyptian Thoth, who speaks but the Emerald of the Wise or the Emerald Table itself.'

9 The most violent string of abuse is aimed by Khunrath at his detractors and at the learned ignoramuses who scoff at alchemy and the alchemists.

At the centre of the plate (which is the last in Khunrath's sequence) are most of the classic hieroglyphs of the Secret Art: the Green Lion, the Serpent Ouroboros which bites its own tail, the Green River proceeding from the rock struck by Moses' wand, and the Crystal of Saturn, the Universal Quintessence, which lends body to the celestial influence.

Most of the calumniators are given animal or devilish features. The first one on the left, wearing the dunce's cap, is depicted as the Egyptians (according to Horapollo) depicted Ignorance. The two Philosophers in the foreground, who defend the principles of the Hermetick Philosophy, are also symbols of the Fixation of the Volatile. The one on the left steps on the Snake's head and holds it with his tongs; his opposite number steps on the Scorpion's tail, while on both sides dead Birds plummet to the ground.

10 The door of the Amphitheatre of Eternal Wisdom, the gate to the All in All, is hidden from the profane, who are warned to remain far hence. The seven steps on the Stairway of Wisdom lead the Adept into the shining Divine Light of Revelation. Khunrath's emblems have the inestimable merit of showing that the ultimate aim of alchemy is indeed the Ultimate, wherein man transcends the limitations of mortality to 'walk into immortality' and, by becoming One with God, becomes God.

According to the caption, the only true way is narrow but sublime (*angusta sed tamen augusta*); one can accede to it 'Christian-Kabbalistically, divine-magically or physico-chemically'.

The top inscription warns the profane to stay away, the second below proclaims All in All. On the left is inscribed: 'A truly divine Mystery which shall rightly claim the love and admiration of all those who shall penetrate it.' Seven recommendations are displayed: 'I. Wash yourselves and be pure. II. Have with you the Lord who effects all things, and the other powers that serve him. III. To the First vows and prayers [should be addressed], and hymns to the inferior [powers]. IV. If the petition is first addressed to those inferior powers, it should be because of the delegation [of power] which they receive from the First [the Lord]. V. May reverence and fear of God be Angels [messengers] flying from us to the Lord and back to us. VI. That joyous obedience be toward them according to the experience received. VII. The sacred Mysteries of which you come to treat are open to the worthy and closed to the profane.'

Another inscription on the right states: 'With the help of the Lord: Rightly to will, to know, to be able, and to be.'

11 A scheme of Christian Kabbalism. The outer circle of Ten Commandments represents the Physical World of Asiyyah, the twenty-two letters of the Hebrew alphabet the Formative World of Yetsirah, the Sefirot the Spiritual World of Beriah, and the corresponding Names of God (fiery circle) the Divine World of Azilut.

The nucleus of the Divine Emanations, the En Soph, is occupied by the figure of the resurrected Christ floating above the head of the fiery Phoenix (another symbol of Resurrection and Immortality). 'En Soph! En Soph!' exclaims Khunrath, 'depth of depths, and height of heights!

Amphitheatrum sapientiae · 43

I say it without any blasphemy. The Stone of the Philosophers, servant of the Major world, represents in the Book or Mirror of Nature Jesus Christ crucified, Saviour of humankind, that is to say of the Minor World. Know naturally Christ by the Stone: Christ. I deviate not at all from the Book of the Most Holy Scripture.'

Indeed, the image of Christ with the inscription *In Hoc Signo Vinces* ('In this sign shalt thou conquer') is a hieroglyph of the Stone of the Philosophers (☿), which undergoing the action of Fire within the crucible (symbolized by the Crucifixion) becomes the Philosopher's Stone, the resurrected Saviour or the flaming Phoenix.

12 The Stone of the Philosophers, their *Materia Prima* or Subject, is also called the Chaos of the Wise (**ΧΑΟΣ**) because despite its vile and useless aspect it contains the essence and substance of the Universal First Matter in an undifferentiated state akin to that of the world prior to the Creation: 'And the earth was without form, and void; and darkness was upon the face of the deep. And the Spirit of God moved upon the face of the waters.' (Gen. 1.2.)

This Stone is called Triune, since it is one body with a spirit and soul. It contains the three Principles, ☿ Mercury, ⊖ Salt and ♃ Sulphur, which correspond to various states of fluidity or volatility: the Saline or crystalline state, the Volitile or humid state, and the Fixed or dry state, which the Matter will assume in repeated turns.

The first *modus operandi* is to dissolve and coagulate – *Solve et Coagula* – as one may read on the androgynous figure, the Rebis (from *res bina*, the double thing). The second, **ΧΑΟΣ**, occurs once one has realized a perfect Solution and 'conjoined' the opposites which initially clash violently. The Matter assumes the darkness of night and is also called the Raven. Once the Raven is slain it turns into the Peacock displaying its tail – that is the stage at which all sorts of varied colours can briefly be seen in the vessel. Then the Matter takes on the wings of the Swan, for it is whitened before being brought to the Solar Redness, and Perfect Fixity is attained when the Stone of the Philosophers has at last become the Philosopher's Stone.

13 Syzygy or conjunction of the macrocosmic Unity with the microcosmic triunity. The entire process of the elaboration of the Philosopher's Stone is symbolized here. This elaboration finds its perfect counterpart in the Creation of the World, in the formation of mankind, male and female, and in their deplorable fall from grace. It is exemplified by a most excellent and perfect Marriage, whose mysterious offspring is likened to the Divine Logos, redeemer of all humanity, conceived by the Holy Ghost in the womb of the Blessed Virgin. The Divine Stone, like Christ, is crucified, descends into hell, is resurrected and ascends gloriously into heaven with its transmuted body. Khunrath sees therein 'the infallible proof of the Last Judgment which must be a trial by fire for the living and the dead even for the whole world ... the testimony of the Resurrection of our flesh renewed and in glory, and even the truest example of the conjunction of each Soul with its own Spirit and Body indissoluble in Eternity. [The Stone] is the formula of our spiritual and corporeal Regeneration, and the most perfect and clearest mirror of the Sabbath of Sabbaths and in consequence of eternal beatitude; [it is] the Living Image of the mystery of the indivisible union of the Divine Holy Trinity.'

This most recondite of Khunrath's emblems will greatly reward the reader who takes the trouble to go beyond the mere words and to seek to elucidate its complexities further.

Andreas Libavius
Alchymia, 1606

Alchymia Andreae Libavii, recognita, emendata, et aucta, tum dogmatibus & experimentis nonnullis; tum commentario medico physico chymico: qui exornatus est variis instrumentorum chymicorum picturis; partim aliunde translatis, partim planè novis: in gratiam eorum, qui arcanorum naturalium cupidi, ea absq[ue] involucris elementarium & aenigmaticarum sordium intueri gaudent. Praemissa defensione artis: opposita censurae Parisianae: Cum Gratia & Privilegio Caesareo speciali ad decennium. Francofurti, Excudebat Joannes Saurius, impensis Petri Kopffii. Anno CIƆ. IƆ. VI.

The Alchemy of Andreas Libavius, revised, emended and augmented, with a number of new teachings and experiments and with a medical, physical and chymical commentary; which has been adorned with divers pictures of chymical instruments, in part drawn from elsewhere and in part entirely new; for the sake of those who, eager for the secrets of nature, wish to behold them free from elementary wrappings and enigmatic accretions. Prefaced by a defence of the art against Parisian censure: By Imperial Grace and Special Privilege for ten years. Frankfurt, printed by Joannes Saurius for Petrus Kopffius, 1506 [*sic*].

Andreas Libavius was born at Halle in Saxony in 1540, and graduated in medicine. In 1588 he taught at the *Gymnasium* in Rottenburg and in 1607 was headmaster of the *Gymnasium* in Coburg, where he died on 25 July 1616. An enthusiastic chemist, author of numerous works, he was no blind follower of Paracelsus and in fact carried on controversies with both Galenists and Paracelsians. Among the first to explain chemical reactions in plain language, he has been credited with writing the first real textbook. He attempted the analysis of mineral waters and described several substances which he discovered.

Georg Keller (born at Frankfurt 15 September 1568, died Frankfurt *c*. 1640), who signed the engraved title-page (dated 1605), was a painter as well as an engraver. He was the pupil of Jost Amman and of Philipp Uffenbach. He painted a notable *Coronation of the Emperor Ferdinand III* (1627) and numerous religious subjects.

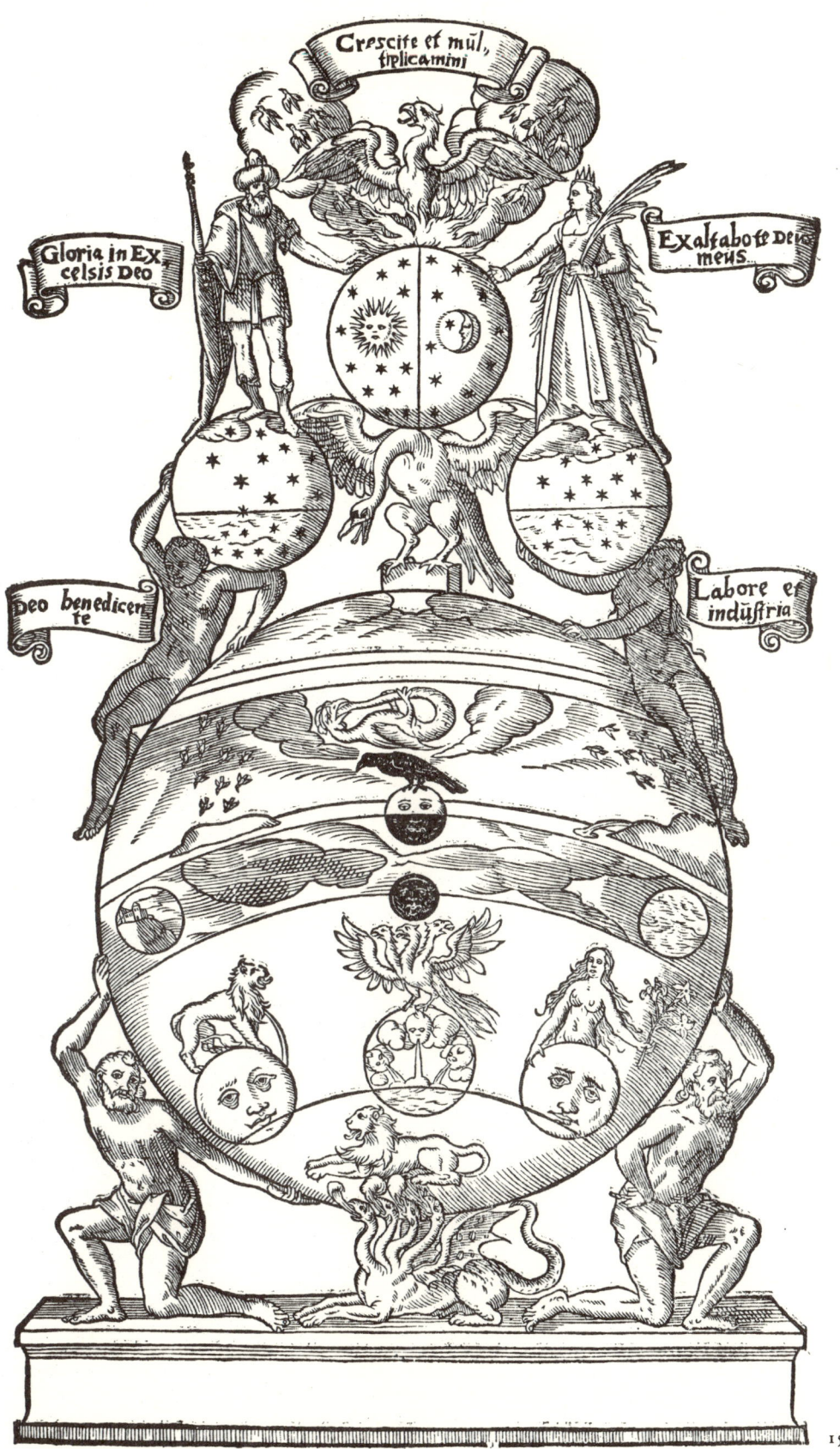

16

14 The title-page, crowned with the Tetragrammaton or Name of God, is flanked by Hippocrates and Galen (for medicine), Hermes Trismegistus and Aristotle (for alchemy). The operations depicted in the lower part of the page include hints as to the nature of one of the twin components of the Secret Fire: a winepress and an outhouse.

15 The four-headed winged Hydra is the Dragon or Subject of the Wise. Above the recumbent Lion, which stands for the Earth, are the triple-headed Eagle, for the Air; the Lion on the Moon, for Fire and Sulphur; the naked Lady with the lily, for Water, *Lac Virginis* or Mercury. Above the black Moon of Putrefaction, the half Moon and the Raven correspond to the second and third cycles of Dissolution, which is why Ouroboros eats his tail. The swooping Birds on the left signify Fixation; those soaring on the right, with water flowing from the rock, signify Solution. The Swan with outspread wings is the Philosophick Mercury; above, the King and the Queen show the union of the opposing Principles, culminating in the Multiplication or Phoenix, which is an emblem of the Philosopher's Stone.

16 Libavius ascribes this diagram to a manuscript of 1421, by Heinrich Kuhdorfer, drawn in turn from 'an ancient book of the year 1028'. Unable to draw the image in every detail, he supplies a lettered key to the items left blank – which, he says, the reader may complete as he thinks fit. As for the interpretation: 'What each and every one of these may mean, is not easy to say, as the applications are diverse, and there is diversity in the Work itself.' His key is summarized below.

  A. Fire of the Philosophers, Motor of the Work.
  B. Dragon or Subject of the Wise.
  C. Mercurial Eagle or Volatility.
  D. Raven or Putrefaction.
  E. Red Rose in silver field: Sulphur.
  F. White Rose in red field: Mercury.
  G. Lady: Mercury.
  H. Lion: Sulphur.

The King and Queen are the Principles united at their base; notice how their feet make them one.

17 A second diagram of the Philosophick Work. Here it may be useful to summarize the whole of Libavius' key.

  A. Plinth: the Earth upon which the Work is founded.
  B. Atlantes: the twin Mountains supporting the Work.
  C. Dragon, Subject of the Art, breathing the four Fires.
  D. Mercury the mediator or Salt of Harmony.
  E. Green Lion: the Dissolvent.
  F. Volatile Dragon: the Subject to be dissolved.
  G. Tricephalic Eagle: Triple Solution.
  H. Sea of the Philosophers.
  I. Celestial Influx or Wind.
  K. Blood of the Red Lion or Fixation.
  M. Mountain: first Solution, Coagulation and second Solution.
  N.N. Darkness: the Artist must cut off the Raven's Head by washing with Fire.
  O. Ablution, Silver Rain. Washing of Latona and second Solution.
  P. Clouds.
  Q. Second Coagulation: Ouroboros.
  RR. Darkness in the Second and Third Works.
  S. Pure Silver Sea: the Philosophick Mercury.
  T. Swan: Whiteness.
  V. Eclipse of the Sun.
  XX. Sunrise and Solar Eclipse. Rainbow or Peacock's Tail.
  YYY. Eclipse of the Moon. Rainbow and preparation of the White Stone.
  Z. Moon sinking into the Sea.
  b. White Queen: first stage of Fixation of the Volatile.
  a. King, in purple robe and golden crown, with the Lion of perfect fixity.
  c. Phoenix: Multiplication.

18 A. The bicorporate Lion, from whose mouth proceeds a liquid that the *Spiritus Mundi* colours green, is the first Dissolvent. This Green Lion is the result of the first Work, which consists in the union of our Subject ☿ with our Mars ♂; and so he has two bodies but one head.
  B. The Lions flanking the seven steps are the results of alternating *Solve et Coagula* operations. The steps correspond to the days of Creation, since alchemy is a microcosmic re-Creation.
  C.D. Sun and Moon, Sulphur and Mercury.
  E. From the alchemical Bath, in which recline the King (F) and the Queen (G), emerges the Single Unity of the Tree of Life, bearing the golden apples of the Hesperides, a symbol of the Philosopher's Stone.
  G. The six Stars are the Multiplication.

Alchymia · 51

Steffan Michelspacher
Cabala, 1616

Cabala, Spiegel der Kunst und Natur: in Alchymia. Was der Weisen uralte Stein, doch für ein ding sey, der, da dreyfach, und nur ein Stein ist. Welches allen mühseligen liebhabern der Kunst zu Ehren, mit hilff Gottes, so klar als ein Spiegel fürgestellt: Davon vil bisshero geschrieben, aber wenigen bekandt. Gantz offenbar mit kurtzen worten, der gantzen Warheit, durch die beyligenden Figuren, erklärt und an tag gegeben. Durch einen unbekandten, doch gewandten, wie ihm das Signet in diser ersten Figur zeugknuss gibt. Gedruckt zu Augspurg, bey David Francken, in verlegung Steffan Michelspachers auss Tyroll. 1616.

Cabala, mirror of Art and Nature: in alchemy. What the ancient Stone of the Wise is, which is threefold, and yet one Stone. Which to the honour of all laborious lovers of the Art is set forth, with God's help, as clearly as a mirror; of which much has hitherto been written, but known to very few. Quite openly in brief words of entire truth explained and brought to light through the accompanying figures, by one who is unknown but knowledgeable, as the seal in this first figure testifies. Printed at Augsburg at the press of David Francken for Steffan Michelspacher from Tyrol. 1616.

Steffan Michelspacher was a physician from Tyrol about whom little is known. In 1615 he collaborated on an anatomical work, *Pinax microcosmographicus*, with its main author, Johann Remmelin, to whom the present work is dedicated.

The plates, designed by Michelspacher, were engraved by Raphael Custos, or Custodis, the grandson of the Dutch painter Pieter Balten and the son of Dominicus Custos, who adopted the name Custos when he moved from Antwerp in 1584. Raphael was the eldest of Dominicus' three sons and his pupil. The date of his birth is uncertain, but he died in Frankfurt in 1651. Le Blanc lists some 70 portraits, views of towns and religious subjects by his hand.

A rare first edition of this book appeared in 1615; in it Michelspacher's name appeared as 'Müschelspachen'. The first of the three Latin editions appeared at Augsburg in 1654, the second in 1667 and the third in 1704. The Latin titles contain an interesting reference to the Rosicrucian fraternity which is absent from the German editions: *Rosae Crucis fraternitati dicata edita, quo hac in materia amplius nil desideretur*: 'Published [and] dedicated to the Brotherhood of the Rosy Cross; than which in this matter let no fuller statement be desired.'

I found in the Department of Manuscripts of the British Library a manuscript translating the *Cabala, Spiegel der Kunst und Natur in Alchimia* (Sloane 3676, ff. 1–36). I quote from it here, as there are hidden pearls which the reader might wish to discover.

'But these things doe only concerne the students of the true and solid Alchymy, and Spagyrick art, and those that are expert in Chymicall operations to whom even the least occult and arcana of nature will be clear by the help of the degrees or order of the scales which are often made use of in operation. As for example the figure by the number *I* doth declare the degree of calcination under which also reverberation and commendation are understood. The second figure doth shew the degree of exaltation which doth comprehend sublimation and elevation together with distillation. The third figure doth note conjunction together with putrefaction, solution, dissolution, resolution, digestion, circulation. The fourth figure doth contain multiplication under which are latent ascension, lavation, imbibition, cohobation, as also coagulation, fixation, augmentation and tincture. They who are to pass this way must ascend by these degrees, to wit, of these three glasses to make one by means of the four chiefest pillars which are Philosophy, Astronomy, Alchymy, and the Virtues; and by the alphabet of the second figure in the circumference of the circle declaring plainly and perspicuously from letter to letter the true matter of this art wherefor when ABC and the characters are in order known you will easily see what is to be seen even as in the first and third figure the foure qualities and the elements which are the hot, dry, cold, and moist which truely shew the first and last matter, by which you shall attain to all as I have briefly described them but I forbear to adde more . . . For much writing yeelds little profit seeing all the four things are sufficiently cleare (I trust) here in figures.'

54 · STEFFAN MICHELSPACHER

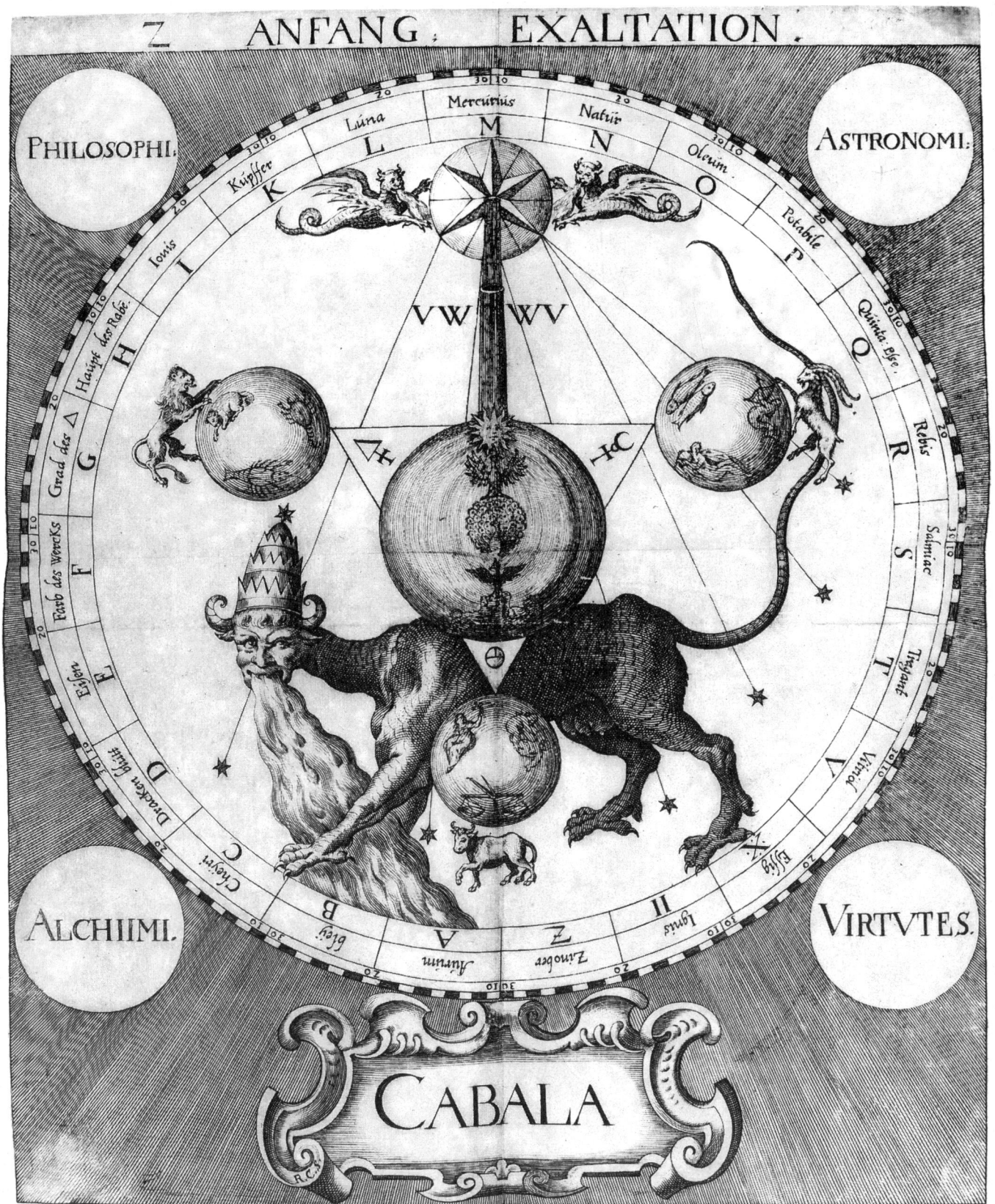

Cabala · 55

19 I. SPIGEL. The *Prima Materia*, or Subject of the Wise, is provided by nature (see the man top left), whereas the Philosopher's Stone, the *Ultima Materia*, is a production of the Art of Hermes, which helps Nature to achieve its ideal end. The volatile Eagle pertains to the first, whereas the Lion pertains to the last, that is to say to Fixity. But at the same time both animals are hieroglyphs of the first Principles initially in opposition. The coat of arms displays the alternation of the three colours: black, white and red.

The middle section contains complex diagrams. At the top of the Caduceus, between the twin heads of the Twofold or Philosophick Mercury, is the emblem of our Subject ☿ conjoined with the martial agent ♂ thus ☿. In the circle we read *VITRIOL* (the O being the circle itself and the A of *AZOT* being formed by the symbol of the Air, △).

Below we see in the laboratory the two classic methods of performing the Great Work: one alchemist is at work with distillation equipment on the Wet Way, while another handles the crucibles of the Dry Way. In the two medallions at the top is written:

> *Cabala and Alchemy*
> *Give thee the medicine most high.*
> *Also the Stone of the Wise,*
> *In which alone the foundation lies,*
> *As is plain before thine eyes*
> *Betimes in these effigies.*
>
> *O God help us to be grateful*
> *For this gift sublime and pure*
> *The man whose heart and mind Thou openest,*
> *Who is perfect herein,*
> *To prepare here this Work,*
> *To him may all strength be given.*

20 II. ANFANG. EXALTATION. This plate shows the entire process of Perfection of the Stone from the beginning (*Anfang*) to the end of the alchemical Great Work or *Magnum Opus*. The fearsome horned beast (which refers to the biblical Book of Revelation) is a hieroglyph of the *Materia Prima*, Subject of the Wise, which assumes the steganographic hieroglyph of Aries; hence the horns. The Triple Crown indicates that this very Subject, once perfected, becomes the Philosopher's Stone, which then dominates the three Realms or Kingdoms of Nature (Animal, Vegetable and Mineral). The Elaboration is shown as taking place within the Vessel or Alchemical Egg. From the destruction of two Bodies proceeds the Raven (Blackness and Putrefaction), followed by the Peacock (varied colours), the mercurial Eagle (Whiteness) and finally the Solar Perfection.

The three Principles of this Work, Sulphur ♃, Mercury ☿ and Salt 🜨, are shown in the triangle. Salt is a Dissolvent; hence it is confined within a downward-pointing triangle, symbolic of the element Water. This dissolves the Earth below, indicated by a sphere, beneath which in turn is the zodiacal Earth sign Taurus. The Dissolvent is a double Fire, hence the dual sign of Gemini; it is applied in right proportion, hence the scales of Libra. The result of this dissolution is *Lac Virginis*, the Virgin's Milk which is the Mercury of the Philosophers; hence the sign of Virgo (governed by the planet Mercury).

21 III. MITTEL: CONIUNCTION. The blindfold figure in the foreground indicates ignorance of the basic Principle, i.e. of the *Materia Prima*. His opposite number, on the other hand, who remembers the axiom: *Visita Interiora Terrae Rectificandoque Invenies Occultum Lapidem Verum Medicinalem*, 'Visit the interior of the earth and by rectifying thou shalt find the hidden true medicinal stone', ferrets out the Hare, a symbol of the sought-after First Matter, which comes running to him.

The central temple leads up seven steps (corresponding to a deliberately deceptive order of Operations) to the conjunction of the purified (hence naked) Principles of the Work, from whose union the Philosophick Mercury will be obtained. Once again the composition is extremely complex, with every detail strictly meaningful; I point out only the solar mask brandished by Venus.

22 IV ENDT. MULTIPLICATION. Mercury on top of the fountain wields, besides his Caduceus, the six-pointed Star of Harmony, indicating the type of Water here symbolized. The three Operations are represented by the three steps of the fountain; the middle one charitably indicates, by the figures of Mars and Venus, what metal and what Matter must be conjoined. The provenance of the two saline substances composing the Secret Fire is revealed. Christ is the Philosopher's Stone, flanked on either side by Luna, the Medicine of the First Degree or White Rose, and Sol, the Fixed Sulphur. Below, the seven metals or Earthly Planets (gold/Sun, silver/Moon, quicksilver/Mercury, copper/Venus, iron/Mars, tin/Jupiter and lead/Saturn) await their Perfection, which is imparted to them by the Perfection of the Work.

MICHAEL MAIER
Arcana arcanissima, 1614

Arcana arcanissima hoc est Hieroglyphica aegyptio-graeca, Vulgo necdum cognita, ad demonstrandum falsorum apud antiquos deorum, dearum, heroum, animantium & institutorum pro sacris receptorum, originem, ex uno Aegyptiorum artificio, quod aureum animi & Corporis medicamentum peregit, deductam. Unde tot poëtarum allegoriae, scriptorum narrationes fabulosae & per totam Encyclopaediam errores sparsi clarissima veritatis luce manifestantur, suaeque tribui singula restituuntur, sex libris exposita. Authore Michaele Maiero Comite Palatii Caesarei, equite exemto, Phil. & Med. Doct. &c. Caesar: Mai: quondam Aulico. Anno salutis humanae M.D.CXIIII.

The most secret secrets, that is, the Egyptian and Greek hieroglyphics, never hitherto known to the public, set forth in six books for the purpose of demonstrating that the origin of the false gods, goddesses, heroes, animals, and institutions, received as sacred by the ancients, lies in one device of the Egyptians, which accomplished the golden medicine of body and soul. Whereby all the allegories of the poets, the fabulous tales of the writers and the errors spread throughout the whole body of knowledge are brought into the clear light of truth and restored to their several tribes. By Michael Maier, Imperial Count Palatine, Free Knight of the Empire, Doctor of Philosophy and Medicine, formerly of His Imperial Majesty's Court. In the year of human salvation 1614.

Michael Maier was born at Rendsburg in 1566, the son of Johann Maier, an official of the duchy of Holstein. A relation of his mother, Severin Goebel, a well-known physician who practised in Danzig and Königsberg, encouraged him in his studies. Maier went to the University of Rostock, then on to Nuremberg and Padua with Goebel's son. By 1592 he had already come to the attention of his principal patron, Emperor Rudolph II. At the university of Frankfurt an der Oder, he held the title of *Poeta Laureatus Caesareus* and wrote elegant Latin verse which he signed 'Hermes Malavici', an anagram of his name. His love for the Hermetick Art was already deeply rooted.

Having received his doctorate in medicine at Basle, Michael Maier moved to Prague where he moved in the Emperor's intimate circle and was elevated to the rank of Imperial Count Palatine. As Maier continued to travel extensively, it is likely that he acted as an imperial secret agent of some kind.

By 1611 he had visited many German towns and had befriended among others the Landgrave Maurice of Hesse and Prince Christian I of Anhalt, both of whom shared his passion for alchemy. Both princes were also connected with the mysterious Rosicrucian Fraternity, and subsequently with the Bohemian coup d'état of 1618 and the fateful adventure of the Elector Palatine Frederick V, whose brief reign and subsequent defeat as the 'Winter King' of Bohemia (1619–20) marked the opening of the Thirty Years War between Catholics and Protestants in Germany.

After the Emperor's death in 1612, Maier appears to have taken refuge for several years in England, where he learnt the language and translated Thomas Norton's *Ordinall of Alchemy* into Latin. In London he published his first work, *Arcana arcanissima*, and he probably wrote several other works there as well. In 1616 he returned to Germany, where the cycle of his many works published by the de Bry family and by Lucas Jennis begins.

The *Arcana arcanissima* is a work of special importance, not only because it was the first of Michael Maier's books to be published, but also because it presented at length for the first time the hermetick interpretation of Greek and Egyptian myths. No place of publication is given, and it was generally believed that this work was published at Oppenheim by J. Theodor de Bry. I was inclined to suppose, on the contrary, that it was printed in England, since I could not believe that the firm of de Bry would have produced so crude a publication. Patient research at long last elicited the evidence that had eluded others: in the catalogue of the Frankfurt Book Fair for 1614 (*Catalogus universalis pro Nundinis Francofurtensibus vernalibus de anno M.D.C.XIV*), under the heading *Libri historici, politici & geographici*, there is the following entry: *Arcana arcanissima . . . Michaele Maiero Med.D. Londini in 4.*

Michael Maier

Lusus serius, 1616

Lusus serius, quo Hermes sive Mercurius rex mundanorum omnium sub homine existentium, post longam disceptationem in concilio octovirali habitam, homine rationali arbitro, judicatus & constitutus est. Authore Michaele Maiero Com. pal. Med. D. Horat. Omne tulit punctum, qui miscuit utile dulci. Oppenheimii ex chalcographia Hieronymi Galleri sumptibus Lucae Jennis Bibliop. 1616.

The serious game, in which Hermes or Mercury, after a long debate in the Council of Eight, with rational Man as judge, was deemed and constituted king of all existing earthly things inferior to Man. By Michael Maier, Count Palatine, Doctor of Medicine. Horace: 'He who combined the useful with the pleasurable earned all the applause.' Oppenheim, printed at the copperplate press of Hieronymus Galler for Lucas Jennis, bookseller, 1616.

Maier's dedication is of interest: *Clarissimis politissimis excellentissimisque viris D.N. Francisco Antonio Londin. Anglo, Seniori, D.N. Jacobo Mosano Illustriss. Mauritii Hassiae Landgravii Archiatro digniori, D.N. Christiano Rumphio Electorali Palatino ad Rhenum Med. ordinario circumspecto . . . Valete, dabam Francofurti ad Moenium ipso ex Anglia reditu, Pragam abituriens,*

Anno 1616 mense Septembri. He salutes his three dedicatees – Francis Anthony of London, Jacob Mosanus, physician to the Landgrave of Hesse, and Christian Rumpf, physician to the Elector Palatine – from 'Frankfurt, by the city wall, on my return from England and about to leave for Prague, September 1616'. The Elector Palatine had married Elizabeth, daughter of King James VI and I, in London in 1613, and was elected king of an insurgent Protestant Bohemia in Prague in August 1619.

MICHAEL MAIER

Examen fucorum, 1617

Examen fucorum pseudo-chymicorum detectorum et in gratiam veritatis amantium succincte refutatorum, authore Michaele Maiero, Com. Pal. Eq. Ex. Med. D. Francofurti typis Nicolai Hoffmanni, sumptibus Theodori de Brij, Anno M. CDXVII [sic].

The swarm of drones: the false alchemists detected and succinctly refuted for the sake of lovers of truth, by Michael Maier, Count Palatine, Free Knight of the Empire, Doctor of Medicine. Frankfurt, printed by Nicholas Hoffmann for Theodor de Bry, 1617.

The engraving is by Johann Theodor de Bry. The dedication (dated Frankfurt, September 1616) is to Joachim Hirschberger, Doctor of Medicine, who is described as 'a most diligent chemical student and the author's particular friend'.

MICHAEL MAIER

Jocus severus, 1617

Jocus severus, hoc est, Tribunal aequum, quo noctua regina avium, phoenice arbitro post varias disceptationes et querelas volucrum eam infestantium pronunciatur, & ob sapientiam singularem, Palladi sacrata agnoscitur; authore Michaele Maiero Com. Pal. M.D. Francofurti, typis Nicolai Hoffmanni, sumptibus Theodori de Brij, Anno MDCXVII.

The earnest game, that is the just tribunal whereby the Bird of Night is pronounced queen of the birds, the Phoenix being judge, after sundry arguments and objections from the birds attacking her, and on account of her unmatched wisdom is acknowledged to be sacred to Pallas. By Michael Maier, Count Palatine, Doctor of Medicine. Frankfurt, printed by Nicholas Hoffmann for Theodor de Bry, 1617.

The dedication reads as follows: *Omnibus verae chymiae amantibus, per Germaniam notis et ignotis, et inter hos, Nisi nos Fama fallat, adhuc delitescenti, at FAMA FRATERNITATIS & CONFESSIONE SUA admiranda & probabili in genere manifestato, ascribo, dico & dedico*: 'To all lovers of true chymistry in Germany, known and unknown; and among these, if Fame deceive us not, to one who remains concealed at present but who, by the *Fame of the Brotherhood* and by his admirable and pleasing *Confession*, has manifested himself in this connection, I address, indite and dedicate.'

The works referred to in the title are, of course, the famous Rosicrucian manifestos, the *Fama Fraternitatis* and the *Confessio*, both believed to have been penned by the theologian Johann Valentin Andreae (1586–1654). These manifestos were widely circulated in manuscript form (as early as 1610 in the case of the *Fama*) before being first published by Wilhelm Wessel of Kassel in 1614 and 1615 respectively. The works in question claimed to emanate from a mysterious fraternity of invisible, all-seeing, all-knowing, all-powerful beings calling on all learned men of good will to overthrow the tyranny of ignorance in general, of the Pope in the West and of Mahomet in the East. The movement sought to replace the Catholic Habsburg hegemony by a chosen saviour of the Reformed Faith, who — it was probably hoped — would have been the Elector Palatine, Frederick V.

Michael Maier was one of the staunchest supporters of the Rosicrucian movement. In 1611 he travelled through Germany meeting the Landgraves Maurice of Hesse and Christian of Anhalt, both alchemists, and both sympathetic to the Rosicrucians' political and mystical aims. In a stay of two years in England, 1612–14, Maier seems to have rallied many people to the cause, including Robert Fludd. In 1617 he published his *Silentium post clamores* . . ., an apologetic treatise in which are explained not only the causes of the revelations of the German Rosicrucian Brotherhood but also the reasons for its subsequent silence or 'failure to respond to the wishes of everyone', together with a 'refutation of the evil-minded'. The following year he published his *Themis aurea, hoc est de legibus Fraternitatis R.C.*, which set forth the laws of the mysterious Brotherhood.

For further information I refer the reader to Frances A. Yates' fascinating, if tentative, book, *The Rosicrucian Enlightenment*.

The dedication is dated from Frankfurt, 'by the city wall', on the way from England to Bohemia (*transitu ex Anglia in Bohemiam*), which means that this work was readied for printing at the same time as the *Lusus serius* which Jennis published a few months ahead of it. The engraving is by J.T. de Bry.

LVSVS SERIVS,
QUO
HERMES sive MERCVRIVS
REX
MUNDANORUM OMNIUM
SUB HOMINE EXISTENTIUM,
post longam disceptationem in Concilio Octovirali
habitam, homine rationali arbitro, judicatus
& constitutus est.
AVTHORE
MICHAELE MAJERO Com. Pal. Med. D.
HORAT.
Omne tulit punctum, qui miscuit utile dulci.

OPPENHEIMII
Ex Chalcographia HIERONYMI GALLERI;
Sumptibus LUCÆ JENNIS *Bibliop.* 1616.

EXAMEN FVCORVM PSEVDO-CHYMICO-RVM DETECTORVM

ET

IN GRATIAM VERITATIS AMAN-
tium succincte refutatorum,

AVTHORE

MICHAELE MAIERO,

Com. Pal. Eq. Ex. Med. D.

FRANCOFVRTI

Typis Nicolai Hoffmanni, sumptibus Theodori de Brij,
Anno M.CDXVII.

JOCVS SEVERVS,
HOC EST,
TRIBVNAL ÆQVVM,
QVO
NOCTVA REGINA AVIVM,
PHOENICE ARBITRO
POST
VARIAS DISCEPTATIONES ET QVErelas Volucrum eam infestantium pronunciatur, & ob sapientiam singularem, Palladi sacrata agnoscitur:
AVTHORE
MICHAELE MAIERO COM. PAL. M. D.

FRANCOFVRTI
Typis Nicolai Hoffmanni, sumptibus Theodori de Brij,
Anno M.DCXVII.

23 *Arcana arcanissima*. Osiris and Isis are the opposite Principles, Sulphur and Mercury, while Typhon, an anagram of Python, is the Chaos or *Materia Prima*. Awoken from his sleep by the sharp bite of the double-headed serpent Amphisbaena, Dionysus kills it with the vine-branch growing at his side. The incisive action of the Secret Fire spurs the potential power of Sulphur within the Mercury of the Wise. When Sulphur attains perfect Fixity, he has killed the Volatile Mercury. A by-product of the grape is, one may note, one of the saline components of the Secret Fire. Hercules (i.e. the alchemist) pursues the iron-hoofed, golden-horned Hind. The Hind is the White Stone — iron-hoofed because of the part played at the beginning of the Work by the martial agent, and golden-horned because the White Stone needs but one further elaboration to reach the golden Perfection of the Philosopher's Stone — symbolized here by the golden apples of the Hesperides (see the title page of *Atalanta fugiens*, p. 69). The Ibis, an aquatic bird revered by the Egyptians, is a great destroyer of snakes and the symbol of dissolution. Apis, the Black Ox sacred to the Sun God, had a lunar crescent on his robe. He was ritually drowned after forty days. Thus the Compost in the alchemist's vessel dissolves into darkness and putrefies for a similar period before yielding the 'promise of Dawn' expressed by the lunar crescent: that is to say by the seed or essence of Sulphur, promising the Ultimate Fixity of the Philosopher's Stone. Revered as a symbol of Osiris, the *Cynocephalus* or Baboon is a hieroglyph of maleness and Fixity.

24 *Lusus serius*. After a heated debate, in the Great Amphitheatre of the World, as to who was to be acknowledged as sovereign, it was eventually agreed that representatives should be elected from all parts of nature — two from the quadrupeds, and one each from the birds, fish, insects, creeping things, plants and minerals — and sent to be judged by Man. At length the eight representatives foregathered: a cow, a sheep, a goose, an oyster, a bee, a silkworm, the flax plant, and lastly Mercury. Each in turn harangued the judge, and Mercury, having given the lengthiest account of his own usefulness, was at length awarded the golden crown. 'Thou', said the judge to Mercury, 'so much exceedest thy competitors as the Sun the Planets; thou art the miracle, splendour, and light of the world.'

25 *Examen fucorum*. False alchemists, carrying symbols of their useless knowledge, approach the practising Philosopher, with whom rests Wisdom in the shape of the owl (Pallas Athena's bird). Maier likens their activities to those of drones in beehives. Lazy and greedy, the drones are like the pseudo-chymist, 'pretending but useless bees'.

26 *Jocus severus*. The assembly of the birds, convened to determine the most meritorious among them, includes the owl, the crow, the goose, the crane, the raven, the nightingale, the jackdaw, the heron, the swallow, the sparrowhawk, the cuckoo, the magpie, the jay and the parrot. Presided over by the Phoenix, the assembly eventually awards the crown of Wisdom to the owl.

Michael Maier
Atalanta fugiens, 1618

Atalanta fugiens, hoc est, Emblemata nova de secretis naturae chymica, accommodata partim oculis & intellectui, figuris cupro incisis, adjectisque sententiis, epigrammatis & notis, partim auribus & recreationi animi plus minus 50 fugis musicalibus trium vocum, quarum duae ad unam simplicem melodiam distichis canendis peraptam, correspondeant, non absque singulari jucunditate videnda, legenda, meditanda, intelligenda, dijudicanda, canenda & audienda: Authore Michaele Maiero Imperial. Consistorii Comite, Med. D. Eq. ex. &c. Oppenheimii ex typographia Hieronymi Galleri, sumptibus Joh. Theodori de Bry, MDCXVIII.

Atalanta fleeing: that is, new chymical emblems of the secrets of nature; fitted partly to eyes and intellect, with figures engraved in copper and additional maxims, epigrams and notes, and partly to the ears and the recreation of the soul, with some fifty musical fugues in three parts, of which two are to correspond to one simple melody suitable for singing in couplets; the whole to be seen, read, meditated, understood, judged, sung and heard with extraordinary pleasure. By Michael Maier, Count of the Imperial Consistory, Doctor of Medicine, Free Knight of the Empire, &c. Oppenheim, printed by Hieronymus Galler for Johann Theodor de Bry, 1618.

The dedication, which is to Christoph Reinhart of Mühlhausen in Imperial Thuringia, Doctor of Laws and Senator, is dated Frankfurt, August 1617. The work was first published later that year; its success inspired a reissue in 1618 with the addition of the author's portrait on p. 11, and this has led us to use a copy of this second printing for reproduction. There was a subsequent edition in 1687 under the title *Secretioris Naturae secretorum scrutinium chymicum*, which omitted the music, and this was translated into German in 1708. The plates were definitely engraved by Johann Theodor de Bry and not, as has been erroneously suggested in recent years, by Matthäus Merian.

President Jean d'Espagnet, another famous alchemist, praised the emblems of *Atalanta fugiens* 'because they depict with sufficient clarity for clairvoyant eyes what is most secret and hidden in the Great Work'.

TRES SCHOLA, TRES COESAR TITVLOS DE:
DIT; HÆC MIHI RESTANT,
POSSE BENE IN CHRISTO VIVERE, POSSE MORI.
MICHAEL MAIERVS COMES IMPERIALIS CON:
SISTORII etc. PHILOSOPH: ET MEDICINARVM
DOCTOR, P. C. C. NOBIL: EXEMPTVS FOR: OLIM
MEDICVS CÆS. etc.

29

30

Atalanta fugiens · 71

31

32

33

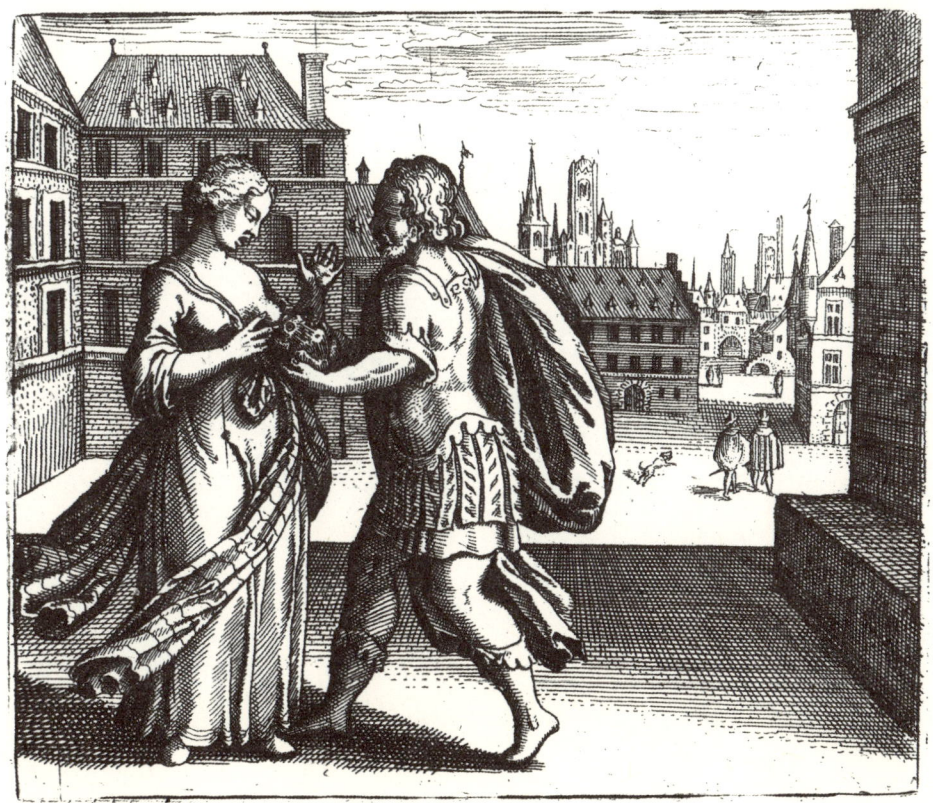

34

35

36

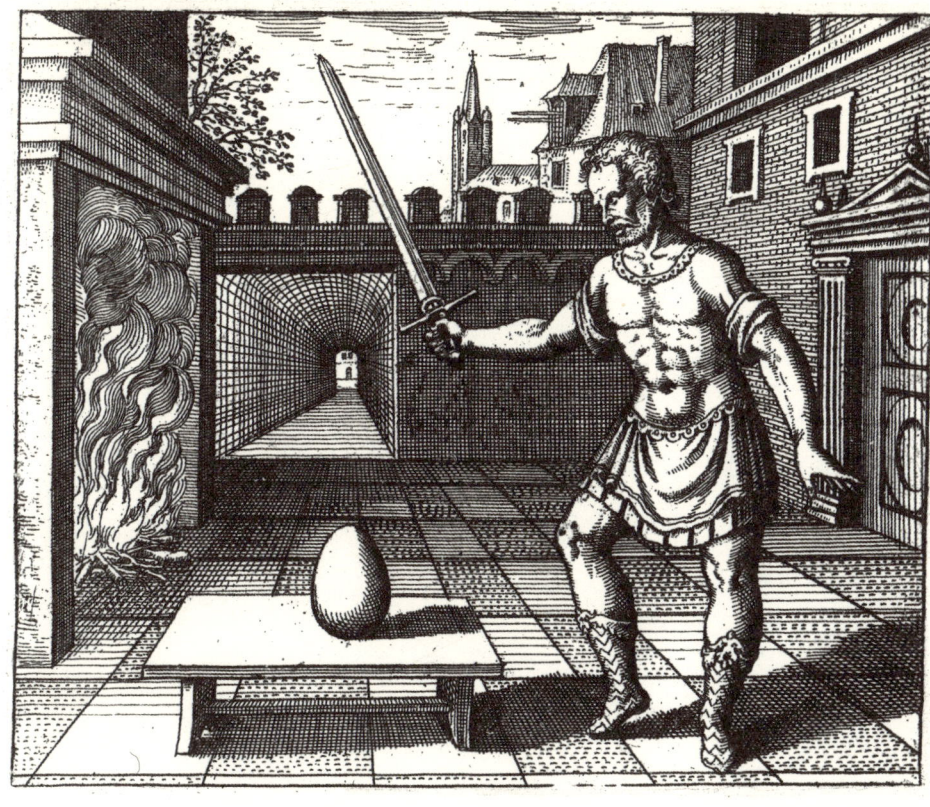

37

38

Atalanta fugiens · 75

39

40

41

42

Atalanta fugiens · 77

43

44

45

46

Atalanta fugiens · 79

47

48

49

50

51

52

82 · MICHAEL MAIER

53

54

Atalanta fugiens · 83

55

56

84 · MICHAEL MAIER

57

58

59

60

61

62

Atalanta fugiens · 87

63

64

65

66

Atalanta fugiens · 89

67

68

90 · MICHAEL MAIER

69

70

Atalanta fugiens · 91

71

72

92 · MICHAEL MAIER

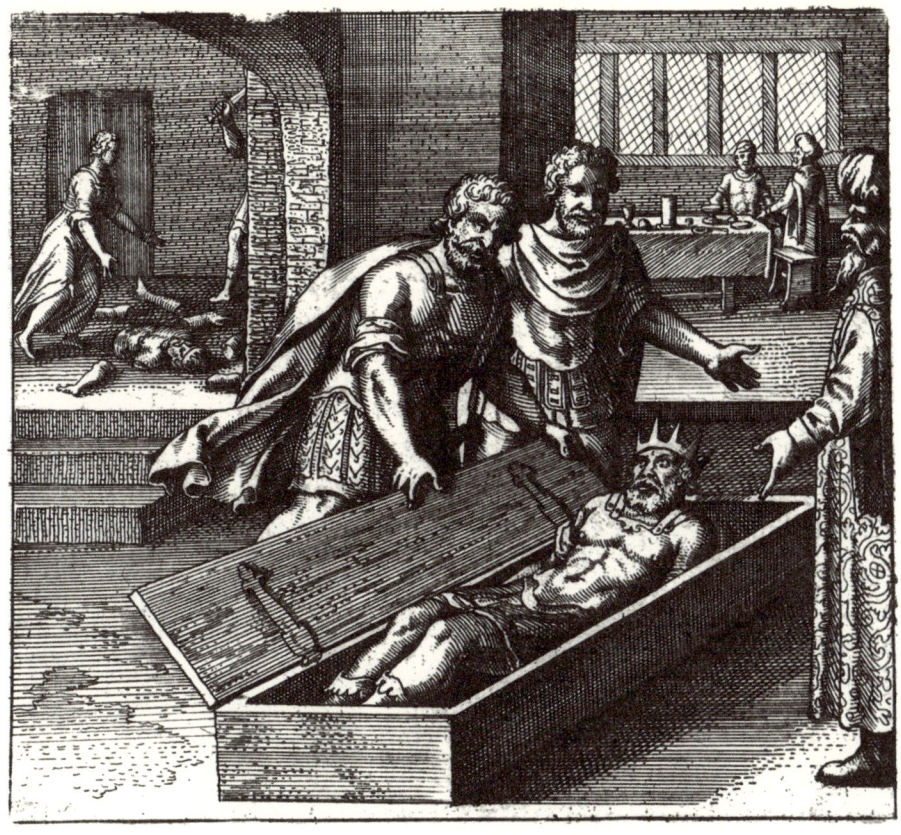

Atalanta fugiens · 93

75

76

79

27 The enigmatic Hesperides, Aegle, Hespertusa and Arethusa (to whom a fourth is sometimes added: Erytheis), were, according to one tradition, the daughters of Zeus and Themis. Their Garden lay, significantly, beyond the Red Sea (with its purple sands and glittering waters wherein Helios the sun god bathes), beyond the western confines of the world, hidden by golden clouds. The way thither was a secret impossible to discover without Divine guidance. Hercules had to wrestle with the Old Man of the Sea, the Triton Nereus, before the way was revealed. Within the Garden grew a tree bearing golden apples, a wedding gift from the Earth to Hera, the Queen of the Gods, and guarded by an unwinking dragon. Hercules killed the guardian and won the apples which, according to an important esoteric tradition, were given to Venus.

The tale of Atalanta is told by Venus to Adonis (Ovid, *Metamorphoses*, x.560). Atalanta, whose beauty was matched by her fleetness of foot, had been warned to resist all suitors lest she should lose her own nature. She warned her suitors they would have to win a race against her or be killed. Young Hippomenes, great-grandson of Neptune, obtained from Venus three golden apples which she instructed him to throw at crucial moments in the race. Each time Atalanta was about to catch him he dropped an apple, and she stopped to pick it up; thus he won the race. Hippomenes savoured his triumph — then, seized with desire for Atalanta, he entered a temple and yielded to its prompting therein. The offended Mother of the Gods then turned them both into lions.

The tale, in alchemical terms, illustrates the rivalry of Male and Female, Sulphur and Mercury, the initial domination of the Female, the victory of the Male, and the conversion of both principles into Fixity (the Red Lions). The vivacity of the Mercury of the Wise is therefore fixed by the action of its own Sulphur, which is of the same nature and of the same origin (both Atalanta and Hippomenes were of royal and divine ancestry).

28 Portrait of the Adept in 1617, at the age of forty-nine. 'Three titles I have from Caesar, three from the School. These things remain to me: that I can live well and that I can die well in Christ.'

29, 30 Emblema I. *Portavit eum ventus in ventre suo.* 'The wind has carried it in his belly.' This first emblem of *Atalanta fugiens* illustrates one of the famous sentences of Hermes in the Emerald Table. The infant, the future Philosopher's Stone, is Sulphur — Fire or Spirit — carried by Mercury (first of the twin Principles of the Work) in its volatile form, therefore 'in the belly of the wind'.

Each of Maier's fifty devices is accompanied, as shown here, by a bilingual epigram and a fugue (*fugire*, to flee), and followed by a prose discourse.

31 Emblema II. *Nutrix ejus terra est.* 'The Earth is its nurse.' This emblem again alludes to the Emerald Table. In the discourse, the words CUR VERO TERRA ('Why indeed the Earth?') are written in capital letters, suggesting the reading *Cor verum terra* ('The Earth is the true heart'). Indeed, the Philosophick Earth is the Matter (*mater* or mother) of the Work, whose milk, the *Lac Virginis* (Milk of the Virgin), feeds the infant Sulphur.

32 Emblema III. *Vade ad mulierem lavantem pannos, tu fac similiter.* 'Go to the woman washing sheets, do thou likewise.' This injunction means that the Subject of the Wise must be 'laundered' (purified) by a fiery laundry. Indeed, the Philosophers stress that their Fire is a water (that does not wet the hands) and that their Water is a fire (burning without flames). This Secret Fire is essential to penetrate and wash the darkness from the Philosophick Body.

33 Emblema IV. *Conjuge fratrem cum sorore et propina illis poculum amoris.* 'Unite the brother with the sister and offer them the cup of love.' The necessity of incest, stressed throughout alchemical literature, serves the purpose of highlighting the close kinship of the two opposite but complementary Natures. The Brother is ardent, dry and 'choleric'. The Sister, cold and moist, contains much 'phlegmatic' matter. Their tumultuous union must however be at once stimulated and 'tempered' by means of a love philtre proffered by the third figure in the picture, who incarnates the Secret Fire, the saline mediator or Salt of Harmony.

34 Emblema V. *Appone mulieri super mammas bufonem, ut ablactet eum & moriatur mulier, fitque bufo grossus de lacte.* 'Place upon the woman's breasts a toad, so that she may feed it and die, and the toad grows fat with milk.' (This in the order of operations should precede rather than follow Emblema IV.) In the First Work, this sinister injunction, here illustrated, translates as the feeding of the Sulphur (the Toad-Child) of the Philosophers with the milk (Mercury) of the Matter or Subject. The death of the woman, corresponding to the important axiom 'Kill the living to revive the dead', signifies that the initial Matter dies in the Dissolution that produces the Milk (Mercury) upon which feeds the embryonic Sulphur — hitherto described as dead because initially it (Sulphur) was but a latent potentiality within the grave of Matter.

35 Emblema VI. *Seminate aurum vestrum in terram albam foliatam.* 'Sow your gold in the white foliated earth.' Alchemy (often called 'Celestial Agriculture') borrows numerous analogies from farming. Below the present image the epigram (drawn from *Rosarium philosophicum*, Frankfurt 1550) stresses the need to observe 'as in a mirror' the lesson of the grain of wheat, which teaches how the Gold of the Wise is sown in the white foliated Earth. Reference is made in Maier's discourse to the excellent treatise (*Secretum*) published in Leyden in 1599 by Jodocus Greverus, who compared the operations of wheat farming in detail to the operations of the alchemical Work.

As a seed is needed to obtain wheat (*nisi granum frumenti*), so is it necessary to obtain the metallic Seed to multiply the metal. The Seed, which every natural product contains, is obtained by the entire decomposition of the substance. But any seed needs the right soil, and the Artist will have to prepare the required Earth, which work will (in comparison to the actual sowing) take considerably more time.

36 Emblema VII. *Fit pullus à nido volans, qui iterùm cadit in nidum.* 'There appears a fledgling flying from the nest, which falls into the nest again.' Maier says: 'If you join the head of one to the body of the other, it will not be a futile work.' The Eaglet (the Volatile Principle) attempts to take wing, from the eyrie 'hollowed in the rock'. His unfledged sibling (the Fixed) holds him back, and thus the Volatile falls back into the nest. To 'join the head of one to the body of the other' is to make the Fixed volatile and the Volatile fixed.

37 Emblema VIII. *Accipe ovum & igneo percute gladio.* 'Take the egg and strike it with a fiery sword.' The egg is the Subject of the Art, which must be struck by the martial igneous agent wielding the 'double-edged sword' of the Secret Fire. Mars thus comes to the help of Vulcan, and from the ensuing darkness of Putrefaction (*Nigredo*) the hermetick chick will hatch. Raymond Lull, quoted here by Maier, stresses in several places that the fiery sword is a sharp lance, because Fire, like a lance, pierces bodies, rendering them porous and permeable, so that Water may penetrate them and turn their hardness into softness.

38 Emblema IX. *Arborem cum sene conclude in rorida domo, & comedens de fructu ejus fiet juvenis.* 'Enclose the old man and the tree in a house of dew, and eating of its fruit he will be made young.' A double allusion is made here: the first is to the rejuvenating power of the Panacea or universal medicine (one of the degrees of perfection of the Philosopher's Stone); the second is to the Work itself. The Subject of the Art (the old man) is placed in the alchemical vessel and made to 'sweat' the corrupting superfluous humidity which subli- mates and rises to the top of the vessel, then falls like dew upon the desiccated Matter (at the bottom of the vessel) which drinks it avidly.

39 Emblema X. *Da ignem igni Mercurium Mercurio & sufficit tibi.* Give fire to fire, Mercury to Mercury, and it suffices thee.' This is based upon the alchemical axiom attributed to Democritus (see Berthelot, *Collection des anciens alchimistes grecs*, I, 43). Nature rejoices in nature; but, Maier warns, the Philosophers consider several Fires and several Mercuries. The external Fire (kindled by any combustible substance) must be applied in the proper degree to excite the inner (or secret) Fire hidden within the Subject. Similarly, Mercury (the primordial Principle of the Work) transmits its own vitality to Sulphur, giving its own life in the process. Philosophick Sulphur is then united, in the correct proportions, to the same living Mercury; and the product of that operation is Philosophick Mercury.

40 Emblema XI. *Dealbate Latonam & rumpite libros.* 'Whiten Latona and tear up the books.' This axiom is attributed to Morienus — who quotes in turn a Hebrew source. The discovery of Latona's identity as mother of Diana and Apollo — who are Sun and Moon, but also the Mercury and Sulphur of the Philosophers — corresponds to the discovery of the identity of the Subject of the Wise or *Materia Prima*. The injunction to whiten or purify this Subject encompasses the whole Work; while the destruction of the books means that the way to do so is by Dissolution. Violence of any kind, in alchemy, means the alchemical application of Fire. The leaves of the books are a further indication of the nature of the Subject or Matter. The ancient Sages called it *Liber*, a book, because its crystalline, laminated or foliated texture is formed of superimposed leaves, like the pages in a book.

41 Emblema XII. *Lapis, quem Saturnus, pro Jove filio devoratum, evomuit, pro monumento in Helicone mortalibus est positus.* 'The Stone that Saturn devoured instead of Jupiter his son, and vomited up, was placed upon Mount Helicon as a monument for mortals.' The Saturn of the Wise is the Stone of the Philosophers, which has a dark colour, and to which the biblical 'I am black, but comely' (*Nigra sum sed formosa*) applies fully. Further, Saturn is also the *Nigredo*, i.e. the Blackness of Putrefaction which is the first important sign of success. It vomits the stone (which Saturn was deceived into swallowing in place of the infant Jupiter) because the first colour to follow Blackness is the grey of Dawn — the colour of Jupiter. So in the order of operations it is said that Saturn begets Jupiter, who in turn begets Diana (Whiteness) and Apollo (Perfect Redness) upon Latona.

The reader has here an example of how a symbol can change its meaning by a shift of application to another phase of the Work.

42 Emblema XIII. *Aes Philosophorum hydropicum est & vult lavari septies in fluvio, ut Naaman leprosus in Jordane.* 'The Ore of the Philosophers is dropsical and needs to be washed seven times in the river, like the leper Naaman in the Jordan.' The dropsy of 'our Stone' is the superfluous humidity which adheres to its Mercury. Such a problem has but one alchemical remedy: to dissolve and sublimate the Subject seven times over, so that in the waters of the Dissolution the dropsy may be drawn and sublimated, to return as beneficent dew. Maier prescribes great care in order to avoid either an over-desiccation, which will burn the Body, or the further dropsy which results from the use of too much water.

43 Emblema XIV. *Hic est Draco caudam suam devorans.* 'Here is the Dragon that devours his own tail.' This Dragon, Ouroboros, is perhaps the oldest hermetick hieroglyph, symbolizing the Unity of Matter and the Subject of the Wise; or more precisely the Mercury of the Wise, in which, assert the Philosophers, everything is found: 'From the One to the One by the One.'

44 Emblema XV. *Opus figoli consistens in sicco & humido, te doceat.* 'Let the work of the potter, which consists in [combining] dry and wet, teach thee.' Another favourite analogy to the work of the Hermetick Artist is that of the potter. As he combines Water and Earth, Air and Fire, so in both Works there is great affinity between the wet and the dry, or Water and Earth (Mercury and Sulphur).

45 Emblema XVI. *Hic leo, quas plumas non habet, alter habet.* 'This Lion has no feathers, the other has.' The fixed Sulphur seeks to prevent the flight of its volatile counterpart. This picture is, in a sense, a variant of Emblema VII. The Lioness is shown as winged, because the first Mercury (the initial Dissolvent) communicates to Sulphur a volatile quality (during the Reincrudation and Decomposition of the metal) without which their union would not be possible.

46 Emblema XVII. *Orbita quadruplex hoc regit ignis opus.* 'The fourfold sphere rules this Work of Fire.' Here are shown the relations of the four Fires of the Work, which, says the epigram, 'like a chain should guide thy hand'. The first is the Elemental Fire which provides heat and the first motion; the second and the third are the composite principles of the Secret Fire excited into a reaction by the heat of the first. The fourth – belonging to the sphere of Apollo – consists of the electromagnetic dynamism whose indispensable action upon the whole Work sets alchemy apart from chemistry. In the foreground, on the left, the old outhouse privy building constitutes a clue as to the nature of one of the components of the Secret Fire. The presence of water in the picture further indicates that the 'Fires' of the Philosophers are, as Maier says, waters; but 'waters that do not wet the hands'. 'These four Fires', states Maier, at the conclusion of his discourse, 'are locked in spheres or circles, which is to say that each has its own centre, from which, or toward which, tends its motion; however, they are seen as related in part by Nature and in part by the Art, in such a way that one without the other achieves little or nothing, and that the activity of the one is the passivity of the other and vice versa.'

47 Emblema XVIII. *Ignire ignis amat, non aurificare sed aurum.* 'Fire loves to ignite, but gold does not love to make gold.' Vulgar gold is useless in the Work, unless it be turned to Philosophick Gold, which is achieved through Reincrudation, or return to rawness: a very ambiguous term. The 'dead' metal must be re-animated by a 'spirit', taken as Basil Valentine recommends from the 'metallic root': this process revitalizes gold and makes it useful to the alchemist. When the so-called Wet Way is adopted, this Philosophick Gold serves as a Subject; and in all alchemical operations it is employed as a ferment in the last part of the elaboration. The Dog is a symbol of Sulphur, the fixed Seed or the latent embryo.

48 Emblema XIX. *Si de quattuor unum Occidas, subito mortuus omnis erit.* 'If thou killest one of four, all at once will die.' The destruction of gold is reputed in alchemical literature to be more difficult than the making of it. The four brothers are the Four Elements, which, alchemically speaking, compose a substance. Therefore the destruction of one causes the death of all. 'Kill therefore the live, but so as to resuscitate the dead, or else the death of the victim will have been in vain', warns Maier in his discourse. Avicen, quoted by our author in the preceding discourse, writes: 'Of Water is made Earth. Water is vanquished by the qualities of Earth and conversely.' By this one should understand that the Reincrudation means a liquefaction through Dissolution, and a return to the bosom of the Earth. The goal of this operation is the acquisition of Sulphur and its revivification through the death of the initial Mercury.

49 Emblema XX. *Naturam natura docet, debellet ut ignem.* 'Nature teaches Nature to vanquish fire.' 'The way of Nature when it seeks the perfection of any work', writes Maier, 'consists in making one thing come out of another, the most perfect from the least perfect, and to activate its potential.' This is exactly what we see in the gesture of the mercurial heroine speeding the Knight on his way to do

battle against the tyranny of Fire. The Knight is the Fixed Sulphur that the flame can no longer vanquish.

50 Emblema XXI. *Fac ex mare & foemina circulum, inde quadrangulum, hinc triangulum, fac circulum & habebis lap[idem] Philosophorum.* 'Make from the male and female a circle, then a square, afterwards a triangle, from which make a circle, and thou shalt have the Philosophers' Stone.' The alchemical Squaring of the Circle consists in taking a microcosmic sphere to which a cross is added (notice it at the foot of the Artist) which is then converted into a square (the four elements), then into a triangle (body, spirit and soul). The man and the woman are Sulphur and Mercury, the Principles of the Work, and the triangle is finally converted into the macrocosmic greater sphere which is the Philosopher's Stone. The compasses — whose points not only measure and compare distances but trace the perfect circumference of the hermetick cycle — act as an invaluable teaching-aid, indicating the proportions of Weights in the Art.

51 Emblema XXII. *Plumbo habito candido fac opus mulierum, hoc est, COQUE.* 'Once you have the white lead, do women's work, that is, COOK.' 'You need but one thing', writes Alphidius, 'our Water and a single decoction' (coction or decoction means 'cooking'). He adds 'there is but one vessel for the White and the Red'. This alchemical coction can be said to be the whole Work, as it constitutes its main part; then, as in the kitchen, only patience and attention are required. The Subject is first resolved into its own Water (dissolved), which is why Maier's epigram here says that the trout must be liquefied in its own waters. Hence the window opened upon the river. 'By coction', writes Maier, 'we mean the ripening of raw parts which thanks to Vulcan is achieved within the vessels of Philosophy.' The Philosopher, like the woman who brings to maturity the fish in the water, resolves in Air and Water their superfluous humidity. His Subject macerated in its own Water (stronger than the strongest vinegar) is liquefied and dissolved in it. Eventually it is coagulated and fixed by the same 'Water' in the same hermetically sealed vessel. Notice, among the host of significant details, the Cat, emblem of the Secret Fire.

52 Emblema XXIII. *Aurum pluit, dum nascitur Pallas Rhodi, & Sol concumbit Veneri.* 'Gold rains down, while Pallas is born in Rhodes and Sol lies with Venus.' Vulcan (Fire), with one blow of his axe, opens the head of Jupiter, relieving him of a tremendous headache, and giving birth to Pallas Athena (Mercury sublimated, by the coction, to the highest degree). Jupiter, in this case, is passive, because he represents the innate generative heat of bodies (the Natural Fire) which brings metal to maturity. A rain of gold falls upon the island of Rhodes (the Philosophick Earth) during this event. That is because the volatilized Philosophick Gold falls back like a rain of gold upon the fixed Matter that remains at the bottom of the alchemical vessel. The sexual union of the Sun with Venus, shown in the background, is the union of Fixed and Volatile which produces the eventual perfect Fixity of Apollo, represented as the Colossus of Rhodes.

53 Emblema XXIV. *Regem lupus voravit & vitae crematus reddidit.* 'The wolf devoured the King and, cremated, restored him to life.' The Wolf is the Dissolvent ('Mercury') which devours the 'inanimate' King (i.e. the Gold of the Philosophers) which is useless to the Work until it is reincrudated. The Wolf yields his own life in the Solution (see Emblema XIX), communicating his own vitality to the hitherto latent potentiality of the King, and the latter, having absorbed the life of his assailant, steps from the fire with 'restored health, youth and beauty'. In short, the emblem is another illustration of the hermetick axiom: 'Kill the live to revive the dead.'

54 Emblema XXV. *DRACO non moritur, nisi cum fratre & sorore sua interficiatur, qui sunt Sol & Luna.* 'The Dragon does not die unless it is slain with its brother and sister, who are Sun and Moon.' The death of the Dragon consists in its Dissolution by its own Mercury or sister (drawn from its own blood); therefore the emblem shows Cynthia the Moon slaying the hunter Orion, and his subsequent Fixation (*Coagulatio*), symbolized by Apollo killing the serpent Python (which is the very same Dragon).

55 Emblema XXVI. *Sapientiae humanae fructus Lignum vitae est.* 'The fruit of human Wisdom is the Tree of Life.' Wisdom comes forth bearing in one hand 'Health and length of days', in the other 'Glory and infinite riches'. If someone, in deed and thought, accedes to Wisdom, 'she shall be unto him like the fruit from the tree of life'. 'Those who are her kin attain eternity', says Solomon, 'while those who are her friends possess true delight, and whosoever diligently seeks her shall partake of great delight. For with Wisdom, there is no sorrow in living, neither is there weariness; on the contrary there is happiness and joy. However sweet the pleasures of music and the taste of wine, Wisdom is sweeter still. For those who seize her she is a tree of life: those who keep her are blessed.' The Philosophers enjoin the Sons of the Art to seek Wisdom, penetrating the arcane Knowledge of God. However, it is a Gift of God, bestowed upon those chosen to receive it.

56 Emblema XXVII. *Qui Rosarium intrare conatur Philosophicum absque clave, assimilatur homini ambulare volenti*

absq[ue] pedibus. 'He who tries to enter the Rose-garden of the Philosophers without the key is like a man wanting to walk without feet.' Without the required knowledge no man can penetrate the Garden of the Philosophers, as the door is secured by solid locks. The (first) key consists in the knowledge of the proper Matter. He who fails to gain it 'is like a man without feet, hard put to stand on even ground' who strives to climb the steep Parnassus. (The figures on Parnassus are well worth close study.)

57 Emblema XXVIII. *Rex balneatur in Laconico sedens, Atrâque bile liberatur à Pharut.* 'The King is bathed, sitting in the Laconian bath, and is freed from his black bile by Pharut.' The present Emblem should follow Emblema XXII – to which the reader is referred. Here the King (the Subject of the Wise) has been recognized, despite 'a vile, despised outer garment'. Black bile (*melancholia*) was clogging up his body, and he desired either death or a cure. A great doctor prescribed the correct vaporous bath, taking care to apply the proper degree of heat. And the King was (in the Sublimation) cleansed of all impurities and made a full recovery.

58 Emblema XXIX. *Ut Salamandra vivit igne sic lapis.* 'As the Salamander lives in the Fire so does the Stone.' The hieroglyph of Fire, the Salamander is the symbol, at once, of Sulphur and of the Secret Fire. The Secret Fire, hidden under a saline aspect, is indispensable so that the prepared Matter, or Subject of the Philosophers, may fulfil its calling as a mother. Each form of generation seeks the aid of the proper agent. As animals are born of a fecundated egg, and vegetables from a seed that has been made prolific, so minerals and metals have their origin in a Seed, a metallic liquor, fertilized by the mineral Fire. The spiritual Secret Fire, corporified as a Salt, is the hidden Sulphur which, as Maier points out, is the Philosophick Tincture, and which fixes all flying Spirits.

59 Emblema XXX. *Sol indiget lunâ ut gallus gallinâ.* 'The Sun needs the Moon as the cock needs the hen.' This theme derived from the *Rosarium philosophorum* – one of the basic axioms of the Hermetick Philosophy – shows that the twin Principles of the Work are complementary and must be united. The mercurial, volatile Moon will have to be exalted to the sublime degree of the Sun for a lasting union to be achieved. The Sun (Sulphur) is virtually worthless without the Moon; and, in turn, without the Sun she is vile and despised. Her union with the sun bestows upon this lowly Matter splendour, force and dignity, says Maier: which is to say, firmness of body and soul (i.e. Fixation), The Moon, in turn, provides the receptacle for the Tincture of the Sun, and gives birth to his children, thus ensuring the propagation of his race (i.e. Multiplication).

60 Emblema XXXI. *Rex natans in mari, clamans altâ voce: Qui me eripiet ingens praemium habebit.* 'The King swimming in the sea, crying aloud: Whoever saves me will obtain a great reward.' This emblem illustrates the injunction, attributed to Hermes, to save the vile Subject of the Wise from its miserable condition. Although unrecognized by the ignorant, the Stone of the Philosophers is a King, who, if saved and taken care of, will bestow rich rewards upon his saviour. In another sense the King, desperate to be rescued, is also Sulphur, which after the Dissolution floats upon the 'crystalline' waters of the Philosophick Sea.

61 Emblema XXXII. *Corallus sub aquis ut crescit & aëre induratur, sic lapis.* 'As the coral grows below the waters and hardens in the air, so does the Stone.' Following the second sense of the previous emblem, we see the Artist carefully extracting Coral, the Philosophick Sulphur coagulated from Mercurial Water. The separation or gathering of the Coral is fraught with difficulties. Maier warns that one must 'cut it under the waters, with great prudence, in order to avoid losing its blood and its taste, leaving in consequence nothing but a formless terrestrial chaos'. Maier concludes by warning of another major danger affecting the Stone, that of superfluous humidity, which prevents its progress and must therefore be removed.

62 Emblema XXXIII. *Hermaphroditus mortuo similis, in tenebris jacens, igne indiget.* 'The Hermaphrodite, who lies in darkness like a corpse, needs fire.' In the darkness of Death, the Hermaphrodite (or Rebis) – the Subject – needs heat of the proper degree to guide its evolution toward Perfection. When the cold humidity of the Moon is present in their Subject, the Philosophers call it their Woman; when in turn the dryness and heat of the Sun prevail they call it their Man. When all four qualities are present at the same time they call it their Rebis or Hermaphrodite. The Woman is easily converted into the Man (that is to say the Volatile into the Fixed), by means of the heat of the alchemical coction. The heat drives away, and separates, the superfluous humidity, and the Tincture is obtained: this is an incombustible oil which contains the active power of the Sun.

63 Emblema XXXIV. *In balneis concipitur, & in aëre nascitur, rubeus verè factus graditur super aquas.* 'Conceived in baths, and born in the air, made truly red, he steps on the waters.' Sulphur (the Sun of the Wise) fecundates the Mercurial Moon by immersion. Mercury (the Moon of the Wise) possesses the specific virtue of absorbing the Tincture which Sulphur yields during the immersion (or Bath of the

King). It is this precise analogy with the act of coition that inspired in alchemy the use of erotic imagery.

64 Emblema XXXV. *Ceres Triptolemum, Thetis Achillem, ut sub igne morari assuefecit, sic artifex lapidem.* 'As Ceres made Triptolemus – and Thetis made Achilles – able to stay in the fire, so the Artist makes the Stone.' In the foreground (on the left), Ceres (the Philosophick Earth) foster-mother of Triptolemus (the Subject of the Wise), feeds him with her own Divine Milk (Mercury) and at night lays him in the Fire so that he may mature to immortality, growing impervious to the flames that make others flee. Triptolemus thus becomes the Philosophick Tincture (see preceding emblem). Achilles, son of Thetis, goddess of the Sea, and of Peleus (the Mountain, or Earth) is, after his death, taken by his mother from the pyre on Leuke, the White Island. The Subject of the Art thus reaches Whiteness – the first degree of immortality.

65 Emblema XXXVI. *Lapis projectus est in terras, & in montibus exaltatus, & in aëre habitat, & in flumine pascitur, id est Mercurius.* 'The Stone is projected upon the Earth, and exalted upon the mountains, and dwells in the air, and feeds in the river: that is Mercury.' The omnipresence of the Stone in its various aspects is shown by cubes. The exoteric, and baffling, explanation is that the Stone is everywhere, but ignored, and might be found by anyone. However, a study of the picture shows that one should seek it in the mountains where it is threefold (an allusion to Triple Mercury and to the three principles). Upon the foliated Earth it becomes a quintessence; and in the river a clever shading indicates the Stone to be a compound of four Elements alternatively dissolved and coagulated. Lastly, the nature of the Stone is hinted at by the curious ensign above the rider at the centre of the composition.

66 Emblema XXXVII. *Tria sufficiunt ad magisterium, fumus albus, hoc est, aqua, leo viridis, id est, aes Hermetis, & aqua foetida.* 'Three things suffice for the Work: a white smoke, which is Water; a Green Lion, which is the Ore of Hermes; and a fetid Water.' The snowy vapour or white smoke is the Secret Fire, and the fetid water is the sepulchral Blackness of the dissolved composition. The Greenness refers to the rawness of this product, and to the curious fact that, upon the surface of the bath, the Philosophick Vitriol acquires a green colour, bestowed upon it by the Universal Spirit. The Green Lion is the living and luminous spirit (the Secret Fire) extracted from the crude mineral Subject; it is a green translucent crystal, as fusible as wax, which the Sages call their Vitriol, or Emerald of the Wise. Like Jonah emerging from the belly of the whale, this surfaces on the Waters. It is, as it were, the Seed of Fixity. Basil Valentine points out that the fixed blood of the Red Lion (Sulphur) is made from the non-fixed blood of the Green Lion, because both are of one nature.

67 Emblema XXXVIII. *Rebis, ut Hermaphroditus, nascitur ex duobus montibus Mercurii & Veneris.* 'The Rebis, like Hermaphroditus, is born from the twin mountains of Mercury and Venus.' The Rebis, Hermaphrodite or Androgyne of the Wise is born from the union of the twin Principles (Sulphur and Mercury), who enter the mercurial Bath. This, like the mythical fountain where the nymph Salmacis swam, has the property of turning both sexes into one: that is, it dissolves the Bodies radically in such a way that, once recomposed in the Fixation, they are One.

68 Emblema XXXIX. *Oedypus Sphynge superata & trucidato Lajo patre matrem ducit in uxorem.* 'Oedipus, having overcome the Sphinx and slain his father Laius, takes his mother to wife.' The Sphinx questions Oedipus, posing the famous riddle (What has four feet in the morning, two at noon and three at sunset?) illustrated in the foreground. The well-known answer is Man. But here the answer (which refers to Emblema XXI) is the Philosopher's Stone: the four Elements (square on the baby's head); the twin Principles united as one (see preceding emblem); the Hermaphrodite (or, as the lunar hemisphere on the man's forehead indicates, the Matter having reached the First Perfection); lastly the triangle of Fire (which also indicates Sulphur, Mercury and Salt) upon the old man's brow. The vanquished Sphinx is seen about to cast herself from the cliff. The Blackness, *Nigredo* or Death, will appear. Oedipus kills his father Laius because, as Maier writes, the first agent is destroyed by his effect, or son; then Oedipus marries his mother, i.e. the same effect unites with the secondary cause until they become as one.

69 Emblema XL. *Ex duabus aquis fac unam, & erit aqua sanctitatis.* 'From two waters make one, and it will be water of holiness.' During the Work two Waters, of contrary disposition, are obtained and mingled. Raymond Lull, quoted by Maier, says of the First that it possesses a virtue that hardens, fixates, and coagulates, while the Second is unstable, volatile, and soft. The First Water (First Mercury or Dissolvent) liquefies and dissociates metals in such a way that they regain their natural, original power. The Dissolvent removes their heterogeneous impurities, as well as their infirmities; it revives them and renews them, acting upon them as a veritable Fountain of Youth. Thus the reincrudated metals are said to be living or philosophick metals. The First Water (First Mercury) is the Edenic Eve,

which has a renovative power; the generative power is the preserve of the Second Water (Second Mercury), daughter of the First. When both are united in the correct proportions, the Philosophick Mercury is obtained. This is the direct Subject of the Philosopher's Stone, which is the Fountain of Youth.

70 Emblema XLI. *Adonis ab apro occiditur, cui Venus accurrens tinxit Rosas sanguine.* 'Adonis is killed by a wild boar; Venus, rushing to his side, dyes the Roses with blood.' The death of Adonis was brought about by a wild boar that jealous Mars had placed in his path. Venus scratches her leg on thorns, and her blood colours the White Rose red. The emblem illustrates the Dissolution (Death) of the Subject (dissolved by the martial Dissolvent), which brings about the Blackness (*Nigredo*). According to Maier's text, Venus places her dead lover under tender lettuces, thereby indicating the Reincrudation. Her blood colours the White Rose red, because, beyond the long night of Death, Whiteness is eventually reached, and ultimately Whiteness is tinged with the Redness of perfect Fixity.

71 Emblema XLII. *In Chymicis versanti Natura, Ratio, Experientia & lectio, sint Dux, scipio, perspicilia & lampas.* 'To him who concerns himself with Alchemy, may Nature, Reason, Experience and Reading be guide, staff, spectacles and lantern.' Nature must be the Artist's guide; Reason the staff on which he leans lest he may stumble into foolish errors; Experience the spectacles which, as they allow the myopic to see at a distance, will allow the Artist to discern true from false. Reading must shine within Intelligence like a bright light, without which clouds of obscurity will prevail. The reading of good books must often be renewed; otherwise it is useless. 'He who will be patient,' writes Bacaster in the *Turba philosophorum*, 'and enjoy his patience, will progress upon the right path of this Art; but should someone believe that he can quickly seize the fruit of our books, he is mistaken, and far better for him would it have been that he had never opened them.'

72 Emblema XLIII. *Audi loquacem vulturem, qui neutiquam te decipit.* 'Hark to the speaking vulture, who in no wise deceives thee.' From the Mountain-top (the original Matter) the Vulture (Bird of Hermes) proclaims: 'I am black, white, yellow and red' – which are the main colours of the Subject as it evolves towards the Perfection of the Philosopher's Stone. The Vulture is the symbol of the Philosophick Mercury: partly fixed (therefore shown with his talons firmly gripping the Mountain) and partly volatile (the wings are partly spread). He is born after the Death of the first Mercury (or Dissolvent), killed by the fixative action of the Sulphur that has issued from itself. This earlier process is symbolized by the wingless Crow representing *Nigredo*, the Blackness, Death, or Night of the Work. The Philosophick Mercury is raised to the final degrees of Perfection by the subsequent maturation.

73 Emblema XLIV. *Dolo Typhon Osyridem trucidat, artúsque illius Hinc inde dissipat, sed hos collegit Isis inclyta.* By treachery Typhon slays Osiris and scatters his limbs abroad, but majestic Isis reassembles them.' Typhon (Set), wielding the doubled-edged sword of the Secret Fire, hacks the body of King Osiris (the Fixed) to pieces (Separation). Isis, the mother-sister-spouse, and the mercurial Volatile Principle, appears on the scene, because the dissolving Water, or First Mercury, results from the initial Dissolution of the Subject. She gathers the scattered pieces of the corpse to make Osiris whole again. This is because, as we have repeatedly stated, the mercurial Dissolvent yields its life in reviving Sulphur. The King emerges whole (fixed) from the coffin in the foreground.

74 Emblema XLV. *Sol & ejus umbra perficiunt opus.* 'The Sun and his shadow finish the Work.' The apparent course of the Sun through the sky during the year, and the necessary alternation between day and night, are used in this emblem as symbols of the whole Work. The shadow 'that causes night' refers in Maier's discourse to the Chaos of the Philosophers (i.e. their Matter) and to the *Nigredo*. The necessity to use a fiery remedy to remove the dense shadow (heterogeneous impurities) from the Body is stressed (see the 6th emblem of Maier's *Symbola aureae mensae, 86*). Similarly, we are reminded of the necessity to whiten or wash Latona (see Emblema XI).

75 Emblema XLVI. *Aquilae duae, una ab ortu, altera ab occasu conveniunt.* 'Two Eagles, one from the east, one from the west, come together.' Jupiter launches two Eagles, one eastwards, the other westwards; they will meet at the same point. The two Eagles here symbolize the twin Principles of the Work, which in the next emblem appear under quite a different guise. They are, says Maier, the two Stones that are pleased to unite. The Eagle, states Pernety, was sacred to Jupiter because the Mercury of the Wise is volatilized, bearing the Fixed aloft with itself, as soon as Jupiter (the colour grey) succeeds Saturn (the colour black). (See further the 5th emblem of Maier's *Viatorium, 113.*)

76 Emblema XLVII. *Lupus ab Oriente & Canis ab Occidente venientes se invicem momorderunt.* 'The Wolf from the east, the Dog from the west, savaged each other.' – 'These two then (which Avicen calleth the Corascene bitch and the Armenian dogge),' writes Nicolas Flamel, 'these two I

say being put together in the vessel of the sepulcher, doe bite one another cruelly, and by their great poyson and furious rage, they never leave one another, from the moment that they have seized on one another (if the cold hinder them not), till both of them by their slavering venom, and mortall hurts, be all of a goarebloud, over all the parts of their bodies; and finally killing one another, be stewed in their proper venome, which after their death, changeth them into living and permanent water; before which time, they loose in their corruption and putrification, their first natural formes, to take afterwards one onely new, more noble, and better forme.'

77 Emblema XLVIII. *Rex ab aquis potatis morbum, à medicis curatus sanitatem obtinet.* 'The King receives sickness from water he has drunk, and health on being tended by physicians.' Affected by an excess of waters, the King has grown pale and sick. Doctors from Alexandria (alchemists), having purged him with the aid of remedies, and by making him sweat, effect a complete cure; the grateful King then rewards his saviours. Once the Matter is purged of superfluous humidity and all heterogeneous impurities, it regains 'its health' and in due course becomes the Philosopher's Stone. It then bestows the most precious gifts.

78 Emblema XLIX. *Infans Philosophicus tres agnoscit patres, ut Orion.* 'Like Orion, the Philosophick Child acknowledges three fathers.' Mythographers relate that Orion had not one but three fathers. Most accounts tell how Jupiter, Mercury, and Neptune granted the wish of their host Hyrieus to give him a son. Accordingly, the gods urinated in the skin of a heifer which was then buried. Nine months later, Orion (the name is a pun on the Greek *ouron*, urine) was born. Here, Maier names Orion's fathers as Apollo, Vulcan, and Mercury; but, as usual, circumstances contrary to nature must in alchemy be understood to be the cloak of hermetick allegory. The Stone's first father is Apollo: a celestial occult virtue (of the Sun) which fecundates the Matter of the Philosophers and gives her a son who will, ultimately, grow even more splendid than his father. Vulcan, symbol of Fire, is its second father (or mentor). Its third is Mercury, who lends it his own volatile Matter (or Mercury). To those three must be added the figure on the left, who is the attentive Artist, and as it were the fourth father. Towering above the others is Mars, whose presence is indispensable: without his action, the Body would not be dissolved. He is the symbol of the metal which, joined to the mineral Matter, attracts the magnetic influence of Phanes: Light, Spirit, Fire, personified in Apollo.

79 Emblema L. *Draco mulierem, & haec illum interimit, simulque sanguine perfunduntur.* 'The dragon destroys the woman, and she him, and at once they are drenched in blood.' The Fiery Dragon (Sulphur of the Philosophers) unites with the Woman (Mercury of the Wise). It is said that the blood of the Dragon is mingled with that of the 'Vegetable Saturnia', so called because she is of the race of Saturn; 'which is why', adds Pernety (imparting a very important piece of information which allows the Son of the Art to identify the substance), 'she is by some called Venus'. (See the *Liber secretus* or *Secret Book* of Artephius.)

Michael Maier
Symbola aureae mensae, 1617

Symbola aureae mensae duodecim nationum. Hoc est, Hermaea seu Mercurii festa ab heroibus duodenis selectis, artis chymica usu, sapientia & authoritate paribus celebrata, ad Pyrgopolynicen seu adversarium illum tot annis iactabundum, virgini Chemiae iniuriam argumentis tam vitiosis, quam convitiis argutis inferentem, confundendum & exarmandum, artifices vero optime de ea meritos suo honori & famae restituendum, ubi & artis continuatio & veritas invicta 36. rationibus, & experientia librisque authorum plus quam trecentis demonstratur, Opus, ut Chemiae, sic omnibus aliis antiquitatis & rerum scitu dignissimarum percupidis, utilissimum, 12. libris explicatum & traditum, figuris cupro incisis passim adiectis, Authore Michaele Maiero Comite Imperialis Consistorii, Nobili, Exempto, Med. Doct. P.C. olim Aulico Caes. Francofurti typis Antonij Hummij, impensis Lucae Iennis. M.DC.XVII.

Symbols of the golden table of twelve nations. That is, The Hermetick or Mercury's feast celebrated conjointly by twelve Heroes by virtue of the custom, wisdom and authority of the art of chymistry, in order to confound and disarm Pyrgopolynices or the Adversary who for so many years has hurled at the Virgin Chymistry insults with arguments as defective as his eloquence is calumnious, and to restore the Artists who have deserved well of her to due honour and fame; wherein the continuance of the Art and its unconquered truth are demonstrated by 36 reasons, experience, and the books of more than three hundred authors; A Work most useful to Chymistry and to all others truly desirous of antiquity and of other subjects most worthy to be known; explained and set forth in 12 books, with figures engraved in copper added throughout, by Michael Maier, Count of the Imperial Consistory, Free Nobleman, Doctor of Medicine, Physico-Chymist, formerly of the Imperial Court; Frankfurt, printed by Antonius Hummius for Lucas Jennis, 1617.

The dedication to Ernst, Count of Holstein, Schaumburg and Sternberg, is dated from Frankfurt, December 1616.

After Maier's return to Germany in 1616 (see p. 60) he continued to travel extensively, although he soon became Maurice of Hesse's private physician. After the onset of the Thirty Years War Maier continued to publish many books, and he appears to have been involved with many fascinating figures of the period. The last work known to have been published in his lifetime was *Cantilenae intellectuales de phoenice redivivo*, which appeared in the autumn of 1622. Its dedication to Prince Frederick of Norway is dated Rostock 25 August 1622.

Some biographers believe that Maier died at Magdeburg in 1622, but I do not. I believe that Maier felt the time was ripe to disappear for political and philosophical reasons, and this may well be why his last treatise (1624) was given out as posthumous. This unsubstantiated feeling of mine derives in part from the title of that last treatise: *Tractatus posthumus, sive Ulysses; hoc est Sapientia seu intelligentia, tanquam coelestis scintilla beatitudinis, quod si in fortunae et corporis bonis naufragium faciat, ad portum meditationis et patientiae remigio feliciter se expediat. Una cum annexis tractatibus Fraternitatis Roseae Crucis. Francofurti 1624* (A Posthumous Treatise, or Ulysses: that is Wisdom or Intelligence, like a spark of heavenly bliss, by which if he suffers shipwreck in the goods of fortune or of the body, he reaches port safely by rowing with the oars of patience and meditation. Together with an appendix of treatises of the Brotherhood of the Rosy Cross. Frankfurt 1624).

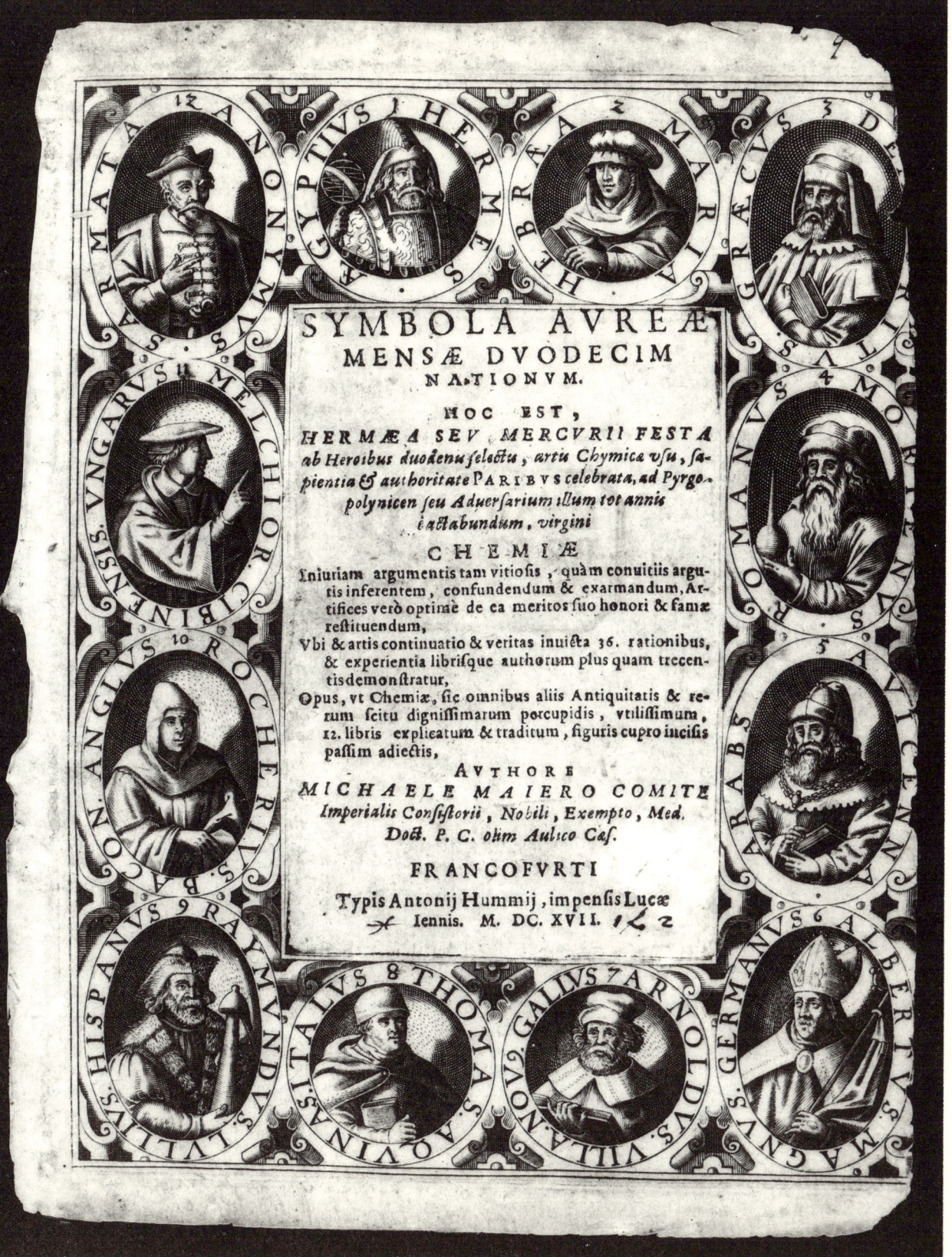

80

Symbola aureae mensae · 107

81

82

83

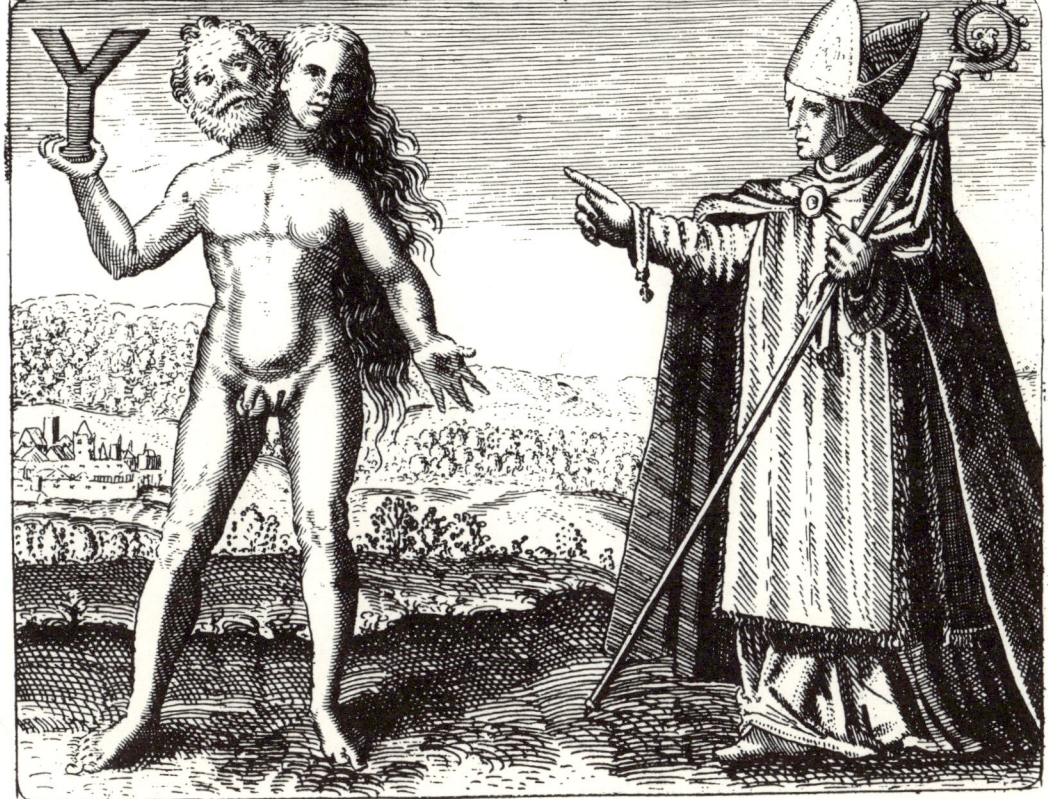

84

Symbola aureae mensae · 109

85

86

87

88

Symbola aureae mensae · III

89

90

Symbola aureae mensae · 113

80 Maier enlists, in refutation of 'vicious and specious arguments' against alchemy, the testimony of twelve of its most famous heroes from twelve different countries: Hermes the Egyptian, Mary the Jewess, Democritus the Greek, Morienus the Roman, Avicen the Arab, Albertus Magnus the German, Arnold of Villa Nova the Frenchman (sic), Thomas Aquinas the Italian, Raymond Lull the Spaniard, Roger Bacon the Englishman, Melchior Cibinensis the Hungarian; the roster is ironically completed by the presence of an Anonymous Sarmatian. The latter's anonymity has not deterred the artist from providing us with two likenesses; the one on the title-page differs in every way from the other in the text.

I am fully aware of a host of critical difficulties connected with the identities of alchemical authors to whom tradition has attributed works which they could not have written. However, in the present context, such considerations are neither relevant nor helpful and are likely to lead only to further confusion. I shall therefore deal with these authors as if they were indeed the authors of the precepts illustrated in these emblems.

81 The legendary Hermes Trismegistus, the Thrice-Great Hermes, has always been regarded by alchemists as the father of their Art, which is, therefore, synonymously called the Hermetick Philosophy. Hermes is always represented in this traditional guise; here he indicates the twin Principles of the Work, Sulphur and Mercury (of the Wise), whose father and mother are the Sun and Moon, joined by the fiery embrace of the twin components of the Secret Fire.

The armillary sphere held aloft is a reminder of the mysterious cosmic agent whose indispensable influence must be received and incorporated before the Subject of the Wise becomes the Philosopher's Stone.

82 Avicenna was the Latin name of a famous Persian doctor, born near Bukhara in 980. Nicknamed the Prince of Physicians, he was one of the most remarkable men of his time, whose genius and knowledge covered an extraordinary range. He died in 1037.

The Volatilization of the Fixed, and the Fixation of the Volatile, constitute the whole of the Work.

83 Morienus the Roman, a Christian hermit of the seventh century, is famous in alchemical lore as the teacher of 'King Calid', actually Prince Khalid ibn Jazid ibn Mu'awijah (673–705), a major figure of Arabian alchemy. Morienus' words derive from the *Liber de compositione alchymiae*, or *De transfiguratione metallorum*, a Latin manuscript translated from the Arabic in 1182 by Robertus Castrensis (Robert of Chester) and printed for the first time at Paris in 1559.

The difficulties of the unprepared seeker are compared, by Morienus, to a man getting stuck in a dunghill of his own making, or else to a man attempting to climb a tower without a ladder, and inevitably falling on his head. Morienus points to the ground in a reminder that the earth shares with the Philosophick Earth or Subject the same spagyrical sign.

84 Albertus Magnus (St Albert the Great), scholar, scientist and Philosopher, was born Albert Count of Bollstädt at Lavingen in Swabia in 1193. He joined the Dominican order at Padua in 1223. His prodigious learning earned him the epithet of Doctor Universalis, while his detractors in turn named him the Ape of Aristotle. He taught at many universities and became Bishop of Ratisbon from 1260 to 1262, then retired to a cloister at Cologne to devote the rest of his life to prayer, writing and study. He died on 15 November 1280.

The androgyne or Rebis (the double thing) results from the conjunction of the twin Principles, obtained with the help of the double saline mediator of which the Y is a symbol; so for that matter is the Bishop himself.

85 Mary the Jewess is described by Zozimos of Panapolis, a Graeco-Egyptian alchemist of the third century, as Maria or Miriam, the sister of Moses. Little survives of her works beyond sayings quoted by others. However, she was a remarkable practician and is credited with the invention of the water-bath – which is still known to every French cook and housewife as the *bain-marie* – and of a clever piece of alchemical apparatus called the *Kerotakis*.

The Mountain, in alchemical symbolism, is the *Materia Prima*, which must first be reincrudated, 'made green again' in order to produce the desired results. The fumes rising and falling between the vessels symbolize the circular process of Dissolution and Fixation (*Solve et Coagula*), preceding the birth of the Quintessence – five flowers on a single stem.

86 Democritus, a Greek sage of the fifth century BC, was called the Smiling Philosopher, laughing at the follies of men; he was the founder, with Leucippus, of the atomic theory. He was widely travelled and according to Diodorus Siculus spent five years among the Egyptians, who instructed him in many secret matters. He died at the age of 109.

The Venus of the Philosophers is their Subject, which must appear in all its splendid nudity. Its dense shadow, formed by heterogeneous impurities, must however be first removed, and that operation requires the fiery remedy yielded by Vulcan. This analysis is confirmed by the closed book under the Philosopher's arm, which symbolizes the unopened or unprepared Matter.

87 Arnold of Villa Nova was not a Frenchman but a Catalan, born near Valencia in 1235. Educated by the Dominicans, he studied medicine at Naples and learnt Arabic in addition to other languages. His genius for medicine brought him fame, and he was the physician of popes and kings. He travelled widely and wrote many books. His most famous alchemical work is the *Rosarium Philosophorum*, first printed in 1556 at Frankfurt.

The Stone is obtained by the marital and incestuous union of Gabritius (from the Arabic *al Kibric*, Sulphur) with Beya his sister (Arabic *al Raida*, Mercury): the twin Principles of the Work. This union is symbolized by the huge ring bearing the Emerald of the Wise. This ring is the Philosophick Fire or Salt, the Fountain of Dissolution in which the King and Queen bathe. It is composed of two salts and like quicklime burns without fire.

88 Thomas Aquinas was born in 1225 at Roccasecca, between Naples and Rome, the son of Landolfo, Count of Aquino. He studied at the University of Naples, then joined the Dominican Order. In 1245 he went to Paris, where he became the favourite pupil and disciple of Albertus Magnus. He received his master's degree in 1256 and returned to a brilliant career at the courts of four Popes. Theologian and philosopher, he was named the Angelic Doctor. His genius and sanctity were soon recognized. Pope Clement IV wished to make him a cardinal and then the Archbishop of Naples, but he declined both offers. He was a prolific writer and died in January 1274. He was declared a saint by Pope John XXII on 18 July 1323.

The emblem illustrates his famous commentary on the third book of Aristotle's *Meteorologica*, where he discusses the generation of metals from the mixture of two vapours, Sulphur and Mercury: one dry, the other moist. Thomas Aquinas says that likewise the alchemists make a true generation of metals from Sulphur and Mercury by making the vaporous exhalation exude from certain bodies through the application of a proportionate heat which is the natural agent. But he stresses that the major difficulty faced by the Artist is the occult operation of a 'celestial virtue'.

89 Raymond Lull or Ramón Llull, known as Doctor Illuminatus, was born at Palma de Mallorca in the Balearic Islands, *c.* 1235. After a dissipated youth he turned to religion in 1266 and soon became convinced that it was his mission to convert the Muslims to Christianity. He spent nine years preparing to do so, studying philosophy, theology and Arabic, and joined the Franciscan Order. He founded a school for Arabic studies and wrote many treatises. For thirty years he travelled far and wide, unsuccessfully seeking help in his endeavours. According to alchemical tradition, he was won over to the Hermetick Art by Arnold of Villa Nova, whose disciple he allegedly became. However, his obsession with his mission led him to journey thrice to Tunis; twice he was imprisoned and the third time he was stoned. Rescued by a Genoese merchant, he was taken on board a ship but died before reaching Palma in 1315.

The emblem shows that the child which results from the union of a man and a woman initially needs the help and support of both his parents; which alchemically means that when the right Principles are conjoined, Sulphur, the future Stone, is born of their union.

90 Roger Bacon was born at Ilchester in Somerset in 1214. He seems to have belonged to a wealthy family ruined in the struggle between Henry III and his barons (1258–65). The pupil of the scholar-philosopher Robert Grosseteste, Bishop of Lincoln, he was persuaded to join the Franciscan Order in 1247. From 1234 to 1250 he studied and lectured in Paris under Petrus Peregrinus, author of one of the first treatises on the magnet. He was devoted to the study of the sciences, alchemy, astronomy and mathematics. He collected occult books in many languages and conducted many experiments. Roger Bacon had an extraordinary acuity, whereby he was able to dismiss most of the nonsensical speculations of the alchemists while retaining that which in practice is essential. He lived for many years at Oxford, where he was buried in 1292.

The emblem indicates that the delicate balance of the right elemental proportions must be achieved before success can be obtained. But which weights are we talking about? Those of Nature or those of the Art? Alchemical texts effectively mask the issue, and the rule must thus be determined: the Weights of the Art apply exclusively to discrete bodies which can be weighed, whereas the Weights of Nature refer to the relative proportions of the component parts of a given body – as for instance of Sulphur and Mercury united in Philosophick Mercury. These latter Weights may not be known to the Artist or rigorously determined by him.

91 Melchior Cibinensis (Nicholas Melchior Szebeni) was a Hungarian from the city of Szeben in Transylvania (known in German as Hermannstadt, in Romanian as Cibiu, and in Latin as Cibinium). Around 1490 he was chaplain and astrologer at the court of King Ladislaus II of Hungary and Bohemia. He continued in his function under Louis II, then in 1526, after the death of the latter, went to the court of Emperor Ferdinand I where he composed his treatise which analyses the alchemical symbolism of the Roman Catholic Mass (as celebrated before the scandalous reforms which have taken place in the wake of Vatican II).

Symbola aureae mensae · 115

Maier underlines the precept: *Lapis ut infans, lacte nutriendus est virginali*: 'The Stone, like a child, is to be fed with Virgin's Milk'. *Lac Virginis* (Virgin's Milk) is a term used by the alchemists to designate the mercurial Water obtained through the Dissolution of our Subject.

92 The Anonymous Sarmatian was identified by Daniel Stolcius, in the *Viridarium chymicum* published in 1624 (seven years after Maier's work), as *Michael Sendivogius Polonus*. Sendivogius was a contemporary of Maier's, born in Moravia in 1566, who owned a house at Cracow and thus was often called a Pole (*Sarmata* or *Polonus*). Maier deliberately omits to name him, because of the events which I shall now relate. Sendivogius befriended an Adept, the Scotsman Alexander Seton, or Sethon, known as the Cosmopolite, who had performed multiple transmutations across Europe in order to convince disbelievers. Towards the end of 1603, Seton (who was on his honeymoon) arrived at Krossen, seat of Christian II, Elector of Saxony. His fame was such that this prince sent for him at once. Seton despatched his assistant William Hamilton, who performed a transmutation before the assembled court. The Elector summoned Seton and with demonstrations of affection tried to persuade him to teach him his secret. The Cosmopolite refused and was imprisoned and tortured – in vain. More dead than alive, he still refused to yield and he was put in solitary confinement in a dungeon.

Michael Sendivogius, a gentleman student of the Hermetick Art, managed through influential friends, to visit him on several occasions. At length he contrived Seton's escape and took him to Poland, where the Cosmopolite died on New Year's Day 1604. On his deathbed he gave Sendivogius a large quantity of his precious transmutatory powder but refused to impart its secret. Sendivogius married Seton's widow, who gave him a manuscript written by her former husband, which he published using an anagram of his own name. Thus the *Novum lumen chymicum* (Cologne 1610) was long believed to be by him.

Sendivogius, who now called himself the Cosmopolite, travelled to the court of Rudolph II in Prague, whom he impressed with a successful transmutation, proceeding thence to Poland where he arrived after many adventures and made more transmutations for King Sigismund III Vasa. Invited by Duke Frederick of Württemberg, he astonished the latter with two more transmutations, and the Duke had him created Count of Neidlingen. However, he was tricked and robbed by a rival and ruined by his own extravagant life-style.

When Maier wrote the *Symbola* Sendivogius had disappeared, and Maier probably suspected that his knowledge came from another. Sendivogius reappeared at Warsaw in 1625 and died, penniless, at Cracow in 1646.

The emblem shows Saturn watering the Earth which bears the flowers of the Sun and Moon. The Matter of the Wise, having first become White Sulphur (the lunar Tree) then Red Sulphur (the solar Tree), is carefully imbibed or soaked, drop by drop, in order to improve its quality and multiply its quantity. Saturn is the gardener, in order to indicate the origin and quality of the mercurial Water that is used.

MICHAEL MAIER
Tripus aureus, 1618

Tripus aureus, hoc est, Tres tractatus chymici selectissimi, nempe I. Basili Valentini, Benedictini ordinis monachi, Germani, Practica una cum 12 clavibus & appendice, ex Germanico; II. Thomae Nortoni, Angli philosophi Crede mihi seu Ordinale, ante annos 140. ab authore scriptum, nunc ex anglicano manuscripto in latinum translatum, phrasi cuiusque authoris ut & sententia retenta; III. Cremeri cuiusdam Abbatis Westmonasteriensis Angli Testamentum, hactenus nondum publicatum, nunc in diversarum nationum gratiam editi, & figuris cupro affabre incisis ornati operâ & studio Michaelis Maieri Phil. & Med. D. Com. P. &c. Francofurti, ex chalcographia Pauli Iacobi, impensis Lucae Iennis. Anno M.DC.XVIII.

The Golden Tripod, that is, Three choice chymical treatises, namely: I. By Basil Valentine, a German Benedictine monk, Practice with Twelve Keys and appendix, from the German; II. By Thomas Norton, an English philosopher, Believe Me or Ordinal, written by the author 140 years ago and now translated into Latin from the English manuscript, retaining the author's every phrase and maxim; III. By a certain Cremer, Abbot of Westminster, an Englishman, a Testament, entirely unpublished hitherto. All now published for the benefit of divers nations, and supplied with figures skilfully engraved in copper, by the labour and study of Michael Maier, Doctor of Philosophy and Medicine, Count Palatine &c. Frankfurt, printed at the copperplate press of Paul Jacob, for Lucas Jennis, 1618.

The identity of Basil Valentine, author of the *Twelve Keys* illustrated here by Maier, remains a controversial enigma. As Antonius Guainerius – who praised him – died in 1440, we can rule out the hypothesis that Johann Tholden, who published Valentine's works in the 1590s, was their author. In his *Currus triumphalis Antimonii*, Valentine himself says that he came from the Rhineland (*in superiore quoque Germania in tractu rhenano patria mea*, p. 21) and spent part of his youth in Belgium and England. He became a Benedictine monk in the monastery of St Peter at Erfurt, but because of his use of a pseudonym no record has been found there. However, on p. 129 of *Historia Erfurtensis Duderstadii*, 1675, Johann Moritz Guden states: '*Eadem aetate (scilicet anno 1413) Basilius Valentinus in Divi Petri monasterio vixit arte medica et naturalium indagine mirabilis*': 'At that time, in 1413, Basil Valentine lived in St Peter's monastery, wonderful for his skill in the medical art and things natural.' His works are highly respected. According to tradition, as his name derives from the Greek *Basileus*, the King, and the Latin *Valens*, powerful, he is the Powerful King, a symbol of the Philosopher's Stone.

TRIPVS AVREVS,

Hoc est,

TRES TRACTATVS

CHYMICI SELECTISSIMI,

Nempe

I. BASILII VALENTINI, BENEDICTINI ORDInis monachi, Germani, PRACTICA vna cum 12. clauibus & appendice, ex Germanico;

II. THOMÆ NORTONI, ANGLI PHILOSOPHI CREDE MIHI seu ORDINALE, ante annos 140. ab authore scriptum, nunc ex Anglicano manuscripto in Latinum translatum, phrasi cuiusque authoris vt & sententia retenta;

III. CREMERI CVIVSDAM ABBATIS WESTmonasteriensis Angli Testamentum, hactenus nondum publicatum, nunc in diuersarum nationum gratiam editi, & figuris cupro affabre incisis ornati operâ & studio

MICHAELIS MAIERI Phil. & Med. D. Com. P. &c.

FRANCOFVRTI
Ex Chalcographia Pauli Iacobi, impensis LVCÆ IENNIS.
Anno M.DC.XVIII.

93

PRACTICA
CVM DVODECIM CLAVIBVS ET APPENDICE,

DE MAGNO LAPIDE ANTIQVORVM
Sapientum, scripta & relicta

à

BASILIO VALENTINO

Germ. Benedictini ordinis monacho.

Tractatus Primus.

FRANCOFVRTI APVD IENNIS.

95

96

97

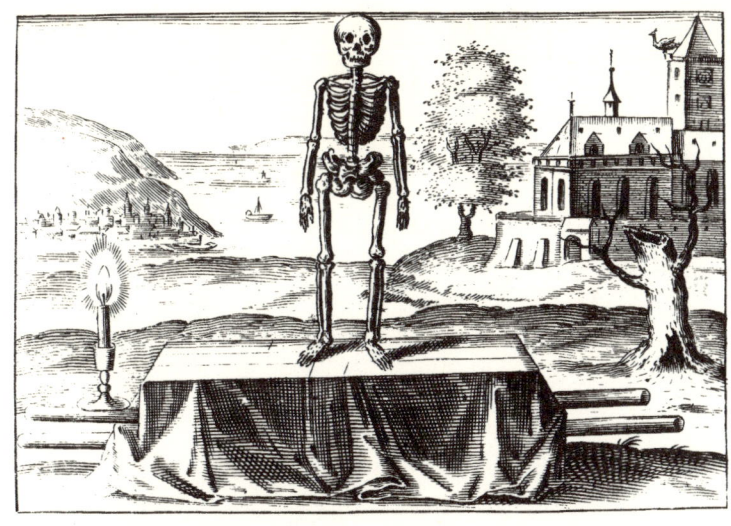
98

99

100

Tripus aureus · 121

101

102

103

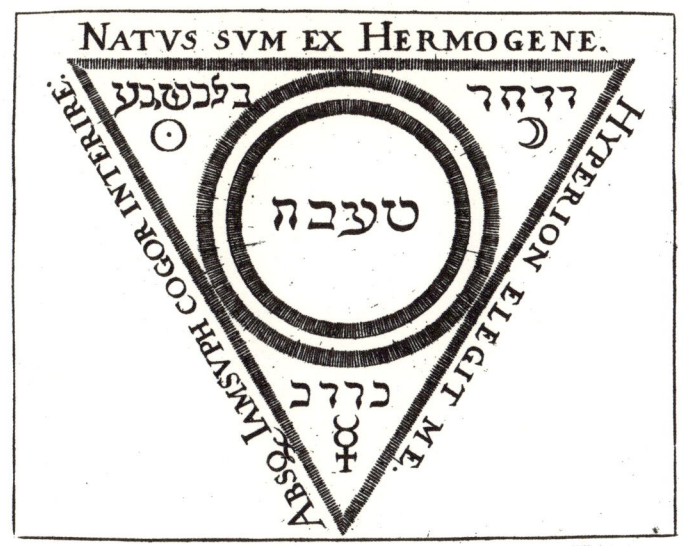

104

105

106

Tripus aureus · 123

93 Title-page. Basil Valentine, John Cremer and Thomas Norton, authors of the three treatises in *Tripus aureus*, in a workshop.

94 Title-page of the Twelve Keys. 'Practice with twelve keys and an appendix, on the Great Stone of the ancient sages.' The disregard for authors' identities in alchemical literature is here once again evidenced. Roger Bacon (90) has now become Basil Valentine.

95 The First Key. The King and Queen, twin Principles of the Work, are extracted from their ore by Dissolution (*solve*), the grey Wolf of Antimony leaping over the crucible while Sulphur is carefully brought out by the action of Saturn. Read in another way, the emblem precisely illustrates the opening sentence of the *Liber secretus* of Artephius: *Antimonium est de partibus Saturni & in omnibus modis habet naturam eius*. 'Antimony is from Saturn's realm and possesses his nature in every way.'

96 The Second Key. Separation and Solution of Philosophick Gold: 'an operation', Basil Valentine declares (in the *Testament*), 'which has never been described by any of the ancient wise Philosophers who have lived before me and have known this Magistery'. The contenders (Fixed and Volatile) are separated and reconciled in the person of Philosophick Mercury ☿ or Twofold Mercury – so called to differentiate it from the first Dissolvent which is obtained in the First Work. The youthful god's nudity indicates the absence of impurities and the crown his nobility. The double Caduceus coupled with the Sun and the Moon on either side shows his twofold power. The wings in the foreground designate the goal of the operation: the Volatilization of the pure portions of the Fixed. The Snake on one sword indicates the Dissolvent, and the Eagle on the other the means to be used.

97 The Third Key. The Dragon is the traditional emblem of the *Materia Prima*, First Matter or Subject of the Wise, also known as the Stone of the Philosophers. The fox, running away with a hen, and attacked in turn by the cock, signifies the Fixation of the Volatile and the Volatilization of the Fixed: a circular process symbolized by the axiom *Solve et Coagula*, 'Dissolve and coagulate.'

98 The Fourth Key. First and foremost of alchemical operations is the Dissolution – called 'Death' by many an ancient author. It is through this Death that the Matter is purified by the Spirit (or Fire), symbolized by the burning candle. The Peacock on the steeple indicates that the Blackness of Putrefaction – a black blacker than black, *Nigrum nigrius nigrâ* – is followed by the many colours of the stage known as the Peacock's Tail. The importance of the Dissolution is further underlined by the dead Tree on the right, which symbolizes the 'dead' state of the *Materia Prima* when it is first acquired. The Dissolution, being the key or axis of the Work, revives the dead; hence the upright position of the skeleton, and the Tree in full bloom next to the church.

99 The Fifth Key. Venus, the Subject of the Wise, displays her wondrous qualities; everything proceeds from her. The vessel that seems to emanate from her mouth and eyes is the most eloquent symbol of the *Sal Petrae*, (Salt of the Stone), also, because of its whiteness, called Crystal (from *Christou halas*, salt of Christ). As 'Our Salt' it shares with the Mercurial Principle its cold, volatile humidity, and with Sulphur its igneous, fixed quality; it is the mediator between Sulphur and Mercury in the Work. Furthermore, the mixture of the two saline substances, which is the Salt of the Philosophers, is the Fire of the Wise, which needs but the intervention of the Elemental Fire (on the right) to be activated. Eros, blindfolded, shows nevertheless that the magnetic power of the Matter is sufficient to attract the celestial shaft which is the Secret (third) Fire – the celestial dynamism upon which alchemy depends. The crowned Lion is the hieroglyph of the Fixed (Sulphur of the Wise), while the 'Sun in Splendour' is the perfect embodiment of the Perfection of the Philosopher's Stone.

100 The Sixth Key. Marriage – the indissoluble Union of Opposites – is, as we have seen, one of the most frequent of alchemical symbols. Brother and Sister are wed with the help of Salt or the Secret Fire (as mentioned in the Fifth Key). The rainbow heralds the end of the Blackness (*Nigredo*) and announces the future Whiteness (*Albedo*), the Swan, which precedes the Sun. The twofold nature of the Secret Fire is clearly shown by the Janus-headed furnace or Athanor. Neptune is the mercurial Water which washes the darkness of Putrefaction, by means of repeated Sublimations, in the three parts (of the Great Work) symbolized by his trident.

101 The Seventh Key. The Salt of the Philosophers is an igneous water (Aqua within the Triangle of Fire) which leads Chaos to Perfection of the Wise. It is their vessel or *Sigillum Hermetis* which dissolves their metal and lends body to its Soul, holding it in so tight an embrace that if the Four Seasons of Fire are correctly applied it is impossible for it to flee. The scales and double-edged sword respectively symbolize the weights of Nature and the Secret Fire.

102 The Eighth Key. 'Verily, verily I say unto you, Except a corn of wheat fall into the ground and die, it abideth alone: but if it die, it bringeth forth much fruit.' (John 12.24.)

'Thou fool, that which thou sowest is not quickened, except it die; and that which thou sowest, thou sowest not that body that shall be, but bare grain, it may chance of wheat, or of some other grain: But God giveth it a body as it hath pleased him, and to every seed his own body.' (I Corinthians 15.36–38.)

From these biblical texts was evolved the alchemical axiom: 'No generation without prior corruption.' The target, Key of the Work, is the Dissolution, leading to Putrefaction, and preceding the glorious Rebirth.

103 The Ninth Key. The shape of this figure is that of the hieroglyph of the *Prima Materia*: ☿. Upon its three Principles, Salt, Sulphur and Mercury, and the three degrees of Perfection, are the two Opposing Principles, Man and Woman. The Raven of the first stage (Blackness) is upon Man's feet; the Peacock's Tail, the following stage, is under Woman's feet. The Swan, corresponding to the Whiteness, is upon her head, while the Red Eagle is on his head.

104 The Tenth Key. The three operations of the Great Work are presented as an enigmatic formula composed of three sentences, written on the sides of the triangle of Water: 'From Hermogenes am I born. Hyperion elected me. Without Jamsuph I am compelled to perish.' Hermogenes, the prime mercurial substance, combined with the second initial Principle, produces an offspring of mixed quality: this offspring, symbolized by the Griffin, is the first step towards the Philosopher's Stone. Hyperion, father of the Sun, is the means by which the purest part, the Soul of the Griffin, is captured as it rises from the second Chaos (the Chaos of the Art) as a clear liquid: the Mercury of the Wise. Jamsuph is the Hebrew name for the Red Sea; and the Red Sea, in alchemical parlance, is the mercurial Water which is red because it contains its own Fixity. This last sentence is a reference to the Fire of Life, the invisible Light – or Spirit – without which the Stone cannot endure.

105 The Eleventh Key. In order to multiply in weight, volume and Perfection, the Fixed Stone re-absorbs a new quantity of Mercury, being in the process redissolved, that is 'dying' again. At each Multiplication the speed of elaboration increases and its power augments tenfold.

106 The Twelfth Key. 'All our laundries are fiery ones'; declares Fulcanelli; 'all our purifications are done in fire, by fire, and with fire – which is why several authors have described such operations as calcinations.' The flaming barrel is a most precious hieroglyph of the Secret Fire, indicating the origin of this mysterious substance, found in old wine barrels and then prepared according to the rules of the Art. The Lion (Sulphur) eating the Snake (Mercury) indicates Fixation of the Volatile.

107 Here is the Athanor, the alchemical furnace. Within is the vessel, with the Snake symbolizing the Mercury of the Philosophers. Below is the hermetick bestiary: the Lion, symbol of the Fixed Sulphur; the Eagle symbolizing Mercury, Volatility and Dissolution; the Snake, the mercurial Dissolvent; the Dragon which is the Subject of the Art; the Raven of *Nigredo* or Putrefaction; the Peacock, the varied colours; the Swan, the White Stone; and the Phoenix, symbolizing the Philosopher's Stone and the Multiplication.

MICHAEL MAIER

Viatorium, 1618

Michaelis Maieri Viatorium, hoc est De montibus planetarum septem seu Metallorum; Tractatus tam utilis, quàm perspicuus, quo, ut Indice Mercuriali in triviis, vel Ariadnêo filo in Labyrintho, seu Cynosurâ in Oceano Chymicorum errorum immenso, quilibet rationalis, veritatis amans, ad illum, qui in montibus sese abdidit De Rubea-petra Alexicacum, omnibus Medicis desideratum, investigandum, uti poterit. Oppenheimii, ex typographia Hieronymi Galleri, sumptibus Joh. Theodori de Bry. MDCXVIII.

Michael Maier: The Wayfarer's Guide; that is, Of the Mountains of the seven planets or metals, a treatise as useful as it is clear, which, like the finger of Mercury at a fork in the road, or the thread of Ariadne in the Labyrinth, or the Pole Star over the vast ocean of chymical wanderings, any rational lover of truth may use to investigate the Prophylactic Medicine of the Red Stone which has hidden itself in mountains and which is desired by all physicians. Oppenheim, printed by Hieronymus Galler for Johann Theodor de Bry, 1618.

Dedicated (September 1618) to Christian I, Prince of Anhalt, with a reference to the author's long abstention from publication ('while I sweat under chymical as well as medical labour'); the group of works he published in 1617–18 must have been written over a long period. The title-page is engraved by Johann Theodor de Bry. An edition with altered plates appeared at Rouen in 1651.

The dedicatee of the *Viatorium*, Christian of Anhalt (1568–1630), who employed Oswald Croll, the Hermetick Philosopher and author, as his physician, was the commander-in-chief of the Bohemian forces which on 8 November 1620 were utterly defeated by those of Emperor Ferdinand II at the battle of the White Mountain. This fact has led Frances Yates in her work *The Rosicrucian Enlightenment* to venture on some interesting speculations concerning Maier's possible connection with the adventure of the Winter King.

MICHAELIS MAJERI
VIATORIUM,
hoc est,
DE MONTIBVS PLANETARVM
septem seu Metallorum;
TRACTATUS tam utilis, quàm perspicuus, quo, ut Indice Mercuriali in triviis, vel Ariadnêo filo in Labyrintho, seu Cynosurâ in Oceano Chymicorum errorum immenso, quilibet rationalis, veritatis amans, ad illum, qui in montibus sese abdidit DE Rubea-petra Alexicacum, omnibus Medicis desideratum, investigandum, uti poterit.

OPPENHEIMII
Ex typographia HIERONYMI GALLERI,
Sumptibus JOH. THEODORI de BRY.
M DC XVIII.

109

110

111

112

130 · MICHAEL MAIER

113

114

Viatorium · 131

108 The traditional correspondences between planets and metals have led many seekers — as well as the majority of critical scholars — into grave errors. Maier, charitably, shows a new and illuminating set of correspondences. Foremost is the relationship between Mars and Venus (to whom the hieroglyph ♂ is attributed); Venus bears, revealingly, a flaming heart. Basil Valentine, speaking of the 'Sulphur of Venus', says that her body is almost all Tincture and colour similar to that of the Sun which, because of its abundance, is almost red. Yet, because her body is leprous and sick, the fixed Tincture cannot dwell therein. The death of her body occasions the death of the Tincture, unless she is joined to a fixed Body where she can dwell permanently. However, Mars possesses the required qualities and proves to be 'Ares mightier than Aries'.

109 The Combat between Fixed and Volatile (twin Principles of the Work), whose shared Death and subsequent Putrefaction give birth to the First Mercury.

110 Agathocles, Tyrant of Sicily, caused an idol of Jove to be cast from an old golden chamberpot, which was then worshipped by his subjects. He then revealed the origin of the material to the worshippers, mocking those who had spitefully spoken of his own humble origins (before his accession he had been a potter). This obscure allegory concerns the vile origin of the *Materia Prima* in a substance dismissed by the ignorant as worthless. The statue made from the chamberpot refers to the origin of the mysterious Fire of the Philosophers, which is partly composed of a substance found in outhouses and old barrels.

111 Democritus, visiting Egypt, the 'Mother of all Sciences', laughed a great deal at the misunderstood allegories of the priests. He studied the anatomy of man and animals. The Chameleon and the Crocodile, says Maier, he considered well worthy of his attention.

112 Mucius Scaevola stabs the secretary of King Lars Porsenna, whom he mistakes for the tyrant. This indicates that a substance other than regal gold is dissolved (in fact by choice rather than by mistake). The killer is Mars; the victim is the Philosophick Earth ♂ . These two are the twin Principles likened by Avicenna to the Corascene Bitch and the Armenian Dog.

113 The flight of the two Eagles launched by Jupiter from Delphi, to prove that spot to be the centre of the earth, seems as incongruous as the presence of Magellan upon his ship after circumnavigating the globe. Yet the island Jupiter stands on (see *Atalanta fugiens*, Emblema XLVI, 75) is in fact Delos, which had sunk almost entirely beneath the waves at the time when Latona landed there to give birth to her twins Diana and Apollo. The composition therefore clearly refers to the Coagulation or Birth of Sulphur, which first appears like skin upon milk. Hermes thus describes this event: 'When I saw this Water, little by little, growing thicker, and when it began to harden, I rejoiced, because I knew that I would certainly find what I sought.' The ship indicates the presence of the Remora (called *echeneis* in Greek), the fish which, according to hermetick authors, could stop a ship dead in its course: another allusion to Fixation.

114 Androcles and the Lion. This well-known story was first told by Aulus Gellius, a Latin author of the second century AD. The man heals the lion, and the lion later succours the man: the arcane meaning is that knowledge of the Stone of the Philosophers — which, like the lion in pain, cries out to be rescued — leads the Artist to purify it by the work of his Art. Then, transformed into the Philosopher's Stone, it provides its rescuer with health, wealth, wisdom and long life.

Johann Daniel Mylius
Opus medico-chymicum, 1618

Ioannis Danielis Mylii Vetterani Hassi M.C. Opus medico-chymicum: Continens tres Tractatus sive Basilicas: quorum prior inscribitur Basilica medica, secundus Basilica chymica, tertius Basilica philosophica. Francofurti, apud Lucam Jennis, 1618.

Johann Daniel Mylius, of Wetter in Hesse, Medico-Chymist: The Medico-Chymical Work, containing three treatises or Basilicas: first the medical, second the chymical, third the philosophical. Frankfurt, published by Lucas Jennis, 1618.

This colossal work, of about 3,000 pages, concludes with an index which Jennis published separately in 1630. The three treatises have separate title-pages, with vignettes taken from Basil Valentine's *Twelve Keys* (already published in Maier's *Tripus aureus*). There is an enormous wealth of material in these volumes, but for present purposes we retain only the title-page, the author's portrait, and the symbolic emblems of *Basilica philosophica*, all engraved by Matthäus Merian. The advanced student of the Art of Hermes will want to look at the fine pictures of equipment in book II of *Basilica philosophica*.

The third book of *Basilica philosophica* contains the so-called Seals of the Philosophers, one hundred and sixty hermetick emblems attributed to the heroes of alchemy, historical and mythical, famous and anonymous. Composed and freely adapted from manuscript sources, as well as from previously published engraved work, the iconography of these 'Seals' constitutes an extraordinary repertory of alchemical symbolism; the association of mottoes with images in these miniature emblems is meant to perform a didactic and mnemonic function.

The 'Seals' were later included in the *Dyas chimica tripartita*... published by Lucas Jennis in 1625. Two years later Daniel Stolcius produced his *Hortulus hermeticus* (1627), a booklet entirely devoted to these emblems, printed four to a page with a transcription of each motto and versified commentaries. This work, again published by Jennis, has led many authors to attribute the composition of the 'Seals' to Stolcius himself.

Johann Daniel Mylius (1585–after 1628[?]), was born, like Oswald Croll, at Wetter on the Ruhr. He was a prolific writer on spagyrical medicine and Hermetick Philosophy, but the facts of his life have proved elusive. Even Johann Christoph Mylius, biographer of countless memorable and unmemorable bearers of the name Mylius or Müller, leaves him out of his *Historia Myliana* (Jena 1751–52) on grounds of space. It is of no help to us that Johann Christoph promises to append the life of Johann Daniel to a forthcoming biography of the Reformation preacher Georg Mylius; this work seems never to have appeared.

Mylius enjoyed the patronage of the leaders of the Protestant party, Maurice and Frederick Henry of Nassau, dedicatees of his *Philosophia reformata*. The main dedicatory epistle of *Opus medico-chymicum* is addressed to no less than God Almighty; it ends with a prayer that the hearts of ill-disposed readers may be converted, and the signature is *Ego, Homo*.

115

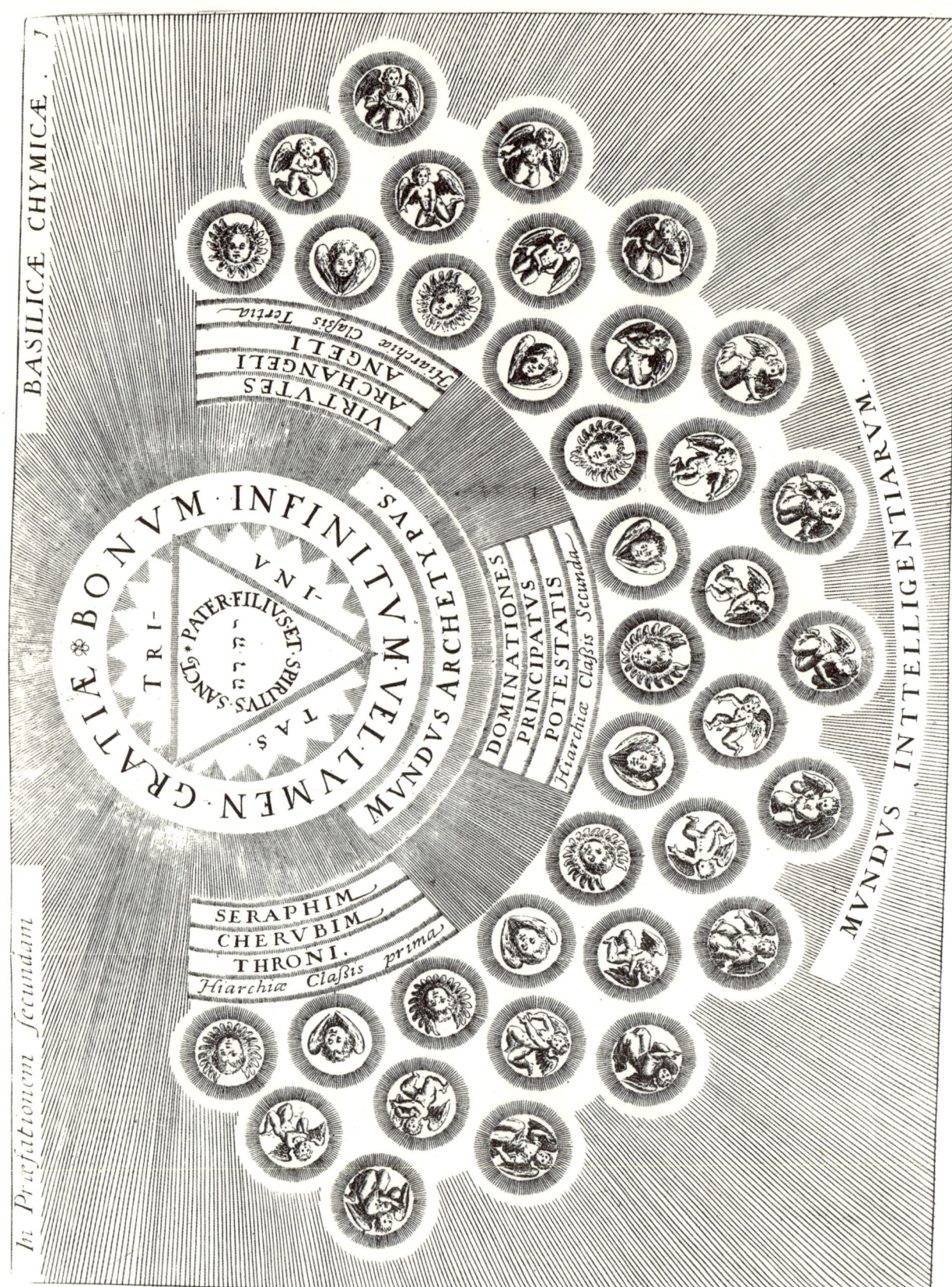

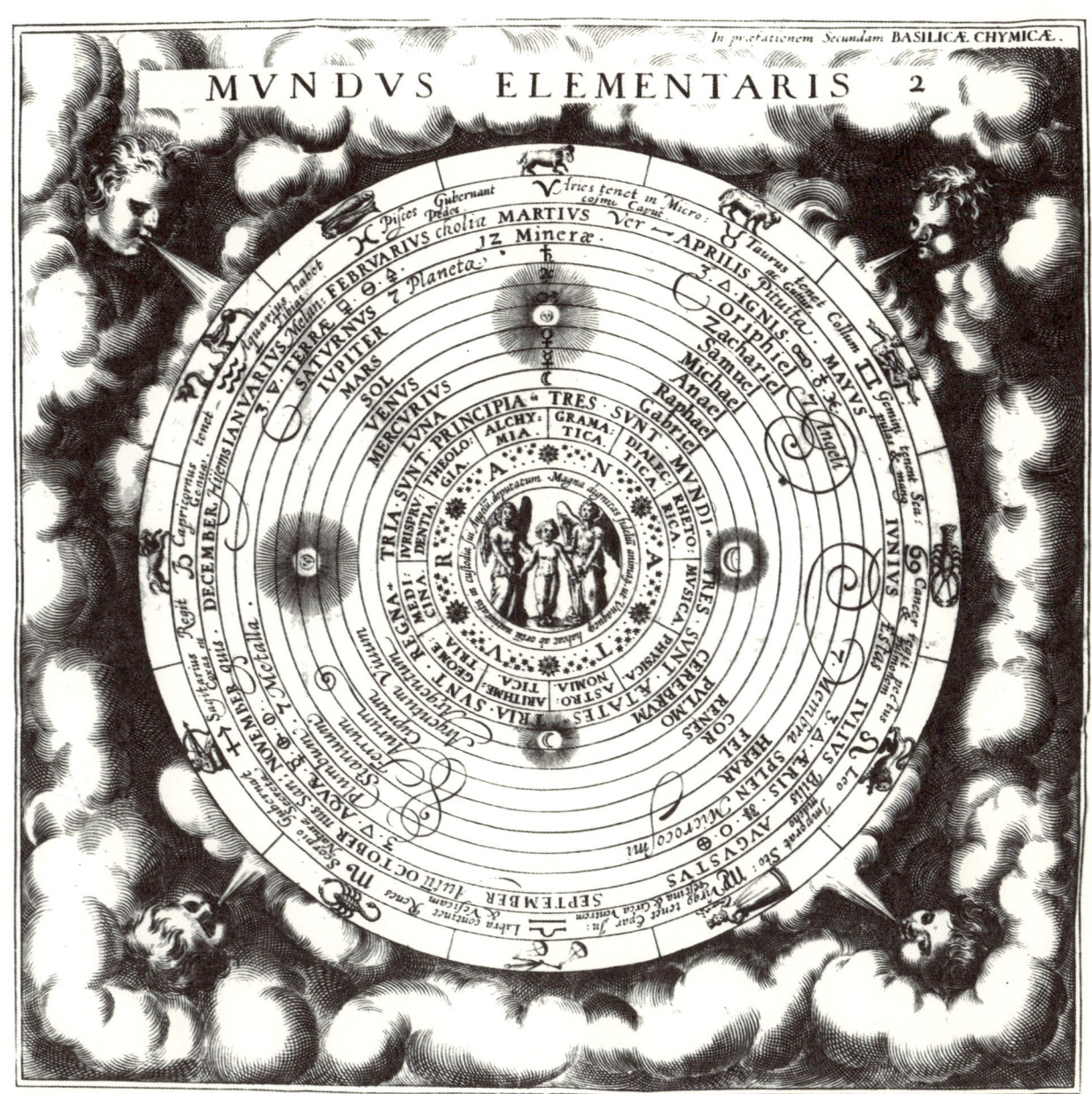

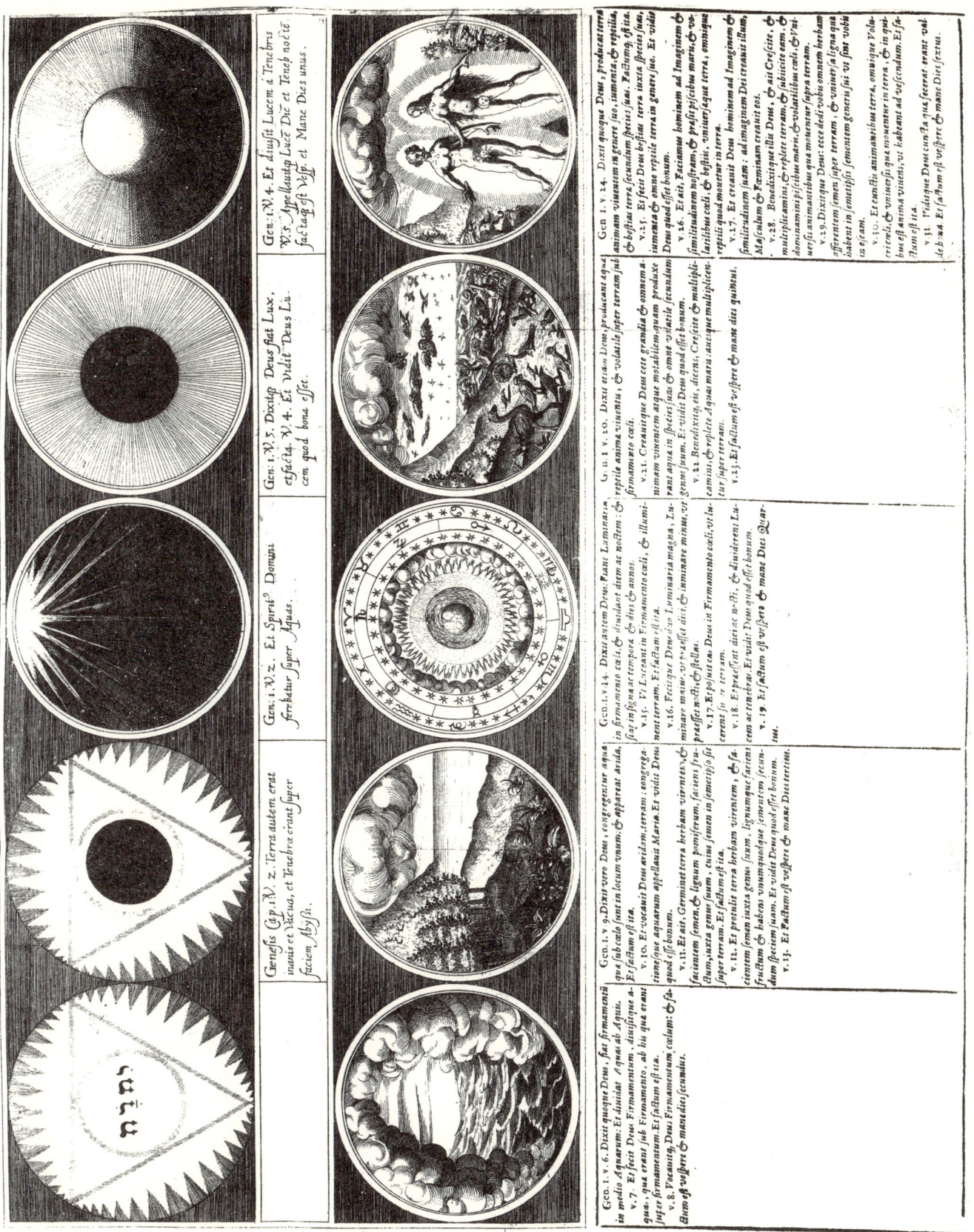

Opus medico-chymicum

Opus medico-chymicum · 149

115 Flanked by Hermes and Hippocrates, Mylius' glyph of threefold and fourfold correspondences has at its core the Adamic Earth. Four emblems represent the Elements. Fire (Salamander) is the Dwelling of the Stars: 'As above, so below.' Air (Phoenix and Toad) is the Dwelling of the Elements: 'By the conversion of Elements [and] the Threefold Purification let the One be made.' Water (Mermaid) is the Dwelling of the Minerals: 'All things natural are in Sun and Salt.' Earth (Lion and Dragon) is the Dwelling of the Microcosm: 'Separate them and bring them to maturity.'

116 Merian's engraving shows Johann Daniel Mylius in 1618, aged thirty-three, between laboratory and library. 'Reader, wilt thou have the mirror of Paracelsus and Galen? Behold, Mylius is certainly the mirror of both to thee.'

117 From the Holy Mystery of the Trinity, Divine Intelligence, as radiant light, descends through the Archetypal World and three classes of angelic hierarchies: Seraphim, Cherubim and Thrones the first; Dominations, Princes and Powers the second; Virtues, Archangels and Angels the third.

118 The Elemental World: here are shown all the correspondences between the signs of the Zodiac, the Months of the year, the human Organs, the Virtues, the Metals, the Minerals, the Elements and the Angels. The twelfth ring proclaims: Three are the Worlds, Three are the Ages, Three are the Realms, Three are the Principles. The names of twelve sciences, including alchemy, are in the next ring. Nature has a ring with six stars, a reminder of the six-pointed Star which floats upon the Night of the Work, like the Star of Bethlehem. At the centre is the purified Man, or Subject of the Art, in the custody of two Angels.

119 In this magnificent composition by Merian, the correspondences of Macrocosm and Microcosm are beautifully symbolized. Above, the Holy Tri-Unity and The Angels of Light influencing the Zodiac; below, the Raven of *Nigredo*, the Swan of *Albedo*, the Dragon, Subject of the Art, the Pelican (Mercury) and the Phoenix (Sulphur). Every conceivable symbol of the archetypal Opposites, Sol and Luna, Mercury and Sulphur, is here displayed. The central figure symbolizes the indissoluble mighty Unity of the Golden Stone. See Psalm 104, which accompanies this plate in the *Musaeum hermeticum* (1677) along with the text of the Emerald Table of Hermes (*8*, p. 36) which it illustrates.

120 The Biblical account of Creation is taken by alchemists as a model of their own microcosmic 're-creation', and each stage receives a complex interpretation which can best be summarized thus: From Divine Unity proceeds Spirit, Fire or Light, which materializes into the diversity of Matter. By isolating and purifying its essential principles, the Artist redeems Matter from the Fall that followed the creation of the human race.

THE 'SEALS OF THE PHILOSOPHERS'

121 Hermes Trismegistus, the Egyptian: That which is above is as that which is below.

122 Adfar the Alexandrian, teacher of Morienus: The Sun is the father of our spouse, but the Mother is the white Moon.

123 Calid, Saracen King of Egypt, disciple of Morienus: A third, who is the ruler of Fire, succeeds the Father and Mother.

124 Mary the Jewess, Sister of Moses: A smoke embraces a smoke, and the grass of the mountain absorbs them both.

125 Cleopatra, Queen of Egypt: The Divine is hidden from the people according to the Wisdom of the Lord.

126 Medera, the woman Alchemist: Whoever does not know the rule of truth does not know the Flask of Hermes.

127 Thaphuntia, the woman Philosopher: A marriage is made between two Gums, the White and the Red.

128 Euthica, the Arabic woman Philosopher: What fights against Fire is Sulphur, what sustains it is Mercury.

129 Calid the Jew, son of Gazichus: The creator's magistery is derived from adoration of God, not from your strength.

130 Musa, from the school of Calid: The teachers of the devout are the middlemen of the Divine Wisdom.

131 Democritus, the Greek Alchemist: The shadow of the solid Body is removed by the fiery medicine.

132 Pythagoras, the Greek Philosopher: In Nature you must study that from which God created all.

133 Anaxagoras, the Chazomoenian Philosopher: The burning Sun, the Soul of the Moon, the Spirit in the centre, are nothing but Mercury.

134 Zamolxis, the companion of Pythagoras: With God and Piety as my companions I come from narrow straits to glory.

135 Heraclitus, the Philosopher: Fire is the beginning of all things.

136 Apollonius of Tyana, the Philosopher: No Prophet is ever born wise in his own country.

137 Michael Psellus, the Philosopher: Mind and Nature bring God down from heaven.

138 Morienus, the Roman Philosopher: The essential starting requirement is in the manure-heap of our Putrefaction.

139 Avicenna, the Arab Philosopher: The Eagle flying in the air, and the Toad walking on the ground, are the Magistery.

140 Geber, the Arab Philosopher: Everything in Nature is in Sun and Salt.

141 Artephius, the Arab Philosopher: Three things comprise the Wisdom of the world, Soul, Body and Spirit.

142 Alphidius, the Arab Philosopher: It is not bought for a high price, but thrown out in the street by rich and poor.

143 Gilgil, the Moorish Philosopher: Nature does not produce the Tincture in the absence of Sulphur and Quicksilver.

144 Hamuel, the Philosopher: Reason and experience build up the firm and stable foundation of the Work.

145 Senior, the Philosopher: The Lunar Son's generation is stronger than its whole parentage.

146 Rasis, the Philosopher: Gum thickens the Milk, and our Milk dissolves Gum, whence comes Redness and the Eastern Blood.

147 Rosinus, the Philosopher: An ignorant fellow unknowingly strikes the gourd, and hopes to get the honey of misfortune thence.

148 The Philosopher of Massara: The dirtiness of the Stone makes men esteem it lightly and not separate it.

149 Mitigo, the Philosopher: Although men and beasts despise the Stone, yet is it loved by the Wise.

150 Malus, the Philosopher: This Stone is beneath you, above you, beside you, and around you.

151 Dante, the Philosopher: Prepare and dissolve the Bodies, and with the Water carry out Imbibition on the washed Spirits.

152 Galienus, the Philosopher: Prepare, cleanse, dissolve, coagulate the Bodies, and project them on the Body.

153 Mahomet, the Philosopher: The Stone required for this Work comes from living Matter.

154 Hercules, the wise King and Philosopher: The Magistery comes from one root, expands into several, and turns back into one.

155 Arsianus, the Philosopher: Our Water has Our Earth above it, great, clear and pure.

156 Datin, the Philosopher and Chymist: Our red Lato is useless: it is extremely powerful when it turns white.

157 Euthices, the Philosopher: We took away the Blackness with Natron Salt and Almizadir, and fixed the Whiteness with Borax.

158 Adarmath, the Philosopher: The beginning of this is connected with its end and its end with its beginning.

159 Azinabam, the Philosopher: The Philosophical Matter is by its nature called Vulphi, that is, Animal.

160 Elbo, Assassin and Philosopher: Whiten Latona and destroy your books, or your hearts will be corrupted.

161 Ademarus, the Philosopher: However it may be purified, sublimed, extracted and fixed, still it cannot be poured or mixed, but vitrifies.

162 Belinus, the Philosopher: My father the Sun has all the power that the whole world seeks.

163 Albugazal, the Teacher of Plato the Philosopher: He who is Saturn destroys me, but not my Nature.

164 Helisardes, the Philosopher: He who notes names and Colours, will not stray from the path of Magistery.

165 Plato, the Chymist: First the Egg perishes, then the Chick is born, the Animal is made from decomposition.

166 Yezid, the Constantinopolite: Our Stone is something which Fire does not affect, and from which our Mercury rises.

167 Galud, King of Babylon: 1. The rule of Saturn at first decomposes and tricks the Sun. 2. Recomposition takes four nights.

168 Seneca, the Philosopher: Fire is advantageous for the perfect, and disadvantageous for the imperfect.

169 Albertus Magnus, Bishop and Chymist: Not by my knowledge, but by the Grace of the Most Holy Spirit.

170 Bernard, Count of Treviso: Permanent water from the masculine and feminine seed gives birth to new species.

171 Basil Valentine, the Monk: Gold is the Father of the Tincture, Quicksilver its Mother, Mercury its Grandfather, the Mercurial Water its Grandmother.

172 Alanus, the Philosopher from India: He who knows two and seven knows all there is to be known. Two and seven are the chymical weights.

173 Arnold of Villa Nova, the Chymist: If the Illness has lasted for a month, it is cured in a day; if for a year, then it takes twelve days.

174 Peter of Villa Nova, Arnold's brother: This Medicine is to be greatly sought in the city, above all other Medicines and riches of the World.

175 Vincent, the Monk of Beauvais: The Elixir is called a stone because it can be ground, a non-stone because it melts and runs in the fire without evaporating, like gold.

176 John of Padua, the Philosopher: Waters have countless, marvellous virtues. Nothing is more marvellous than the Water of this Bath.

177 Jodocus Greverus, the Chymist: The Sun always takes Mercury as his companion. The Moon gets her light from the Sun.

178 Author of the Rose Garden of the Philosophers: One goes East, and one goes West.

179 Author of the Brotherly Dialogue Between Sol and the Stone: The Stone made from gold is a poisonous worm; witness the Mercury made from vulgar gold.

180 Author of the Philosophical Rhymes: Thou shalt visit the interior of the Earth.

181 Isaac and Arnold, the Philosophers: God gave two Stones, the first White, the second Red, gratis and for nothing.

182 Philippus Theophrastus Paracelsus: The Medicine is such as can make gold.

183 Isaac Holland, the Elder: It is a material containing both Quicksilver and the lightning flash.

184 Isaac Holland, the younger: These are the flowers that are hidden among so many thistles and thorns.

185 John Pontanus, the Philosopher: This Fire is without flame, but not without light, and is difficult to find.

186 Nicholas Flamel, the Frenchman: He who has lived well, cannot die badly.

187 Dionysius Zacharias, the Philosopher: This Art is held in reserve by the power of God, and is harmful to lay folk.

188 John Fernley Ambiensis: It is for the Wise to investigate the heights of eternity, with uplifted mind and eye.

189 William of Paris, the Philosopher: This knowledge requires a true Philosopher, not a foolish one.

190 John of Mehung, the Philosopher: It is not for Man's industry alone, but in God's hands, to will and encompass All in All.

191 Christopher of Paris, the Chymist: Here is the Brother, there the Sister; here the Husband, there his Wife. Here is the Son, there the Mother.

192 Guido de Montanor, the Philosopher: The final conjunction is that of the Four Elements, and this is called the fourfold Spiritual Philosophy.

193 Philip of Ravilasco, the Philosopher: It dies to the body by decay, and rises to the spirit by fresh growth.

194 Gratianus, Philosopher and Chymist: All things can be made into an ash; from the ash, a Salt; from the Salt, a Water; from the Water, a Mercury; from the Mercury, Gold.

195 Raymond of Marseilles, the Philosopher: We know there are deep secrets in Nature under the earth, and [?] to seek in minerals and not elsewhere.

196 John of Austria, the Philosopher: All that is created and born is made of four simple elements.

197 Stephen, Philosopher and Chymist: Only Man comes forth from Man, and from an animal is born its like.

198 Daniel, the Philosopher, in his 'Retractions': The more the Ore is cooked, the more it darkens, and becomes Spiritual Water.

199 Valerandus de Bosco, the Philosopher: The more our Ore is cooked, the more it reddens, and forms the Tincture of Redness.

200 John de Sacro Bosco, the Philosopher: The more our Ore is cooked, the more it thickens, and gives the Tincture of Whiteness.

201 Thomas Aquinas, the Italian Chymist: Art, like nature, makes metals from Sulphur and Mercury.

202 Petrus Bonus of Ferrara: From the Soul come the beginning and the first motion, and thus, indeed, everything that happens; from the Body comes the execution.

203 Peter de Zalento, Philosopher and Chymist: The Ferment is the marriage-broker. If it is used at the beginning, and in the middle, the Work is brought to completion.

204 John Aurelius Augurellus: I shall liberally bless him who takes me out of the Water, and reduces me to dryness.

205 Marcellus Palingenius, the Philosopher: Take and kill Saturn by immersing him in dark Waters.

206 John de Rupescissa, the Philosopher: Poverty teaches every skill, and the belly bestows cleverness.

207 Augustine Pantheus, the Venetian Priest: This is his triple paternity – created by the Sun, guided by the Artist, and reared by Vulcan.

208 Aloysius Marlianus, the Philosopher: Gold is made from Sulphur and Quicksilver, in a short space of time in the Fire.

209 John Lacinius, the Philosopher: Compared to Chemistry the other arts are as servants to their mistress.

210 John Chrysippus of Fano: The Wise Philosophers' mineral is the hidden work of celestial power.

211 John Theobanus, the Philosopher: In the Redness I have seen the shape of Fire, in the Transparency that of Air, in the Brilliance that of Water.

212 Ludovic Lazarellus, the Philosopher: What we have seen and made with the help of Nature is the perfect Elixir.

213 Efferarius, the Monk, Philosopher and Chymist: The Alchemists have the ability to transmute imperfect metals, in truth and not in sham.

214 Cardinal Gilbert, the Philosopher: He who does not know how to destroy gold, cannot know how it is made in the course of Nature.

215 John of Aquino, the Philosopher: It is easier to make the purest gold than it is to destroy gold.

216 Raymond Lull, the Philosopher: The Body of the Child born of Man and Woman comes forth for action.

217 Aegidius, Master of the Jerusalem Hospital: It is fed with the cheapest tinder, as the foetus is fed with menstrual fluid in the womb.

218 Author of the Abbreviated Rose Garden: The Principles are four, the Colours are four, the Fires are four, but the means are three.

219 The Prior of Alexandria, Philosopher and Chymist: A fire drawn from the Sun's rays, like Elemental Fire.

220 Cardinal Garcia, the Philosopher: A pattern like the circuit of the year descends from the stars, like Prometheus' fennel stalk to mortals.

221 Hugo Apostolicus, the Philosopher: The height of this Magistery is to remove the mortal shadow from the radiance.

222 Peter, Monk and Philosopher: This fiery little light lives in the Earth, and water cannot extinguish it, for it is heavenly.

223 Durandus, Monk and Philosopher: The Stone is at first a pallid Old Man, then a ruddy Youth, and a blood-red Boy.

224 Bishop Androicus, the Philosopher: This is the flame, that is the oil, this is the horse, that the foal, this is the dog, that the hare.

225 Bishop Dominicus, 'Of Weights': Make the Gold alive by sublimation; pour it on the Salt, and put it in a manure-heap in a strong jar.

226 Dominicus Apostolicus, the Chymist: There are two Matters, one for inceration, and one for hardening.

227 John Dastin, the Englishman: Nature freely accepts all that God orders.

228 Roger Bacon, the English Philosopher: Make the Elements equal to each other, and you will have the Magistery.

229 Hortulanus, Philosopher and Chymist: Only he who knows how to make the Philosophers' Stone, understands what they say concerning the Stone.

230 Richard, the English Philosopher: The study of Science removes ignorance, and leads the mind to true knowledge.

231 Thomas Norton, the English Philosopher: Our Matter is a thing of low price, of no value; anyone who finds it hardly even picks it up.

232 George Ripley, the Philosopher: There are three Mercuries of the Sun and Moon, two superficial, and one essential.

233 The Abbot of Westminster, Philosopher: The Stone is transparent to the view, pellucid and of a wonderful starry clarity.

234 Edward Kelley, the doubting Philosopher: The First Matter is bright and somewhat reddish, therefore it is called our Marcasite.

235 Scotus, the most learned Philosopher: The idea occurs in our Work, that once you do well you need not repeat.

236 Aegidius de Vadis, the Philosopher: It is not a stone to touch and sight; rather it is a fine earth, glistening red and not transparent.

237 John Duns Scotus, the Philosopher: When separated and prepared, our Matter is called Philosophick Litharge.

238 Michael Scotus, the Philosopher: That which was ready to our hands is lost by the sins of wicked men.

239 Melchior Cibinensis, the Hungarian Philosopher: The Philosophick Stone of the Philosophers must be nourished like a child on Virgin's Milk.

240 Bavran, the eminent Philosopher: Once our Son is born like a glorious King, he assumes his Philosophick Tincture from the Fire.

241 Brother Albert Bayer, Monk and Philosopher: Given by royal Venus, he appears revived, which signifies the Red Ornament.

242 Rhodianus, the excellent Philosopher: Death is dead, and our Son reigns, endowed with our flesh and heritage.

243 Rachaidibi, Philosopher and Chymist: All that is fed is fed by reduced doses; all that is brought to life is brought to life by twofold doses.

244 Aristotle, the Philosopher of Alchemy: Philosophick bringing to life and feeding, are the start of the Wise and Philosophick Work.

245 Arda, the Philosopher, Disciple of Aristotle: The seed is fed with moisture natural to it, till it is quickened and brought to life.

246 Remark from the letter of Alexander: Death and shadows flee that sea, and the Dragon flees the rays of the Sun.

247 Serapio, the most industrious Philosopher: Now is the time to bring the dead to life and cure the sick.

248 The Philosophers' Book of Saturn: It is brought to life until it is dead, from that metallic form that is the leprous shadow of the Stone.

249 Dumbeleius, Philosopher and Chymist: It is responsible for the melting of metals, yet it is not the Philosophers' metal.

250 Bernard de Gravia, the petty Philosopher: Our dead Son lives, the King returns from the Fire, and rejoices in a secret marriage.

251 Melchior, Cardinal and Bishop: He ought to be killed judiciously, since death will reveal him.

252 Malchamech, Philosopher and Chymist: Marry gum with gum in a true marriage, and make them like fresh water.

253 Aranus, Philosopher of the Medes: Unless one knows how to produce, fertilize and generate the components, nothing can be done, nor anything accomplished.

254 The Philosopher who bears the Palm: Marry the Slave to his perfumed Sister, and they will bring forth a son who is not like his Parents.

255 Anonymous Sarmatian Chymist: Once you have seen the Whiteness, cool your Work, and you will find the Moon taking on the colour of the Sun.

256 Author of The Golden Cymbal: Tarry near the flask, and see marvels, for it turns white and yellow, in less than three hours.

257 Author of The Lesser Rose Garden: This first growth is green, the second white, which is whiter than all the whiteness in the world.

258 The Philosophers' Ladder: Take pure fixed Mercury to be the great Magistery of the hidden Stone.

259 The Game of the Philosophick Children: It may be a thing that most people do not see, though they tread it under their feet.

260 The Dawn Arising: In all things there dwells a Spirit of their own, by which they are animated and grow.

261 The Philosophick Testament of Pythagoras: Without Fire nothing will be wrought, as no warrior should be without arms.

262 The Assembly of Philosophers and Sages: The first deployment is coitus, the second conception, the third pregnancy, the fourth birth, the fifth nourishment.

263 Author of Mirror of the Chymical Art: The bed beneath heaven, which affords our newly-weds great delight, is a grassy sward.

264 Author of The Universal Way of Wisdom: The Nine Muses bestow a crown of brilliant flowers, the Graces beauty and charm.

265 Author of On the Quintessence of Wine: Apollo plays the lute, Diana wears white roses, and Saturn a black gown.

266 Author of The Light Shining in Darkness: Jupiter wears a pale shirt, Mercury a woman's mantle, and Mars a petagium.

267 Author of The Garden of the Riches of Wisdom: Venus wears her vestment or glorious royal dress of gold and purple.

268 Author of The Process of the Philosophick Tincture: The King comes out of the fire crowned with a golden solar diadem.

269 Author of the Tractate on Aurelia: This is arranged so that it is like the Creation of Man.

270 Author of The Splendour of the Philosophick Sun: From the seeds of Sun and Moon, is born he whom thousands seek and rarely find.

271 Author in the Table of Senior the Philosopher: Let us do it again, till he dies and becomes pliable.

272 The Philosophick Allegory of Merlin: Saturn is the planet of death, see, he wears a black gown.

273 Parabolic Allegory to Arisleus: Conception and betrothal are done in decay, and generation of offspring is done in the air.

274 Author of The Riddles of Chymistry: Our Seed is a Quicksilver which is joined to our Earth.

275 The Philosophick Epitome: Unless Quicksilver is put to death with the hidden body, it will have no strength.

276 The Book of the Truth of Philosophick Wisdom: When the Son first lies with his Mother, she kills him with a viperish blow.

277 Sound of the Philosophick Trumpet: The Earth of the Body will be dissolved in the Water of the Seed, and one undivided Water will appear.

278 Author of On the Philosopher's Stone in 12 Chapters: That which caused you Life, the same also caused you Death.

279 Oswald Croll of Wetter, Disciple of the Philosophers: This knowledge is nothing but the secrets of wise teachers and Philosophers.

280 John Daniel Mylius of Wetter, Disciple of the Philosophick Wisdom: That is, To walk in the Divine ways and in the Magistery, with Our Lord Jesus Christ for companion.

Johann Daniel Mylius
Antidotarium, 1620

Johannis Danieli Mylii, Vetterani Hassi, M.C. Antidotarium medico-chymicum Reformatum: continens quatuor libros distinctos. Quorum I. Generaliora in pharmaciam requisita explicat. II. Tractat de quibusdam exoticis in nostris Basilicis omissis. III. Tradit praecepta Galenic [orum] & Chymicorum de praeparatione medicamentorum. IV. Resolvit formas & dividit medicamenta tam Galen [icorum] quam Chymicorum. Francofurti sumptibus Lucae Iennis. M.DC.XX.

Johann Daniel Mylius, of Wetter in Hesse, Medico-Chymist: Revised medico-chymical collection of remedies, containing four separate books, whereof: I explains the general things requisite for pharmacy. II treats of a number of exotic remedies omitted from our Basilicas. III conveys the precepts of Galen's followers and of the Chymists concerning the preparation of Galenic and Chymical medicaments. IV resolves the forms and distinguishes Galenic and Chymical medicaments. Frankfurt, printed for Lucas Jennis, 1620.

The dedication is to the munificent Corporation of the Imperial City of Frankfurt, with a hint that the author has found refuge and succour there in turbulent times.

OSWALD CROLL
Basilica chymica, 1622

Osualdi Crollii Veterani Hassi Basilica chymica continens philosophicam propriâ laborum experientiâ confirmatam descriptionem et usum remediorum chymicorum selectissimorum e lumine gratiae et nature desumptorum. In fine libri additus est autoris ejusdem Tractatus novus de signaturis rerum internis. Cum Gratia et Privilegio S. Caes. Maiest: Francofurti impensis Godefridi Tampachij.

Oswald Croll, of Wetter in Hesse: Chymical Basilica containing a philosophick description, confirmed by the experience of his own labours, and application of the choicest chymical remedies drawn from the light of Nature and of Grace. At the end of the book is added the Author's new Treatise on the Inner Signatures of Things. By Grace and Privilege of His Imperial Majesty. Frankfurt, printed for Gottfried Tampach.

First published in 1608, this work was many times reprinted. This edition bears a Privilege of Ferdinand II issued at Vienna, 5 March 1622. Oswald Croll or Crollius (1580–1609), a Paracelsian physician, studied at Marburg, Heidelberg, Strasbourg and Geneva and devised a number of new remedies. His dedication, signed at Prague, 1608, is to his patron, Christian I of Anhalt-Bernberg.

The Antwerp-born engraver Aegidius Sadeler (1575–1629) was nephew and pupil to Jan and Raphael Sadeler. He was in Italy, engraving plates after Italian painters, when Rudolph II called him to Prague. He later worked for Rudolph's successors Matthias and Ferdinand II. The quality of Sadeler's vast output earned him the title 'Phoenix of engravers'.

Antidotarium; Basilica · 159

281 *Antidotarium*. This very plate by Matthäus Merian, showing three ancient and three modern Adepts, a mine and an apothecary's shop, was used as the title-page of *Hydrolithus sophicus, seu Aquarium sapientum*, one of nine treatises in the original edition of *Musaeum hermeticum* (1625).

282 *Basilica chymica*. The Superior Sphere shows the Divine Trinity, with God, Messiah and Man and the celestial angelic hierarchies. The Inferior Sphere conforms to microcosmical correspondences, with the alchemical trinity Sulphur, Mercury and Salt and at the centre the *Terra Adamica* or the Subject of the Wise. The conformity, albeit in reverse, of the two spheres is emphasized by the words of Hermes Trismegistus (top left):

AS ABOVE, SO BELOW.

MICHAEL MAIER
Septimana philosophica, 1620

Septimana philosophica, qua Aenigmata aureola de omni naturae genere a Salomone Israëlitarum sapientissimo Rege, & Arabiae Regina Saba, nec non Hyramo, Tyri Principe, sibi invicem in modum colloquii proponuntur & enordantur: Ubi passim novae, & verae, cum ratione & experientiae convenientes, rerum naturalium causae exponuntur & demonstrantur figuris cupro incisis singulis diebus adiectis. Authore Michaele Maiero, Imperialis Consistorii Comite, Eq. Ex. Med. D. & Caes. Maiest. olim Aulico, nunc illustris Principis ac Dn. Mauritii, Hassiae Landgravii, &c. Archiatro. Francofurti, Typis Hartmanni Palthenii, Sumptibus Lucae Iennis, 1620.

The Philosophick Week, in which the golden enigmas of every kind in Nature are expounded and unravelled by Solomon, most wise King of the Israelites, Sheba, Queen of Arabia, and Hyram, Prince of Tyre, in alternate discourse after the manner of a colloquy; in which, throughout, new and true causes of natural things, in conformity to reason and experience, are expounded and demonstrated, with figures engraved in copper added to the several Days. By Michael Maier, Count of the Imperial Consistory, Free Knight of the Empire, Doctor of Medicine, formerly of His Imperial Majesty's Court, now chief physician to the Prince and Lord Maurice, Landgrave of Hesse, &c. Frankfurt, printed by Hartmann Palthenius for Lucas Jennis, 1620.

This work was dedicated at Magdeburg to Christian William, Archbishop of Magdeburg, Margrave of Brandenburg, Duke of Prussia, on 2 January 1620 o.s. (The Protestant states of Germany refused to adopt the 'new style' or Gregorian calendar, preferring until 1700 to adhere to the Julian or 'old style' calendar. Thus 2 January 1620 o.s. would be 12 January 1620/21 n.s. In both systems the year still began on 25 March; 1 January was not adopted as the starting date for the year until 1752.) It consists of a debate lasting six days, in the course of which King Solomon, the Queen of Sheba and Prince Hiram of Tyre examine all the mysteries of Nature.

284

285

Septimana philosophica · 163

286

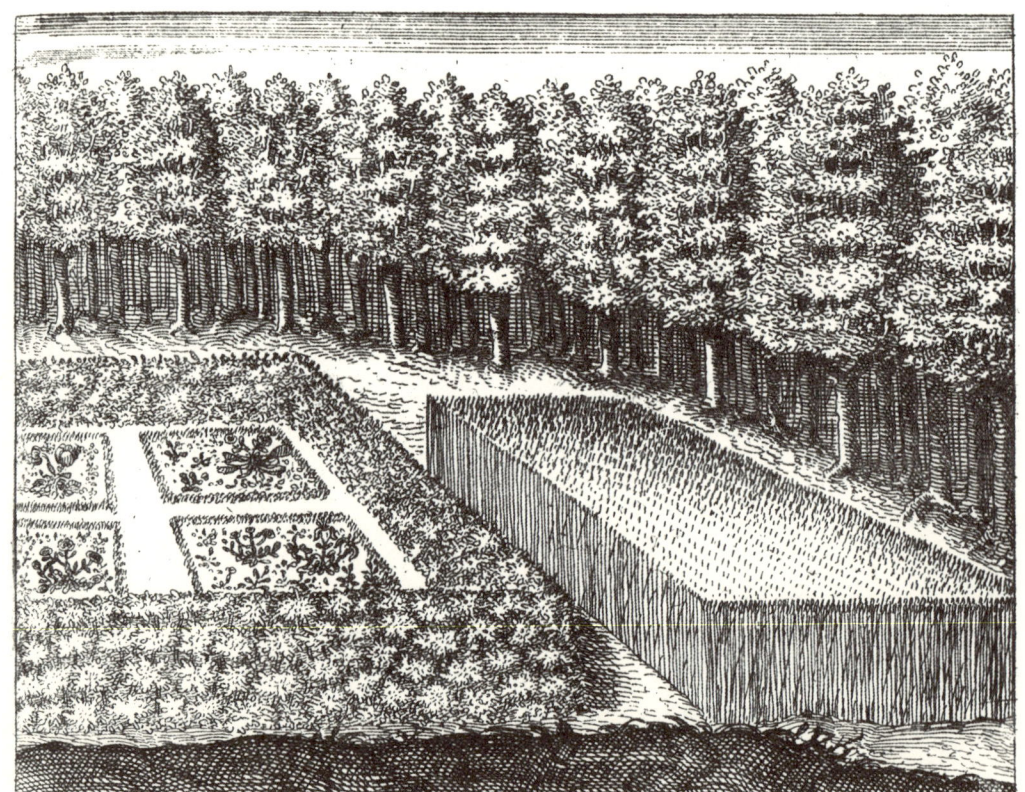
287

288

289

Septimana philosophica · 165

283 The title-page engraving by Balthasar Schwan was used in 1625 as the frontispiece of the fourth treatise of the *Musaeum hermeticum*, entitled *Demonstratio naturae*, by Johannes de Mehung.

284 Alchemical texts, as I have previously stated, are very often deceptive; but hermetick emblems are not. Here, unless one manages to read between the lines, the corresponding text has little to do with the image. Europe can be seen holding the hieroglyph of the Subject of the Wise, and receiving from the Sun, through the mediation of the Moon, the celestial influx which materializes and confers upon the purified crystalline Subject the extraordinary qualities of the Philosopher's Stone. This influx, fire or spirit, perhaps the best-guarded secret in alchemy, can only be received during a few days of the year if favourable weather conditions prevail. The text does mention that some parts of the world are better for that purpose than others, and Europe holds pride of place.

285 Meteors (from the Greek *meteoron*, thing that occurs in the sky) are of many kinds, including storms, rain, snow, aurora borealis, rainbow, lightning, fog, shooting stars and dewfalls. If they occur when one tries to receive the celestial influx mentioned in connection with the previous plate, they are impediments which will prevent success. All these same meteors are also visible in the microcosmic world of the Great Work and can be witnessed through the glass by the alchemist who, depending upon the order of their occurrence, will judge whether he may hope to reach his goal.

286 The reader who has read what I have previously written about the Subject of the Wise will know that this 'inner earth' must be sought in a mine and prepared by the alchemist himself. The main suggestion immediately evoked by the emblem is the axiomatic VISITA INTERIORA TERRAE RECTIFICANDO INVENIES OCCULTUM LAPIDEM: 'Search the interior of the earth and by rectifying thou shalt find the hidden Stone'. Maier in the text provides many indications of great value, and notably warns against the use of the Antimony of the Vulgar. The Saturnine Dragon is the Antimony of the Wise ♄, which, once opened by the fiery sword of Mars ♂, will yield the first ☿ or Mercury of the Wise. The alchemist must extract from the mine the raw ore that contains the Antimony of the Wise.

287 On the fourth day the subject of discussion is the vegetable realm. Maier examines the various species of plants which are connected symbolically with alchemy. The plate shows a garden and a wheat field surrounded by a forest because the conversation deals in turn with gardens, fields, and forests. The study of Nature being an essential discipline to penetrate the Art of Hermes, the principles of gardening, agriculture and forestry will allow one to discover many precious analogies. Maier adduces the hermetick interpretation of such myths as the mulberry-tree coloured by the blood of Pyramus and Thisbe, the esoteric significance of wheat and bread, of vines and wine, the latter of course being linked to the blood of Christ and to the Red Tincture.

Concerning forests, the question is asked: why was the Golden Fleece hung by Aetes, son of the Sun, in the wood of Mars? The Golden Fleece is of course the Philosopher's Stone, obtained after many difficulties and struggles in which Ares must triumph over Aries, that is to say the Subject of the Wise (Aries the Ram) is dissolved in conjunction with the martial agent (Ares or Mars) which yields the principle of Fixity.

288 On the fifth day the conference embraces the animal kingdom. In this emblem all the animals belong to the symbolic hermetick bestiary. In the air are the volatile Eagle or Vulture, the Raven of *Nigredo* or Blackness, the Grey Owl, the many-coloured Peacock and Parrot, the White Swan and the Red Phoenix which we have often encountered before. Within the waters are contending monsters evoking the tumult of Dissolution, the Remora and the Dolphin which are emblems of Sulphur.

On the ground are the Cat, whose whiskers evoke the receptive power of crystals, the Bull, Apis (already encountered in the *Arcana arcanissima*), the Mule, a hybrid showing the Possibility of Nature, the Wild Boar, the Dog, the Camel, the golden-horned Hind, the Unicorn and the Lion.

289 A Philosopher whose noble countenance reminds one of Hermes measures the required proportions to begin the Great Work. The Globe is his Subject, his original Chaos; Death or Dissolution (with its occult Fire) is his recreation preceded by a complete destruction, before the advent of the Philosopher's Stone. Maier, in a text where one must pick and choose carefully, draws attention to the fertilizing action of the Nile, which corresponds in alchemy to Air rather than Water, or more specifically to a nitre drawn from the air which fosters the Earth's fertility and dissolves therein the planted seeds that they may grow and multiply. This, says he, is the pivot of the whole science.

Johann Daniel Mylius
Philosophia reformata, 1622

Ioannis Danielis Mylii T. & Med. Candidati Wetterani Hassi Philosophia reformata continens libros binos. I. Liber in septem partes divisus est. Pars 1. agit de generatione metallorum in visceribus terrae. 2. tractat principia artis philosophicae. 3. docet de scientia Divina abbreviata. 4. enarrat 12. grad[us] sapientu[m] philosoph[orum]. 5. declarat Amb[igua] in hac Divina scientia. 6. dicit de Recap[itulatione] Artis Divinae Theori[ca]. 7. ait de Artis Divinae Recap[itulatione] Practica. II. Liber continet authoritates Philosophorum. Francofurti apud Lucam Iennis, Anno M.DC.XXII.

Johann Daniel Mylius, Doctoral Candidate in Theology and Medicine, of Wetter in Hesse: Philosophy Reformed, containing two books. The first book is divided into seven parts. Part 1 deals with the generation of metals in the bowels of the earth; 2 treats of the principles of the Philosophick Art; 3 teaches of the Divine Science in brief; 4 enumerates twelve stages of the Wisdom of the Philosophers; 5 explains the ambiguities in this Divine Science; 6 speaks of the theoretical recapitulation of the Divine Art; 7 treats of the practical recapitulation of the Divine Art. The second book contains the Philosophers' authorities. Frankfurt, Lucas Jennis, 1622.

With its remarkable emblems, engraved by Balthazar or Baltzer Schwan (a citizen of Frankfurt who died in 1624), the *Philosophia reformata* is the masterpiece of J.D. Mylius. The emblems were re-used by Daniel Stolcius in his anthologies *Viridarium chemicum* (1624) and *Chymisches Lustgärtlein* (1627), both published in Frankfurt by Lucas Jennis. They owe much to Maier and to Basil Valentine.

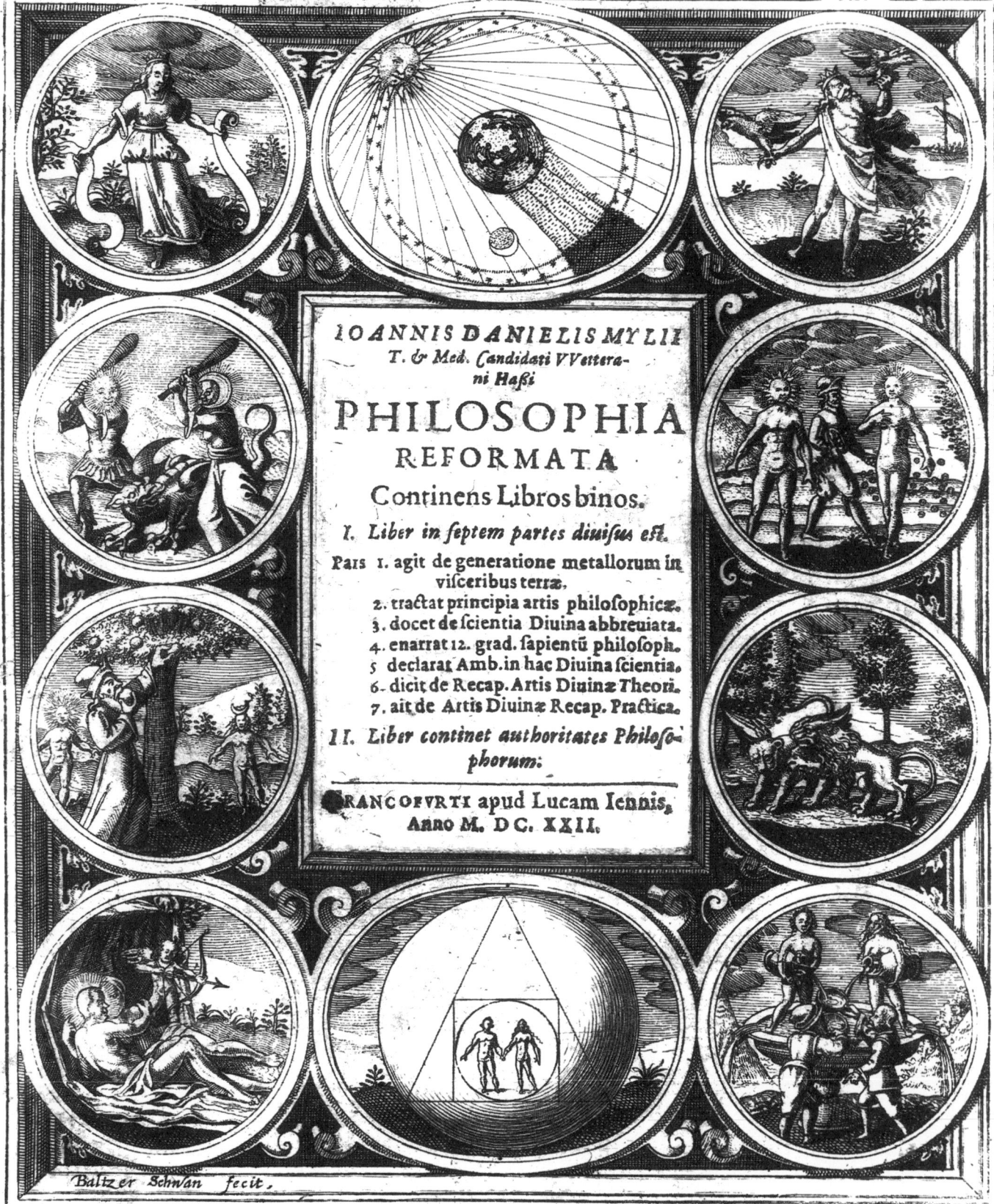

291

292

293

294

295

296

Philosophia reformata · 169

170 · JOHANN DANIEL MYLIUS

303

304

305

306

307

308

Philosophia reformata · 171

172 · JOHANN DANIEL MYLIUS

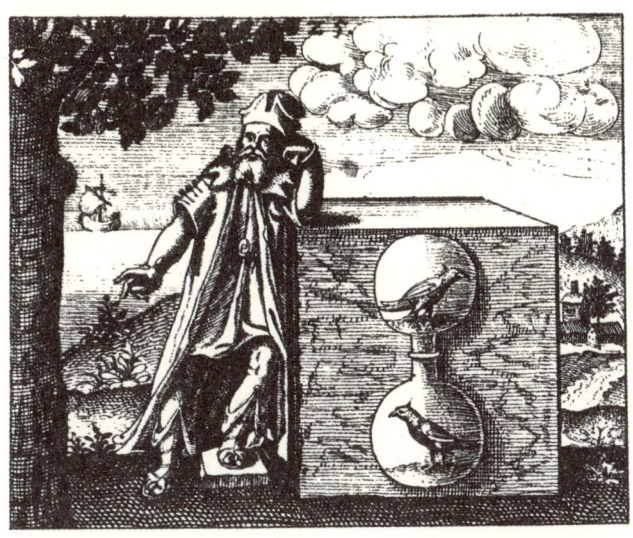
315

316

317

318

319

320

Philosophia reformata · 173

321

322

323

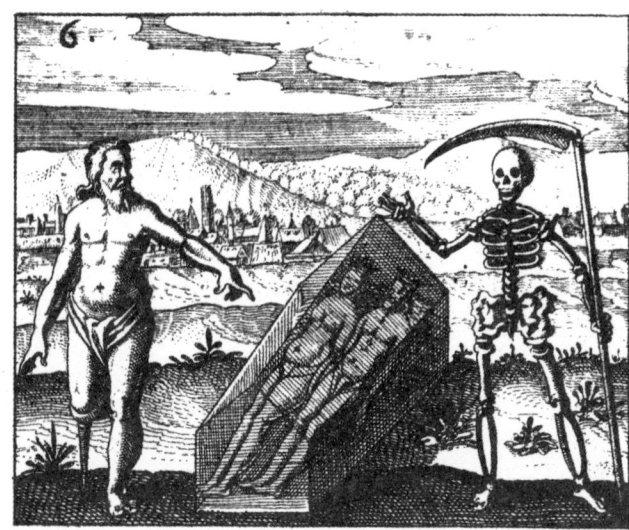

324

325

326

174 · JOHANN DANIEL MYLIUS

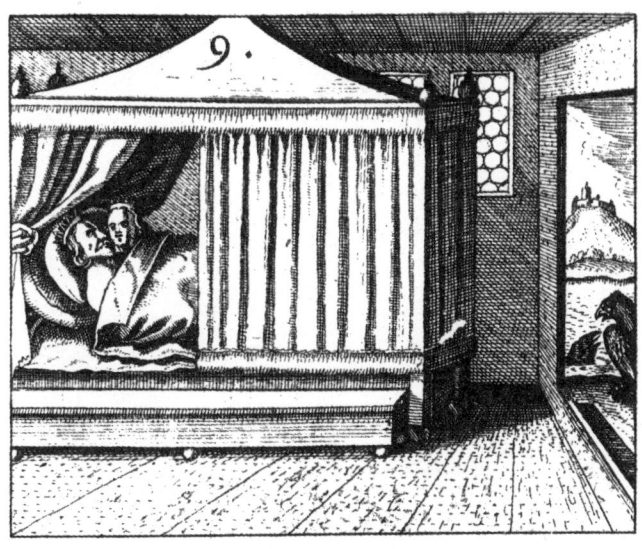

327

328

329

330

331

332

Philosophia reformata · 175

176 · JOHANN DANIEL MYLIUS

Philosophia reformata · 177

178 · JOHANN DANIEL MYLIUS

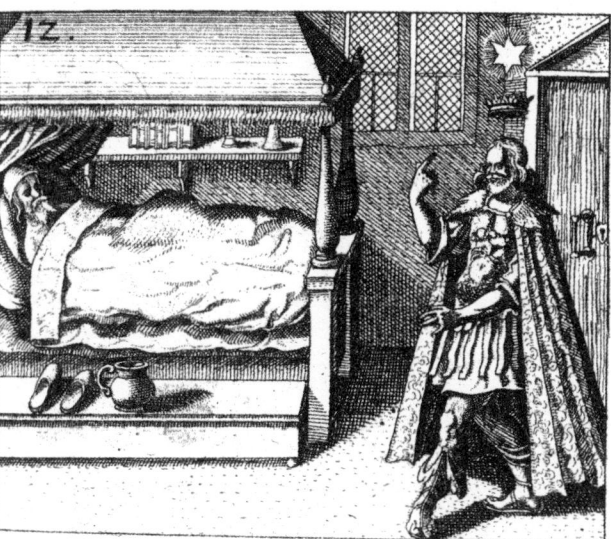

Philosophia reformata · 179

290 Seven of the ten images on the engraved title-page allude to the iconography of Maier's *Atalanta fugiens* (XVI, XXI, XXV, XXVI, XXX, XLV, XLVI). The curious reader will find pictorial analogies to the other three elsewhere in the present book.

291 Inspired by Emblema II of *Atalanta fugiens* (*31*). The Child of Philosophy is nourished by the Milk (Mercury) of the Earth of the Wise.

292 The Four Elements and the corresponding stages of the Work: from left to right Earth, Water, Air and Fire.

293 Sol and Luna with the four main stages of the Work: Raven (*Nigredo*), Peacock (the Peacock's Tail), Swan (*Albedo*), and Red King (Perfect Redness = Fixity). The tricephalic Snake is a reminder that the Great Work is divided into three parts.

294 Mars aiming the arrow of the Secret Fire at the volatile Dragon, the Subject of the Art. The Fixed Lion rests peacefully above.

295 Inspired by the Twelfth Key of Basil Valentine (*106*). The Secret Fire reduces the Bodies to their first Principles without destroying their seminal and generative virtues. The Philosophick Calcination is a Fixation of the quick or Volatile, hence the Lion eating the Snake.

296 The object of this 'Solution' is the acquisition of Sulphur (the Fiery Man), soul of the dissolved metal hidden within the mercurial 'white water' in the glass vessel. The Solution is achieved by the conjugated action of the Secret Fire and the Green Lion, whose mother is the Venus of the Wise. See also the Fifth Key of Basil Valentine (*99*).

297 See commentary to the Second Key of Basil Valentine (*96*). The opposing Principles are reconciled in the person of Philosophick (or Twofold) Mercury.

298 See the Sixth Key of Basil Valentine (*100*). Conjunction: the Mediator marries the opposite Principles. The Philosophick Conjunction is here shown in all its forms. Notice the Janus-headed Secret Fire, and the action of the Trident of Neptune (the Water of the Philosophers) which washes the darkness of *Nigredo*, bringing about the varied colours of the Rainbow or Peacock's Tail, which herald the Light.

299 Putrefaction, Death, *Caput Corvi* (Raven's Head), *Nigredo*, are names for the operation during which the Pure Spirits are separated from the dross.

300 The first grade of the work begins in Aries, the second in Cancer, the third in Libra; while the fourth, beginning in Capricorn, symbolizes both Putrefaction and Fermentation.

301 The Congelation is the reconciliation of the Fixed with the Volatile, brought about by the Mediator who partakes of the nature of both.

302 The Cibation is the feeding of the Philosophick Child with the Virgin's Milk (*Lac Virginis*) extracted from the Matter of the Wise.

303 The Sublimation is a purification of the Matter by means of Dissolution. This operation is repeated several times, which is why Saturn is about to cut the single stem showing the Star, the Moon and the Sun (which are the First, Second and Third Works).

304 Fermentation: the Philosopher sows the Tingent Virtue in the foliated Earth of Hermes, while the Angel of Revelation blows the trumpet of Resurrection. See the Third Key of Basil Valentine (*98*), Emblema VI of *Atalanta fugiens* (*35*), John 12.24–25 and I Corinthians 15.36–38.

305 The Exaltation is the Perfection of the Stone, repeatedly dissolved and coagulated in its own blood, the Mercury which gushes from the single head of the bicorporate Lion.

306 Multiplication: each time the Fixed Stone is redissolved in the Mercury upon which it feeds, it augments in weight, volume and power. Each rebirth of the Stone gives in theory a tenfold increase of power.

307 Birth of the Elemental Quintessence.

308 Inside the Earth, the seven planetary gods incarnating the seven metals, and the four Fires of the Work (concerning which, see *Atalanta fugiens*, Emblema XVII, *46*).

309 Inspired and combined from Emblemata XXI and XLV of *Atalanta fugiens* (*50*, *74*), this figure represents the alchemical Squaring of the Circle, within the microcosm of the Work.

310 Without help from the Volatile, the Fixed is never sublimated; and conversely, the Volatile in growing Fixed grows more and more resistant to the tyranny of the external Fire.

311 Every fixation of the Volatile (the fleeing maiden caught by the monster) is followed by a volatilization of the Fixed until Perfection is reached.

312 See *Atalanta fugiens*, Emblema III (*32*). The Subject is purged of its impurities by a fiery laundry.

313 See *Atalanta fugiens*, Emblema XVI (45). Lion and Lioness (Fixed and Volatile Principles) clash violently.

314 Until the mutual death of the adversaries has occurred, there can be no lasting union between the King and the Queen.

315 The long Coction requires a good deal of patience from the Artist.

316 The resolution of Fixed and Volatile is achieved by a triple operation.

317 See *Atalanta fugiens*, Emblema XXXV (64). Ceres, foster-mother of the Philosophick Child, feeds him. Mars, the complementry initial Principle, looks on. Metal and Subject are in the presence of one another. The brother and sister (Apollo and Luna) are the second Conjunction, from which Mercury, the Philosophick Child and future Philosopher's Stone, is born.

318 The First Perfection allows the Queen to relieve poverty.

319 From the Waters of the Twin Fountains a single Water is made which is the Fountain of Life (see Emblema XL of *Atalanta fugiens*, 69).

320 The Union of King and Queen depends upon a Perfect Solution.

321 A purification by Fire is necessary to remove all heterogeneous impurities.

322 Purified, the Bodies slowly dissolve in the water of the Bath.

323 Now, in the bed of love, the Queen begins to convert the King into her own (volatile) nature.

324 Within the crystal coffin (the vessel of the Art) the reign of Death (*Putrefactio*) has begun. Vulcan is always shown as one-legged, because in this Work his Fire alone does not suffice.

325 The Bodies are passive, while their liberated Spirits take flight.

326 The Spirits return as the celestial rain or Dew, watering the parched Bodies which have merged in the unity of the Hermaphrodite or Rebis (*Res bina*, twofold thing).

327 The lovers lie in the nuptial bed; the Raven's Head (*Caput Corvi*) must be cut off and the Subject of the Art whitened.

328 The First Silver Perfection is reached at the end of the Putrefaction.

329 Fermentation. The Queen has communicated her volatile nature to the King.

330 Now the Fixed Diana turns her (fiery) arrow upon the Sun, Sulphur of the Philosophers, and imparts Perfect Fixity to him.

331 Mercury, like the Hermaphrodite, possesses the double nature of the alchemical Male, hot and dry, and of the alchemical Female, cold and wet: which is why he is the medium of all transformations.

332 All fixed things must be made volatile, and conversely all volatile things must be made fixed.

333 Storms, rain and darkness hide the birth of Latona's children, the hermetick twins – future parents of the Philosopher's Stone.

334 Exalted and multiplied by a re-Dissolution in its own blood (Mercury), the Philosopher's Stone in its Silver and Golden Perfection emerges from the Well of Alchemy.

335 The Philosopher's Stone has the power to reconcile irreconcilable Opposites by virtue of possessing the power of both.

336 Here is the Universal Dissolvent, the Green Lion or Mercury of the Wise, without which nothing can be achieved.

337 The Philosophick Child, born to surpass both his parents in might and splendour, still tugs at his mother's skirts, showing that he has yet to grow in strength and Fixity.

338 After the last trial of Death, here is the Risen King over whom Death has no longer any power; here is the Philosopher's Stone.

339 This image occurs three times in the *Philosophia reformata*, and is used on the title-page (p. 365) of the work's second part, *Liber secundus*. Elsewhere it appears in many treatises, most notably as the frontispiece of *Gloria mundi: alias Paradysi tabula...*, printed in the 1677 edition of the *Musaeum hermeticum*. It derives from two woodcuts (dated 1605) which appeared in *Azoth sive Aureliae occultae philosophorum... in 1613*. In the Tree of Philosophy, the first five degrees of Perfection are shown as six-pointed Stars. The sixth is the Moon (*Albedo*), and the last is the Perfect Sun. The seven Operations appear round the Tree, contrasting for instance, Putrefaction and Resurrection. The King and Queen, besides representing the Opposites, are two of the Four Elements: the Dragon is Earth, the King is Fire, the Queen is Water and the Eagle is Air. In the foreground the alchemists Senior and Adolphus are debating.

340 Three faces of the Stone: the Philosophick Child, the purified Matter; the Old Man in the sphere, the *Materia Prima*; and the union of the three Principles, Mercury, Sulphur and Salt.

341 This emblem (equivalent in significance to the image of a Mermaid or Siren) shows the union of Sulphur (our Fish) and of the first Mercury (the Woman), from which results Philosophick Mercury.

342 The Fixation of the Volatile (the Lion biting the Eagle) produces the Salamander or Sulphur of the Wise.

343 Here is the Quintessential Unity of our Work.

344 The Dissolution resulting in the *Nigredo* is, of all the seven Operations, the one requiring the greatest amount of patience.

345 Here is the King who in power, might and splendour surpasses his parents, who are Sun and Moon.

346 The Sublimation of the King must be renewed up to ten times for the Stone to wield its full power.

347 Yet another emblem concerning the Dissolution and the ensuing Putrefaction, which causes the Spirits to fly.

348 Pointing to herself so that the viewer does not confuse her with the King, the White and Silver Queen may elevate the five base metals to her condition.

349 Wielding the Seal of Solomon composed by the interlocked triangles of fire $\triangle$ and water $\triangledown$, the King incarnates the Philosopher's Stone in all its majesty. It is capable of removing all infirmities and elevating all six other metals to its own golden rank.

350 Only one substance, the Stone of the Philosophers, yields a six-pointed (star) signature.

351 Here are the components of the Secret Fire: the fiery Water and the watery Fire which, excited by the ordinary Elemental Fire, cause the Birds to fly.

Musaeum hermeticum, 1625

Musaeum hermeticum, omnes sopho-spagyricae artis discipulos fidelissime erudiens, quo pacto summa illa veraque Medicina, quo res omnes, qualemcumque defectum patientes, instaurari possunt (quae alias Benedictus Lapis Sapientum appellatur) inveniri ac haberi queat. Continens Tractatus chymicos novem praestantissimos quorum nomina & seriem versa pagella indicabit. In gratiam filiorum doctrinae, quibus Germanicum Idioma ignotum, in Latinum conversum ac juris publici factum. Francofurti, Sumptibus Lucae Jennisii. Anno M.DC.XXV.

The Hermetick Museum, faithfully instructing all students of the Philosophick and Spagyrical Art by what means the supreme true Medicine, by which all things defective in any way may be restored (and which is otherwise called the Blessed Stone of the Wise), may be found and possessed. Containing nine most excellent chymical treatises, the names and order of which the turned page will show. Rendered into Latin and placed in the public domain for the sake of those sons of learning to whom the German language is unknown. Frankfurt, printed for Lucas Jennis. 1625.

As first published, the *Musaeum hermeticum* contains ten treatises: *Tractatus aureus de lapide philosophico*; Henricus Madathanus, *Aureum seculum redivivum*; *Hydrolithus sophicus seu Aquarium sapientum*; Johannes de Mehung, *Demonstratio naturae*; Nicolas Flamel, *Summarium philosophicum*; *Via veritatis unicae*; *Gloria mundi*; *Tractatus de generatione metallorum*; *Liber cuius nomen Alze*; Lambsprinck, *De lapide philosophorum figurae et emblemata*.

It was reissued by Hermann van de Sande in 1677 as *Musaeum hermeticum reformatum et amplificatum*, with the following additions: Michael Maier, *Tripus aureus*; Michael Sendivogius, *Novum lumen chemicum, Aenigma philosophicum, Dialogus Mercurii Alchymistae et Naturae, Novi luminis tractatus alter de sulphure*; Philaletha, *Introitus apertus ad occlusum regis palatium*; Michael Maier, *Subtilis allegoria super secreta chymiae*; Philaletha *Metallorum metamorphosis, Brevis manuductio ad rubinum coelestem, Fons chymicae veritatis*; Johannes Fridericus Helvetius, *Vitulus aureus quem mundus adorat et orat*; *Janitor Pansophus, seu Figura aenea quadri-partita cunctis Museum hoc introeuntibus*.

Hermann van de Sande is someone of whom little is known. He came from the Netherlands and was active in Frankfurt between 1664 and 1688. His son Johann Maximilian succeeded him as head of the firm. The de Sande family were in a minor way the late seventeenth-century successors of the de Bry.

184 · Musaeum hermeticum

352 The fine engraved frontispiece by Matthäus Merian is common to both editions. The central medallion shows Nature bearing the shining symbol of alchemical perfection and the fruits of plenty. Alchemists are following in her footsteps; see *Atalanta fugiens*, Emblema XLII (71). At the sides are Sol, Luna and the Elements. Apollo and the Muses are flanked by Phoenix, Pelican, Athena and Mercury.

353 As above, so below: the four Elements are united. On the left △ Fire, on the right ▽ Water. At the centre the Seal of Solomon, or Star of David, which is the hieroglyph of the Philosopher's Stone wherein all the Elements are reconciled in perfect balance. Below, Apollo strikes the lyre of harmony, and the Muses (six in number corresponding each to a metal and to a celestial counterpart) sit around him.

Lambsprinck
De lapide philosophico, 1625

Lambsprinck nobilis Germani philosophi antiqui libellus De lapide philosophico e germanico versu latine redditus per Nicolaum Bernaudum Delphinatem Medicum, huius scientiae studiosissimum. Francofurti, sumptibus Lucae Jennisi. Anno M.DC.XXV.

The little book of the noble old German philosopher Lambsprinck. On the Philosopher's Stone, rendered from the German verse into Latin by Nicolaus Barnaud of Dauphiné, physician and keen student of this science. Frankfurt printed for Lucas Jennis, 1625.

Lambsprinck's *De lapide philosophico* is a work especially remarkable for the beauty of its emblems, influenced, like so many, by *Atalanta fugiens*. In this form, the work was also published in the same year, 1625, as part of the enlarged edition of the *Dyas chymica tripartita*, by Lucas Jennis who was, it will be recalled, the step-nephew of J.T. de Bry. However, the same Latin translation of the German original had already appeared, without the pictures, in the *Triga chemica* published by N. Barnaud at Leiden in 1599.

LAMBSPRINCK

NOBILIS GERMANI PHILOSOPHI ANTIQVI LIBELLVS

De Lapide Philosophico

E Germanico versu Latinè redditus, per Nicolaum Barnaudum Delphinatem Medicum, huius scientiæ studiosissimum.

Francofurti, Sumptibus Lucæ Jennis I.
Anno M.DC.XXV.

355

356

De lapide philosophico · 189

357

358

359

360

De lapide philosophico · 191

361

362

363

364

De lapide philosophico · 193

365

366

367

368

De lapide philosophico · 195

369

370

354 Title-page. The Philosopher's tunic bears the double Eagle of mercurial Volatility, confirmed by the Cock at the centre of the shield (Mercury's bird and the herald of Light). From his belt hangs a sword, the pommel of which is the head of an Eagle (Fixation of the Volatile, emphasized by the fact that the sword is sheathed). In his hand the Adept holds the double sceptre of the Secret Fire. The Athanor (the philosophick furnace) shows, by its triple structure upon a single arch, that the Work is a single one, divided into three parts. From the topmost roof flies the banner of final victory. The *Spiritus Mundi* or Universal Spirit pours down its fiery celestial influence, the use of which differentiates alchemy from chemistry.

355 The name of the author is an obvious pseudonym, underlined by the coat-of-arms designed to attract attention to Aries and to the spring.

356 'The sea is the Body, the two fish are Spirit and Soul.' (See detail of *Atalanta fugiens*, Emblema XXII, *51*.) Once the two Stones or two Subjects, 'which appear to be one but are in fact two', are made as one (by Dissolution in the Water of their origin), then the Sea of the Wise is obtained. The nautical symbolism, which appears in many hermetick emblems, refers to the arduous voyage of the Great Work upon the mercurial Waters, towards the distant shores of Colchis and the Golden Fleece.

357 The slaying of the Dragon is the Dissolution and Putrefaction of the Stone of the Philosophers or *Materia Prima*. The martial demeanour of the assailing Knight indicates the nature of the dissolving agent.

358 Within the Forest of the Work are found the twin Natures, Mercury the Stag and Sulphur the Unicorn.

359 The Lion and Lioness (see frontispiece of *Atalanta fugiens, 27*) are respectively the Philosophick Sulphur and the Philosophick Mercury; their union produces the Philosopher's Stone.

360 We have already quoted Nicolas Flamel (see *Atalanta fugiens*, Emblema XLVII, *76*) on the two adversaries called by Avicenna the Corascene bitch and the Armenian dog (others, Maier and Lambsprinck among them, call them 'the Wolf and the Dog'). These two are the initial substances, one of which, 'Ares', is stronger than 'Aries': this precious indication means that if the combat is to result in the death of both, the correct proportions must be established and respected. (See Fulcanelli, *Le Mystère des Cathédrales*.)

361 See *Atalanta fugiens*, Emblema XIV (*43*). The perfect hieroglyph of the *Materia Prima*, or Stone of the Philosophers and their Subject, is the Dragon, because its scales, its volatility, and its venomous nature are equivalent to that of the mineral Subject. From a virulent poison, the Stone of the Philosophers becomes the Medicine and the Elixir of the Wise.

362 Fixation of the Volatile; see *Atalanta fugiens*, Emblema VII (*36*). The Bird remaining in the nest prevents the flight of its mate: the Sublimation of 'our Mercury' is repeated until the Fire no longer has any effect upon it. The Volatile is then truly fixed. The Snail (in contrast to the Volatile) is the symbol of the Fixed.

363 The Whiteness or *Albedo* (Body) is overcome by the Redness (Spirit) of Perfect Fixity.

364 Here is the King that Hermes calls Lord of the Forests. From humble origins he has triumphed over the difficulties of the Way, and has, with the help of the Art, attained the highest degree. The King is the Philosopher's Stone, and the seven steps to his level are the seven Operations of Alchemy.

365 The Salamander, which, according to fables, lives in the fire, is the perfect symbol of Sulphur, Fire, Spirit or Light. The Blood of Fire is the Quintessence, which cures all ills in the three Realms.

366 The Father, the Son and the Guide, or Angel, are the Body, the Spirit and the Soul. The Father seeks to shield his Son from the solicitations of the Angel, who will however prevail.

367 Taking the Son (extracted from the Body) to the highest Mountain – i.e. to the top of the Vessel, where he receives the celestial influences from above and is metaphorically purified from the ignorance of matter – the Angel sublimates the Fixed.

368 The Son returns (at the bottom of the Vessel) to the parched, almost lifeless Body of his Father, who avidly absorbs him according to the hermetick axiom: 'Any dry thing avidly drinks its humidity.' (This emblem is in a sense equivalent to the Watering of the Trees by Saturn; see *92*.) The darkness within the King's gaping mouth heralds the Night of the *Nigredo*.

369 The King, under the influence of a severe fever (a new degree of the Fire), sweats profusely, while from the heavens the mysterious celestial dynamism pours down its indispensable influence. With this further Imbibition the Body is dissolved.

370 Lastly, the Three Principles are united as one mighty indivisible whole: The Philosopher's Stone.

De lapide philosophico · 197

Johann Daniel Mylius
Anatomia auri, 1628

Joannis Danielis Mylii, Philosophiae & Medicinae Doctoris, Anatomia auri, siue Tyrocinium medico-chymicum, continens in se partes quinque: quarum I. Tradit concordantiam & harmoniam solis coelestis cum auro terrestri: item Auri definitionem & confusam multorum physicorum de auro opinionem; II. Agit de medicinis aureis & receptis antiquorum ac recentium medicorum, aurum ingredientibus, tam in simplici, quàm preparata forma; III. Tractat de auri potabilis preparatione tam vulgari, quam philosophica; IV. Exhibet usum medicinalem auri potabilis tàm communis, quàm veri & philosophici; V. Demonstrat ideam Lapidis philosophici in duodecim figuris. Francofurti, Sumptibus Lucae Iennisi Bibliop. Anno M.DC.XXVIII.

Johann Daniel Mylius, Doctor of Philosophy and Medicine: The Anatomy of Gold, or Medico-chymical primer, containing five parts, whereof I conveys the concordance and harmony of the celestial Sun and earthly gold, likewise the definition of gold and the confused opinions of many physicians concerning gold; II deals with golden medicines and the recipes of ancient and modern physicians, containing gold, both in simple and prepared form; III treats of the preparation of the Potable Gold, both vulgar and philosophick; IV expounds the medicinal use of the Potable Gold, both vulgar and philosophick; V demonstrates the image of the Philosopher's Stone in twelve figures. Frankfurt, printed for Lucas Jennis, bookseller, 1628.

The *Anatomia auri* was Mylius' last published work, with the exception of the *Pharmacopoea spagyrica,* 1628–29 (and of the copious index to the *Opus medico-chymicum,* which appeared as a separate publication, unsigned, in 1630).

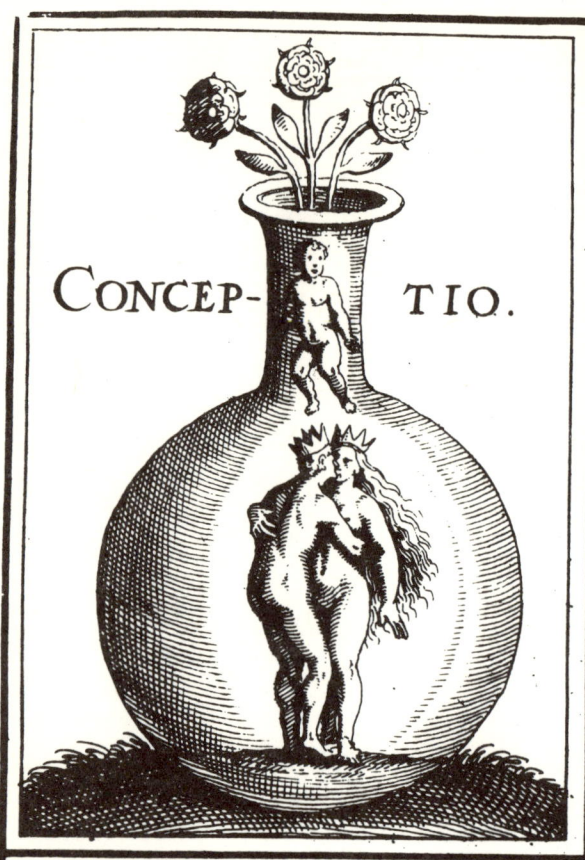 
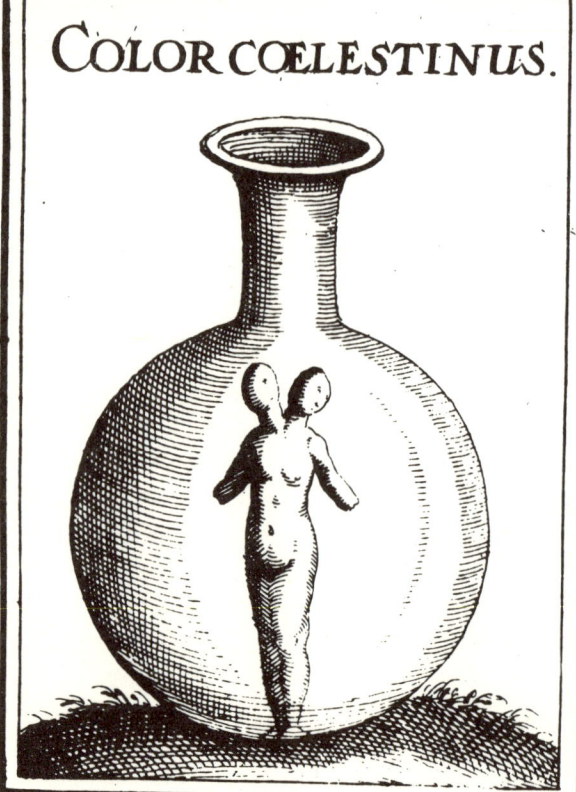 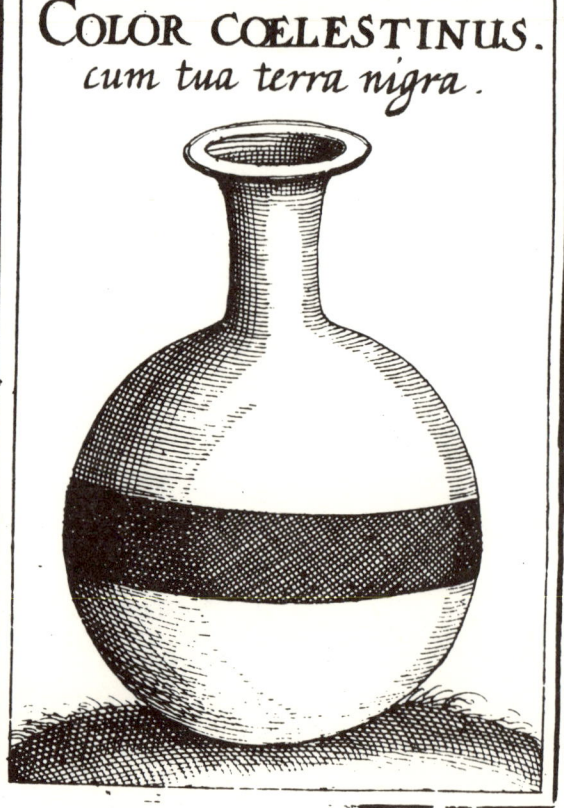

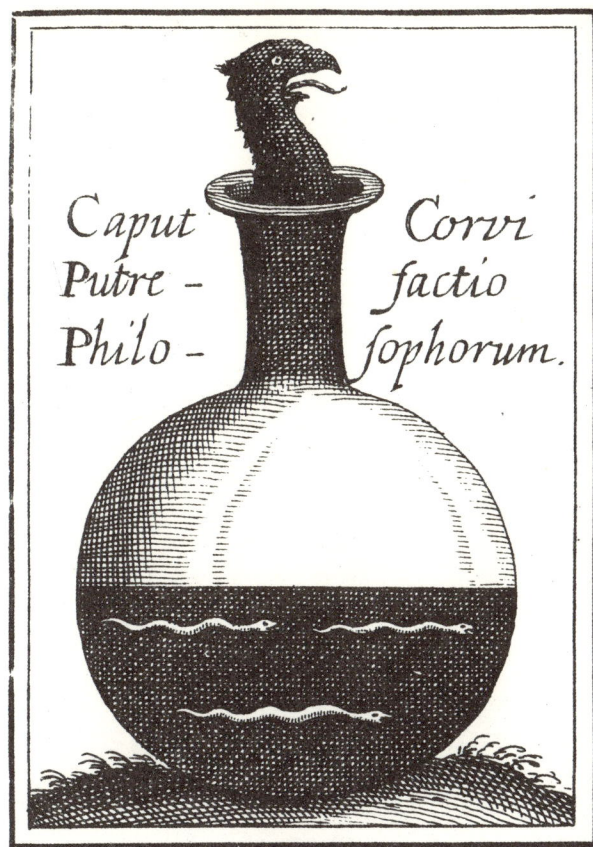

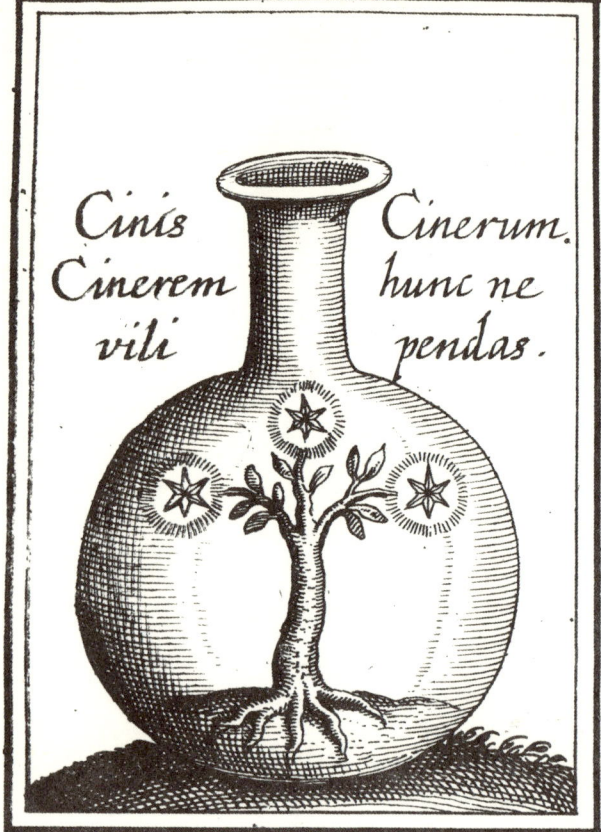

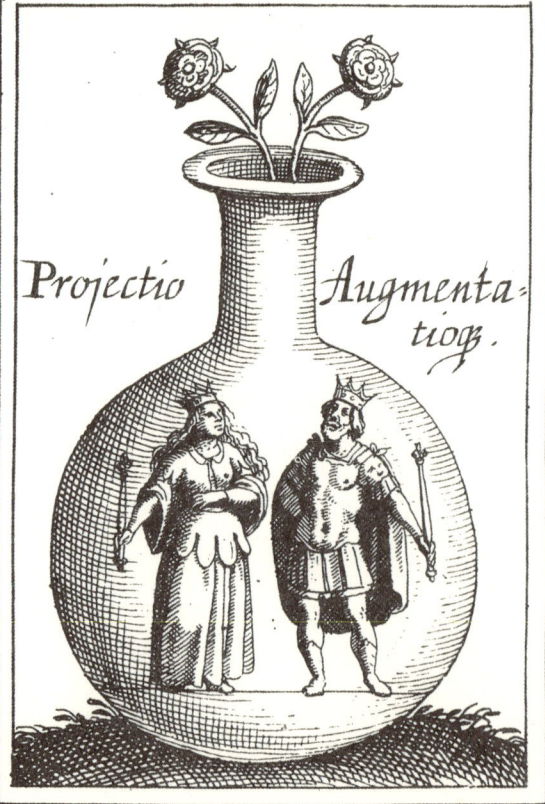

371 The engraved frontispiece shows from the top, left to right: the Physical Distillation or Antique Chaos, a circular figure which indicates Putrefaction (or Death, hence the central skull) to be the key to the 'planetary transformations' of the Subject which corresponds to the metallic transmutation; Sun and Moon, the two Principles in conjunction; the King holding both Eagles to symbolize the Volatilization of the Fixed and the Fixation of the Volatile (see Emblema XLVI of *Atalanta fugiens*, 75); the Queen of Wisdom holding scrolls which correspond to Proverbs 3.16: 'Length of days is in her right hand; and in her left hand riches and honour.' Below the King is seen the Dissolvent (the Green Lion); at the centre the evolution of the Planets towards the Omega-Sun of the Philosopher's Stone; and finally, below the Queen is the melting Lion which is the Philosophick Dissolution.

372 The *Anatomia auri* is here dedicated to Johann Martin Baur von Eÿseneck, an Imperial Counsellor and Chief Magistrate of Frankfurt, whose love for alchemy is underlined by the putto (emblem of the Secret Fire) embracing the two birds symbolizing the Philosopher's Stone, the Phoenix (Exaltation) and the Pelican (Multiplication). Although the plate appears at first sight to be little more than a heraldic device, it is susceptible of a lengthy hermetick interpretation.

373 Across the Chasm the King and Queen (who share identical roots underground) call to each other. The King exclaims: 'Come, my beloved, let us embrace and generate a new son who will not resemble his parents.' The Queen replies: 'Here I come to you, most eager to conceive a son who shall have no equal in the world.' (Their words are quoted from 'Arisleus in Visione' in the *Rosarium philosophorum*.) Both point to a vessel in which a heliocephalic Lady (the Mercury of the Wise) caresses a Youth (the Sulphur of the Wise) whose head rests on her knee.

374 The sexual embrace of the purified Principles causes pregnancy, which, as the winged Spirit at the top of the vessel shows, is a Volatilization of the Fixed. The Female or Mercury absorbs the Male. As their Bodies then dissolve, merging into unity, a bluish colour appears briefly before receding with the onset of Blackness.

375 The Matter, or Dragon, undergoing calcination, dissolves into a dark, stinking liquid whose thick, volatile fumes are extremely toxic. This 'Water', symbolized by the Raven, can only be washed and whitened by Fire, which is why the texts order the Artist to cut off the Raven's Head (*Caput Corvi*). By means of these fiery ablutions, the Water eventually abandons its black colour, and in due course becomes white. The repeated action of Fire upon Water forces the latter to defend its specific qualities while abandoning its superfluities. The Worms, according to Arnold of Villa Nova, indicate that the corruption of one thing is the generation of another. The Dragon, the Subject of the Art, becomes the winged white Mercury which is washed by Fire until all obscurity is removed from it. The Matter circulates at length until a total separation between Body and Soul (that is between the spiritual, volatile parts which ascend to the top of the hermetically sealed vessel, and the Earth or Body which, relieved of its moisture, remains at the bottom) is achieved.

376 The separation of Body and Soul leaves the Matter as powdery Ashes, which, as the inscription points out, 'should not be despised'. Morien calls the Ashes the Diadem of the King, because from them the Sulphur of the Wise is obtained. The White Medicine, or White Elixir, traditionally symbolized by the White Queen and the White Rose (*Rosa Alba*), is the First Degree of Perfection. With the Red King, the Matter has reached perfect Fixity. The power of the Philosopher's Stone is augmented by renewed Sublimations, and its transmutative power of Projection is correspondingly increased each time.

377 Between the candles, corresponding to the complementary Opposites within the art, are the seven Sublimations symbolized by seven six-pointed stars, the mercurial Volatile Eagle, and Ouroboros, whose tail has transpierced it, symbolizing more pointedly, thereby, the need to dissolve the Subject of the Art.

378 On the lower left branch of the Tree of Philosophy sits Mercury, the wing-footed Volatile Principle; its opposite number, the Fixed, sits on the right. From the Dissolution which ensues upon the conjunction of these two, the first Water, or *Lac Virginis*, is obtained (sitting above the Fixed). Opposite, in the order of acquisitions, is the stag-horned Philosophick Mercury; from it is born Philosophick Sulphur (which is the Medicine of the First Order), symbolized here by the King sitting above Mercury. The second Philosophick Calcination produces the Elixir or Medicine of the Second Order, here represented by the Queen waving two crowns on the right. Finally, the third operation produces the Philosopher's Stone itself: obtained in two stages, according to the present emblem, as the White Queen or White Stone and then as the Final Perfection. This is represented by the King with a triple crown, indicating his dominion over the three Realms, as well as the Multiplication of all the qualities of Sulphur and Elixir. The crowns held aloft represent his transmutative and curative powers.

David de Planis Campy
L'Hydre morbifique exterminée
1628

L'Hydre morbifique exterminée par l'Hercule chymique ou les Sept Maladies tenuës pour incurables iusques à present, renduës guerissables par l'art chymique medical, où est traité briefvement de leur definition, causes, differentes signes, pronostic & cure. Le tout selon l'ancienne & moderne medecine, divisé en sept livres. Par David de Planis Campy, dict l'Edelphe, Chirurgien du Roy. Dedié au Tres-Chrestien Roy de France & de Navarre Louys le Juste, XIII. du nom. A Paris chez Hervé du Mesnil, ruë St Jacques, à la Samaritaine. MDCXXVIII. Avec Privilege du Roy.

The Baneful Hydra exterminated by the Chymical Hercules, or the seven maladies hitherto considered incurable, rendered curable by the chymical medical art; briefly treating of their definition, causes, divers signs, prognosis and cure. All in accordance with ancient and modern medicine, divided into seven books. By David de Planis Campy, known as L'Edelphe, surgeon to the King. Dedicated to the Most Christian King of France and Navarre, Louis the Just, XIIIth of that name. Paris, Hervé du Mesnil, rue St-Jacques, by the Samaritaine, 1628. With Royal Privilege.

The engraver Jean Matheus was active in Paris around 1620. He worked above all for booksellers. In 1619 he engraved the thirty-six plates of a French edition of Ovid's *Metamorphoses*. He is known also for religious subjects engraved from his own designs.

David de Planis Campy
L'Ouverture de l'escolle
1633

L'Ouverture de l'escolle de philosophie transmutatoire metallique, où la plus saine veritable explication & conciliation de tous les stiles desquels les Philosophes anciens se sont servis en traictant de l'oeuvre physique sont amplement declarées. Par David de Planis Campy Chirurgien du Roy. A Paris chez Charles Sevestre, ruë des Amandiers, au Pelican, pres le College des Grassins. M.CD.XXXIII. Avec Privilege du Roy.

The Opening of the School of metallic transmutatory philosophy, wherein the soundest and most truthful explanation and conciliation of all the styles which the Philosophers of old have employed in treating of the Physical Work are amply set forth. By David de Planis Campy, Surgeon to the King. Paris, Charles Sevestre, rue des Amandiers, at the Pelican, near Grassins' College, 1633. With Royal Privilege.

380

L'Hydre; L'Ouverture · 211

379 *L'Hydre morbifique*. On the left is the Chaos or Stone of the Philosophers, while on the right the Star, emblem of the Philosopher's Stone, displays the symbols of ♀ Sulphur, ☿ Mercury and ⊖ Salt, which alternate with Hebrew characters. King Louis XIII is the French Hercules, and supposed likenesses of Hippocrates and Paracelsus are below him on either side. On the plinths we have on the left a circular diagram of the Principles of the Great Work. The outer circle contains the *Materia Prima*, the *Magnesia* and the *Lapis*, Stone or Chaos. The four Elements are next followed by the three Operations, Separation, Dissolution and Depuration. Then come the three Principles, Soul, Spirit and Body, corresponding to ♀ , ☿ and ⊖ . The inner triangle contains the Hebrew word YAH or JAH which corresponds to the Divine Celestial Principle. On the opposite side, Sun, Moon and Mercury are found, contained within the Mountain (the Rock or Stone) of the Philosophers.

380 David de Planis Campy (1589–*c*. 1644), counsellor and surgeon to Louis XIII and the child Louis XIV, showed the similarities between the works of Hippocrates and Paracelsus but maintained that only the Hermetick Medicine could cure a host of new and supposedly incurable diseases.

381 *L'Ouverture de l'escolle*. On the base of the left plinth, the famous hermetick axiom, *Ignis et Azoth tibi sufficient*, is inscribed. It means: 'Fire and Azoth [the Mercury of the Wise] will suffice thee.' An inscription on the opposite side warns however that 'Whatever is beautiful is difficult' (*Difficilia quae pulchra*). The Rose of Alchemy is surrounded by thorns. Those students of the Art striving to wrest the precious pearls of Wisdom from the thorny obscurity of alchemical texts will agree with a sigh. Yet, once embarked upon that strange quest, an indefinable charm pervades the hours devoted to study, like the perfume of roses in summer dream gardens. The (Volatile) Eagle faces the (Fixed) Salamander. Above Diana and Apollo, Ouroboros the Dragon bites its tail. The Bull (of Venus) symbolizes Earth, with Fire above it. (Earth must be converted into Fire.) The Dragon (the Stone of the Philosophers) is dissolved and becomes Mercury, symbolized by the Cock (above it), while the Dolphin (Sulphur) arises from Mercury.

The central hieroglyph represents the Chosen Earth and its starry signature: the Mercury of the World or Magnesia (*Mercurius Mundi sive Magnesia*) which adopts, in turn, the attributes of all the planets and eventually reaches the Perfection of the Philosopher's Stone. Fixed and Volatile are indissolubly joined, as represented by the Sun in Splendour and the wings crowned with the crown of achievement. The Pelican and the Phoenix respectively represent the Exaltation of the Stone and its Multiplication.

ELIAS ASHMOLE

Theatrum chemicum britannicum 1652

Theatrum chemicum britannicum. Containing several poetical pieces of our famous English Philosophers, who have written the Hermetic Mysteries in their own Ancient Language. Faithfully collected into one volume, with annotations thereon, by Elias Ashmole, Esq. Qui est mercuriophilus Anglicus. The First Part. Serpens ac Bufo gradiens sup. terra. Aquila volans, ast nostrum Magisterium. London, Printed by J. Grismond for Nath: Brooke, at the Angel in Cornhill. MDCLII.

The British Theatre of Chymistry. . . . Who is the English lover of Mercury. . . . The Snake and the Toad crawling on the earth. The Eagle flying, to wit, our Magistery. . . .

Elias Ashmole (1617–92) was one of the founders of the Royal Society of London, and in 1669 the University of Oxford conferred on him its degree of Doctor of Medicine. A great collector of antiquities with an extremely wide range of interests, Ashmole was, in the words of his contemporary Anthony à Wood, 'the greatest virtuoso and curioso that ever was known or read of in England before his time'. The Ashmolean Museum at Oxford University, founded in 1683 to house his valuable collections, was the first public museum in the British Isles.

His interest in alchemy was stimulated by an alchemical manuscript given to him by a Reading surgeon in 1648. In 1650 appeared his first book on the subject, the *Fasciculus Chemicus*, published under the pseudonym James Hasolle (an anagram of his name), which contained excellent translations of Dr Arthur Dee's *Fasciculus* (1629) and of President Jean d'Espagnet's *Theatrum arcanum hermeticae philosophiae opus* (Paris 1623). The *Theatrum chemicum britannicum*, a remarkable collection of works by British alchemists, annotated by Ashmole, received its *imprimatur* on 21 March 1651. On 21 July the manuscript reached the printer and on 22 September the engraver Robert Vaughan went to stay at Ashmole's house, where 'he wrought and finished all the Cutts' for the book.

'Those of Vaughan's engravings which accompany Thomas Norton's *Ordinall of Alchimy* are of special interest because they are probably the earliest engraved reproductions of miniatures from an illuminated medieval manuscript' (C.H. Josten, *Elias Ashmole*, II.585 n. 5, 586 n. 1). The illuminated manuscript in question is a fifteenth-century copy of Norton's *Ordinall*, now in the Department of Manuscripts of the British Library (Add.10.302), two folios of which were reproduced in my *Alchemy, the Secret Art*, London 1973.

Theatrum chemicum britannicum · 217

382 The Master Adept bestows upon a worthy Son of the Art the secrets of alchemy. 'Receive', says the seated Adept, 'the gift of God under the sacred seal.'

The kneeling disciple then swears to keep secret the secrets of the science of alchemy:

> *Also he must (be never soe loath)*
> *Receive it with a most dreadfull Oath*
> *That as we refuse greate dignitie and fame,*
> *Soe he must needly refuse the same.*
> *And also that he shall not be so wilde*
> *To teach this secret to his owne childe;*
> *For nighness of Blood ne consanguinity*
> *May not be accepted to this dignity:*
> *Sow blood as blood, may have hereof noe part,*
> *But only vertue winneth this holy Arte . . .*

383 Although some people consider alchemy an empirical proto-science, it is on the contrary a precise discipline whose principles must be discovered and applied. The labouring Artist is guided at all times by the *dicta Philosophorum*, the words of the Masters.

384 The alchemist sits at a table preparing 'without repugnance' the correct proportions of the components of the Great Work. The first of his aides is busy, with distilling equipment, separating the Earth from the Fire and the Subtle from the Dense. The second aide is observing the succession of colours, the order of which tells the Artist whether or not he has proceeded correctly.

385 Concordance is of capital importance, stresses Norton, who enumerates five 'Concords':

> *The first Concord is needed to marke*
> *Whether his Minde accorde with the Worke,*
> *Which shalbe Lord to paie for all,*
> *Els all your labour destroy ye shall.*
> *The Second Concord is needfull to kenn.*
> *Between this Crafte and her Workemen*
> *The Third shall serve well your intents,*
> *When Warke accordeth with Instruments.*
> *The fourth Concord must welbe sought,*
> *With the Place where it shall be wrought:*
> *For trewlie it is not little grace*
> *To find a perfect working Place.*
> *The Fift is of Concord and of Love,*
> *Betweene your Warkes and the Spheare above.*

In his notes Ashmole explains that he has had this plate exactly copied from 'the originall' although the planets are not in the order dictated by the rules of astrology. This was, however, done very much on purpose 'to bring them within the compasse of his Rules'.

Ashmole also observes that Norton has redesigned the planetary symbols, 'for he does not exhibit them under the Characters commonly now (or then) Used, but Hierogliphically in Figures agreeable to their Nature'. Thus, Saturn is represented by a spade, Jupiter by a mitre, Mars by an arrow, Venus by a beautiful face, Mercury 'by the figure (in those daies) usually stamped upon the Reverse of our English Coyne'. Only the Sun and the Moon are drawn in the traditional way.

386 The number, the regime and the degrees of Fire must be discovered and established before the alchemist entrusts his Subject to the Athanor. Pontanus and Artephius are the best authorities to be consulted.

387
> *In the name of the holy Triniti,*
> *Now send us grase, so hit be:*
> *Fyrst God made both Angel and Heaven,*
> *Na alleso the World wyth Planets seaven;*
> *Man and Woman wyth gret sensewalite,*
> *Sum of estate, and other in hyr degree;*
> *Both Best and Worme for in the grown crepe,*
> *Everyech in hys kynd to receve hys mete.*
> *Egles and Fowles in the Eyre don fle,*
> *And swemynge of Fycheys also in the See:*
> *Wyth vygital moyster and of the red Grap,*
> *And alleso of the whyte hos can hym take:*
> *Alle meneral thyng that growyth in grownd,*
> *Sum to encrese and sum to make an end:*
> *Alle thes bryngeth now to awre howse,*
> *The mightii Ston that ys so precius,*
> *Thys ryche Reby, that ston of pryce,*
> *The whych wosse send owt of Paradyce:*
> *Thus made the gret God of heven,*
> *Whych alle ben rewled under Planets seaven:*
> *God send us parte of thys secrete,*
> *And of that heven that ys sweet.*

AMEN

Johann Joachim Becher
Oedipus chimicus, 1664

Institutiones chimicae prodromae, id est, Joannis Joachimi Becheri Spirensis Mathem. & Med. Doc. Oedipus chimicus obscuriorum terminorum & principiorum chimicorum mysteria aperiens & resolvens opusculum omnibus medicinae & chimiae studiosis lectu perquam utile & necessarium. Amstelodami, apud Elizeum Weyerstraten. Anno 1664.

Preliminary instruction in chymistry, that is, Johann Joachim Becher of Speyer, Mathematician and Doctor of Medicine, his Chymical Oedipus, opening and resolving the mysteries of the more obscure chymical terms and principles, a little work whose perusal is extremely useful and necessary to all students of medicine and chymistry. Amsterdam, Elizeus Weyerstraten, 1664.

Oedipus chimicus and its author are praised by the fastidious Lenglet Dufresnoy in his *Histoire de la philosophie hermétique*. A Frankfurt edition appeared the same year, published by Hermann van de Sande. I have seen a reference to an earlier edition, Mainz (Moguntiae) 1662.

Johann Joachim Becher (1635–82), physician and alchemist, married (in 1662) the daughter of an Imperial Counsellor, which opened many prospects for him. Court physician and mathematician to the Elector of Bavaria, he later became a Commercial Counsellor to Emperor Leopold I. In Vienna he built an imperial arts and crafts centre with glassworks and a chymical laboratory. He reformed school instruction to provide technical training. He organized an Eastern Trading Company and proposed colonial settlements in South America. He was also alchemical adviser to the Emperor, who was an enthusiastic alchemist. Alongside all his activity, his important *Physica subterranea* appeared at Frankfurt in 1669.

The eventual failure of Becher's mercantile policies resulted in his dismissal and brief imprisonment. By 1678 he went to Holland and submitted a plan for the extraction of gold from the sea through smelting. Although an early test of this process proved encouraging, he soon left for Britain, where he studied mines in Scotland and Cornwall. He died in London in 1682. (See Allen G. Debus, *The Chemical Philosophy. Paracelsian Science and Medicine in the Sixteenth and Seventeenth Centuries*. New York, 1977, II. 445.)

388 *Oedipus chimicus*. The background of the frontispiece shows Oedipus (in the guise of Mercury) questioned by the Sphinx. His 'Solution' to the Sphinx's riddle provokes her to plunge from the cliff to her death; see *Atalanta fugiens*, Emblema XXIX (58).

Joannes de Monte-Snyders
Metamorphosis planetarum, 1663

Metamorphosis planetarum, dass ist Eine wunderbahrliche Verenderung der Planeten, und Metallische Gestalten in ihr erstes Wesen mit beygefügtem Process, entdeckung der dreyen Schlussel, so zu erlangung der drey Principia gehörig und wie dass Universale Generalissimum zu erlangen in vielen Ortern dieses Büchleins beschrieben. Durch Joannem de Monte Snyders. Zu Amsterdam. Bey Johan Jansson 1663.

Metamorphosis planetarum, that is: A wonderful transformation of the planets and metallic forms into their first essence, with the addition of the process, discovery of the three keys which pertain to the attainment of the three Principles and of the Most Great Universal, as described in many places in this little book. Amsterdam, Johan Jansson, 1663.

The *Metamorphosis planetarum* was first published in German (although the author was Dutch) at Frankfurt in 1662, and there were other German editions at Frankfurt and Leipzig in 1678, and at Vienna in 1773.

The value of Monte-Snyders' treatises is in dispute. Isaac Newton esteemed them so much that he copied in his own hand the English translation of the work. The author achieved several successful transmutations, and effected spectacular cures of patients affected with dropsy and arthritis; but as he died in hospital (which means in poverty) at the age of fifty, it has been believed that his transmutation powder was a gift from his uncle Levinus Lemnius.

389 *Metamorphosis planetarum*. The Philosopher's Stone is the mighty royal bearer of the triple crown (triple Perfection and dominion over the three Realms). It is the Stone of the Philosophers after it has evolved through the Metamorphosis of the Planets to the highest degree of Perfection. Its power to resurrect the seven 'dead' metals (or earthly counterparts of the planets), and to bestow its own Perfection upon them, has caused the artist to insert resurrection scenes on both sides of the scroll.

THEODORUS KERCKRING

Commentarius in Currum triumphalem Antimonii, 1671

Theodori Kerckringi Doctoris Medici. Commentarius in Currum triumphalem Antimonii Basili Valentini a se latinitate donatum. Amstelodami, sumptibus Andreae Frisii. M.DC.LXXI.

Theodorus Kerckring, Doctor of Medicine: Commentary on Basil Valentine's Triumphal Chariot of Antimony, rendered into Latin by himself. Amsterdam, printed for Andreas Frisius, 1671.

Kerckring came from a Lübeck family. He was born in Amsterdam, according to some sources, and in Hamburg according to others, but the date of his birth is unknown. A student of Spinoza, he eventually married the daughter of his first medical teacher. Having studied medicine and chemistry, he soon acquired a great reputation and practised at Amsterdam where he was highly esteemed by Leibniz, Clauder, Kirchmacher and others. After travelling for a long time in Holland and France, he went to Hamburg in 1678 and there, while pursuing his medical work, he collected an anatomical museum which is said to have been the admiration of all visitors. He was a Fellow of the Royal Society of London and from the year 1685 bore the title of Resident at Hamburg for the Grand Duchy of Tuscany. His principal work, the *Spicilegium anatomicum*, appeared in 1670. He died on 2 November 1693.

His commentary on Basil Valentine first appeared in 1665, then again at Amsterdam in 1671 and at Geneva in 1671 and 1685. Richard Russell translated it into English (London 1678). German editions were published at Nuremberg in 1724 and 1752. 'Patience in searching, ability in expending, unwearied attention and deep meditation are the requisites to attain the knowledge of what is here contained,' wrote Kerckring. The original work attributed to Basil Valentine was first published in Amsterdam in 1525, with many subsequent editions.

390 *Commentarius in Currum.* The Triumphal Chariot of Antimony is drawn by Mars and Venus, followed in tandem by Apollo and Diana, then Saturn and Juno pushing the wheels. While Vulcan holds the reins, the glorious Lady Antimony (who bears upon her midriff the hieroglyph designating her as the Subject of the Art), joins hands with Mercury through the large ring held by Fame, whose other hand holds aloft the garlanded torch. Eros showers the procession with roses (an allusion to dew and to the Secret Fire). This eloquent emblem is the work of the great engraver Romeyn de Hooghe (1645–1708).

Joannes de Monte-Snyders (?)
Chymica vannus, 1666

Reconditorium ac reclusorium opulentiae sapientiaeque numinis mundi magni, cui deditur in titulum CHYMICA VANNUS obtenta quidem & erecta auspice mortale coepto; sed inventa proauthoribus immortalibus Adeptis, quibus conclusum est, sancitum & decretum ut anno hoc per Mysteriarcham Mercurium, velut Viocurium, seu Medicurium, StatVta oraCVL sVa eX orDIne InoLesCerent et aVrea VerItas perspICaCIorIbVs IngenIIs nVDe breVIterqVe InnotesCeret. Orbe post Christum natum Millesimo, sexcentesimo, sexagesimo sexto, Idibus Majis. Amstelodami, Apud Johannem Jansonium à Waesberge et Elizeum Weyerstraet, Anno 1666.

The hiding-place and disclosure of the wealth and wisdom of the Great Spirit of the Universe, to which is given the title of Chymical Winnowing-fan, obtained and set up by the endeavour of a mortal prophet but discovered by those founding fathers, the Immortal Adepts, by whom it has been decided, appointed & decreed that in this year, by the agency of Mercury the Lord of the Mysteries, otherwise the Guardian of the Way and of the Medicine, their established pronouncements should germinate in due succession and the golden Truth should now be plainly and succinctly known to the keener intellects. In the year of the world after Christ's birth one thousand six hundred and sixty six, on the Ides [15th] of May. Amsterdam, Johan Jansson van Waesberge and Elizeus Weyerstraeten, 1666.

The chronogram (letters capitalized in the title from *Stat Vta* to *Ino Les Cerent*) stands for 1666.

This book was reissued at Leiden in 1696 with the title *Chymiae aurifodina incomparabilis* ... The two editions are virtually identical in all respects. The latter has a resetting of the first sheet and the omission of one engraved plate. The *Commentatio de pharmaco catholico* which is appended is a Latin translation of the tractate *Von der Universal Medicin* by Monte-Snyders. On its title-page he says that the translation from German into Latin was done in London, *celeriter, sed tamen fideliter* ('fast but accurately'), by 'the same translator who previously set up the "Chymical Winnowing-fan"'. In an *Epigramma in Zoilum* he says:

Gelria mia patria est, sed Venloa propria terra,
Me mihi scito datâ non nisi lege loqui.

'Guelders is my father's country, but Venloo is my own; know that I do not speak except by the law entrusted to me.'

Duveen believes Monte-Snyders to be the author of the whole work, 'a supposition which agrees with the Dutch origin of the author as it appears from the verses'.

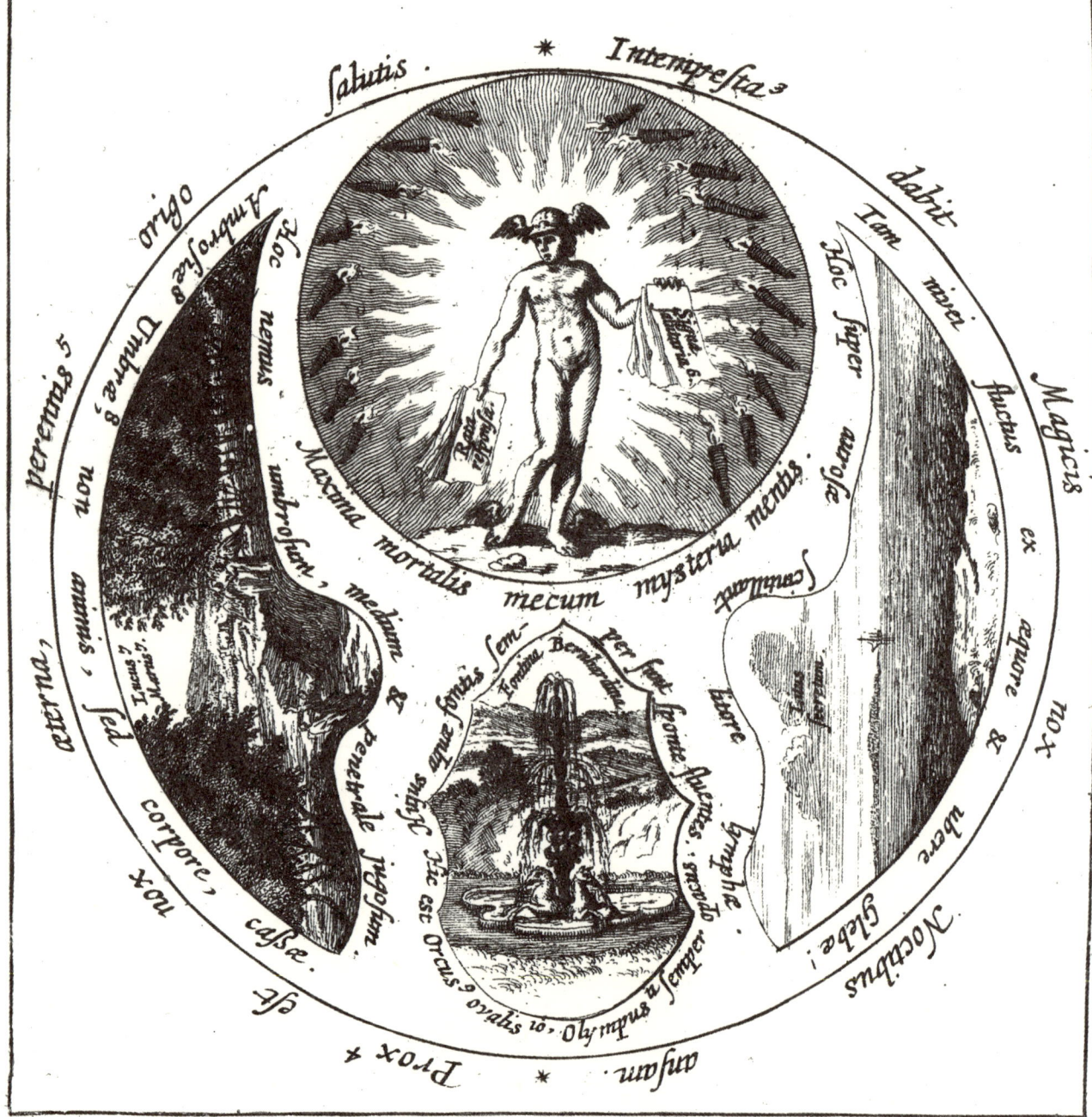

Cavea
SIBYLLARUM[1]
Rem foris in villâ demonstrat dena Sibylla.

nidulari. ✶ *Scala*[2]

Solem — *Sanctum istud Benedictum Pentagrammaton, digitis nostris super linum Terrae, de quo creatus es,* — *Sapientiæ,*

me locuta fuimus, — *in pulvere* — *non*

& penes — *crepitans* — *album*

scrutari, — *volare;*

vero, — *jam simplicissi-* — *sed*

Ecce — *Locus*

sublime[4] — *ignis*

Nobis hic Tellus dissima copia cornu,[3] *humi.*

Ratio ✶ *morari.*

Chymica vannus · 231

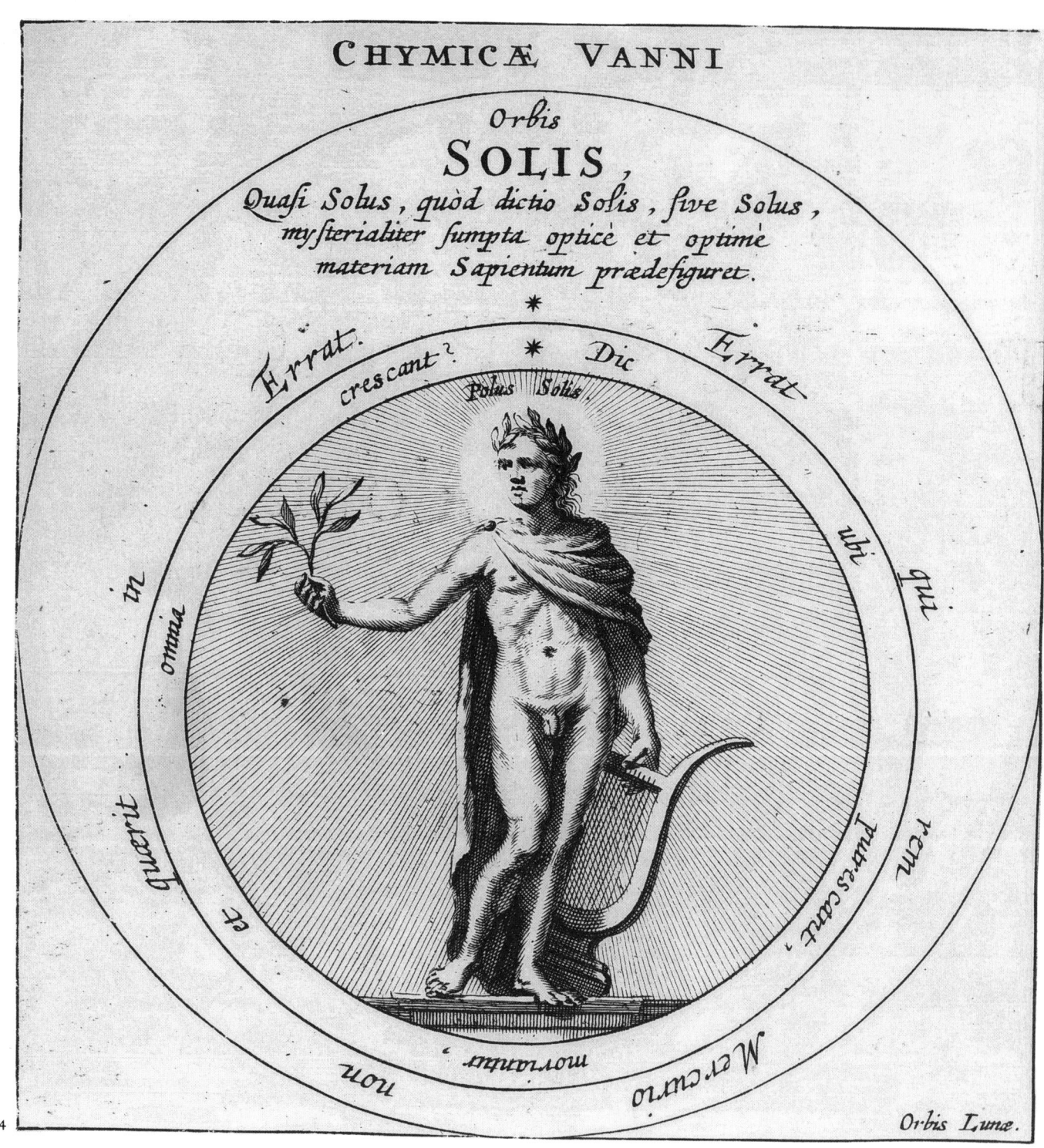

232 · JOANNES DE MONTE-SNYDERS (?)

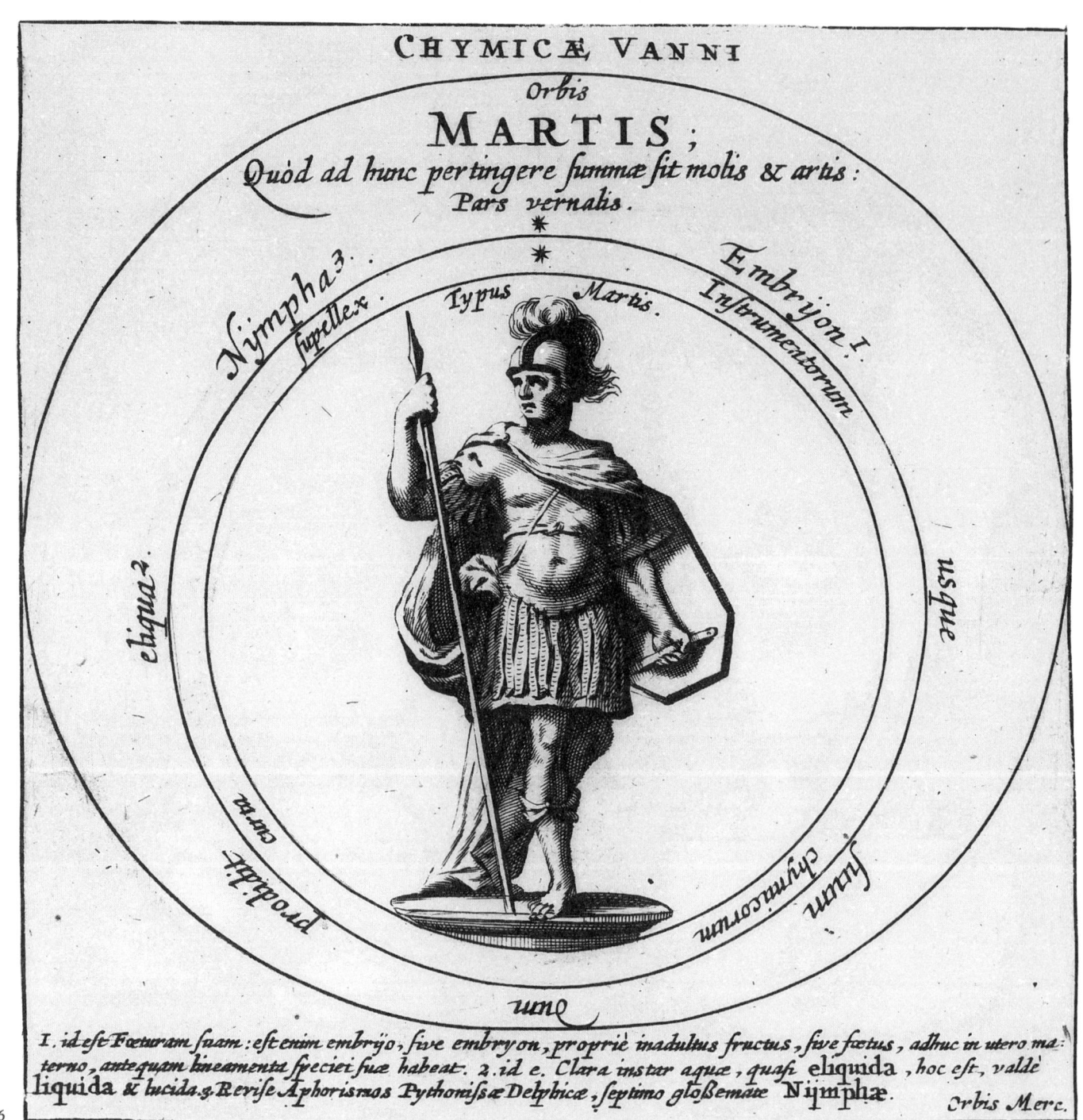

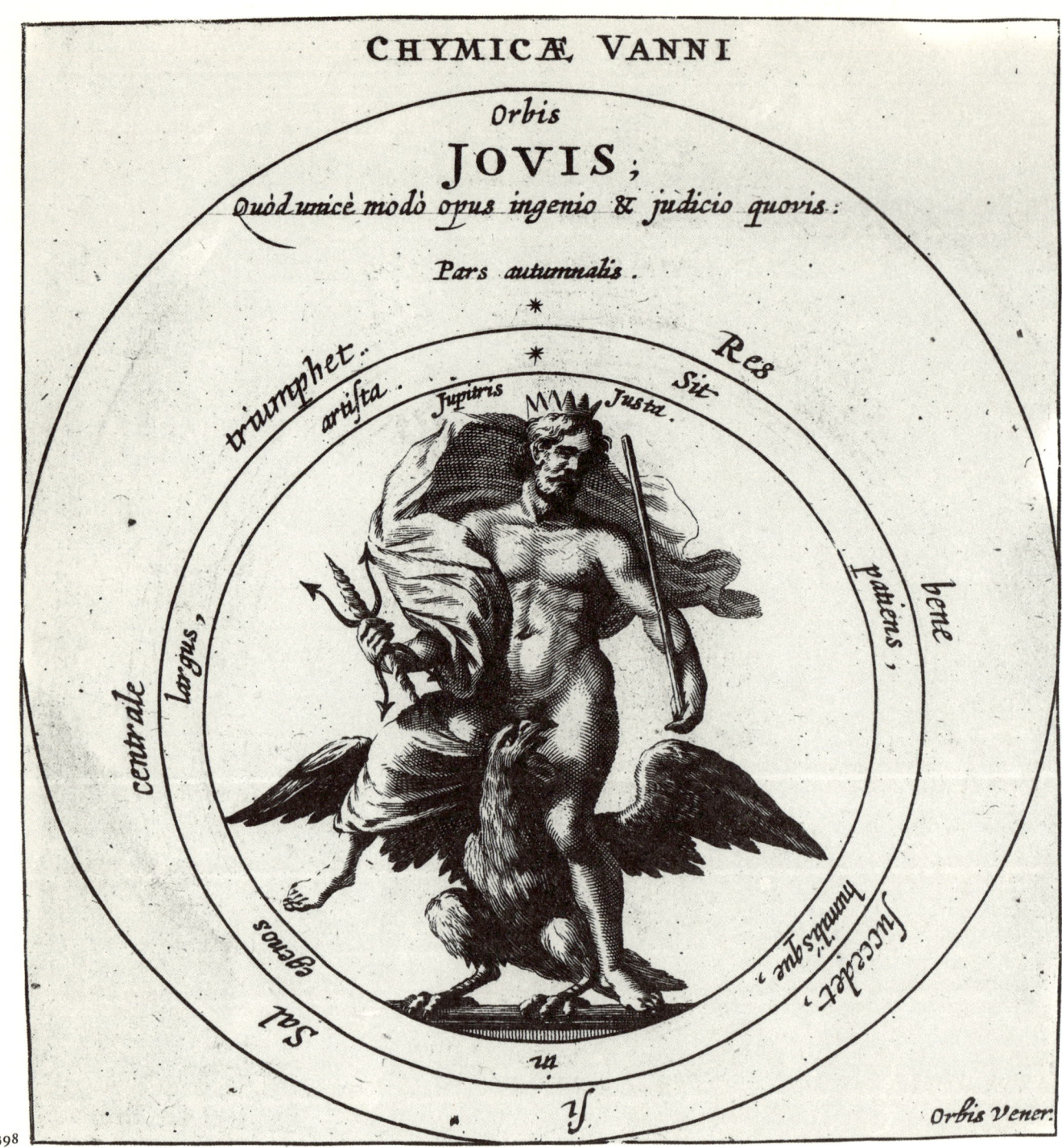

Chymica vannus · 237

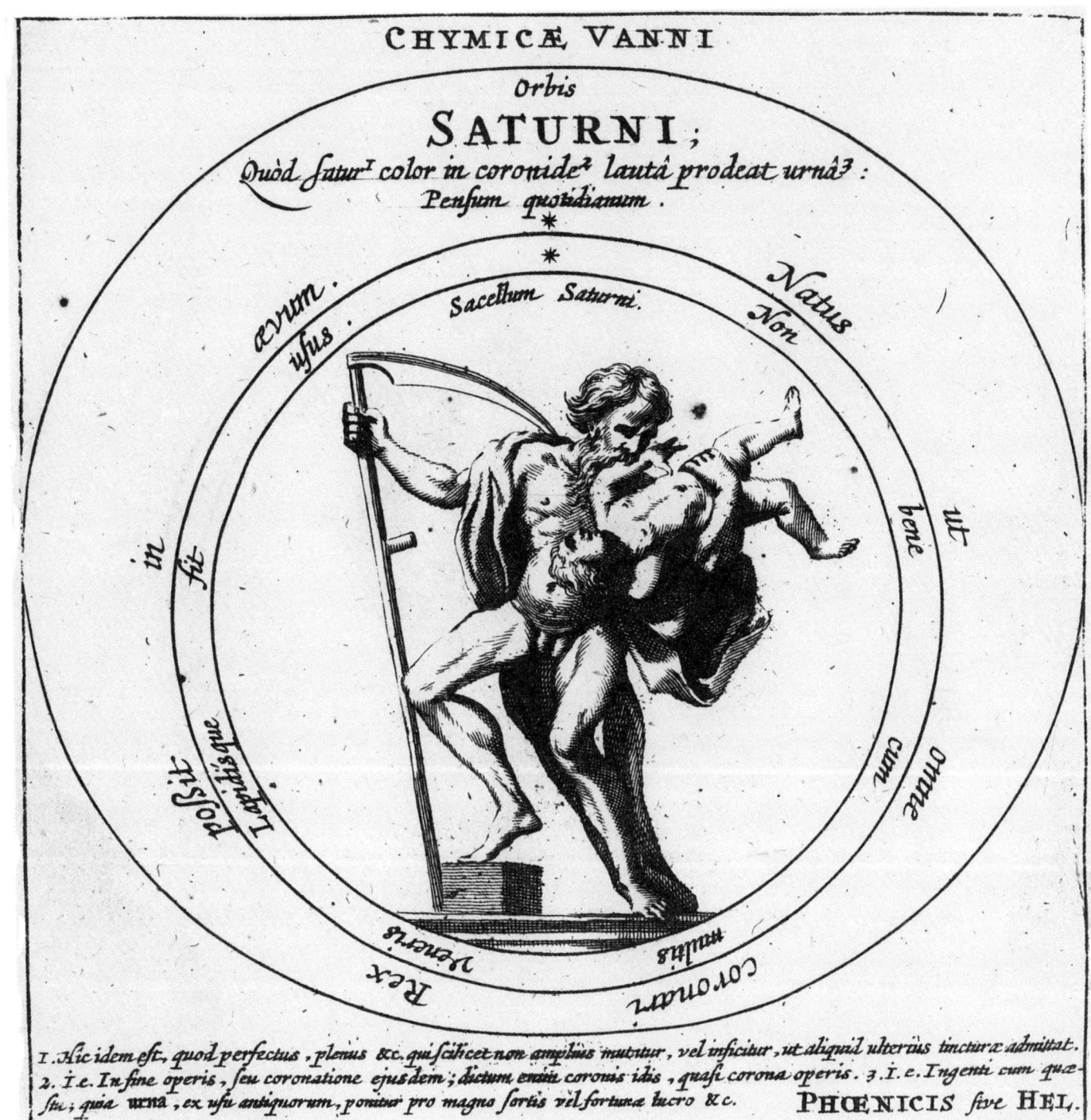

391 One should begin by considering the shape of this emblem ⊕ which expresses the idea of an orb and is a hieroglyph of the Subject of the Wise.

The Philosophick Mercury can only be obtained by the union of two complementary substances, without which one cannot obtain the required Perfection — that is why the little seated figure of the Earth holds the twin Keys. The multiple alchemical similitudes with agriculture are evoked in the background. A proper seed sown in the convenient earth at the required season dies to give birth to the new sheaf of wheat. . . . The Philosopher writing in his secluded cave signifies many things at the same time: the hidden Subject, the Dissolution of the Wise, the darkness of Putrefaction, the darkness of Night in which some of the work must be done. The book is opened as the Subject must be opened. The pen is the sharp fiery means. The oil of the lamp is, at the aftermath of Dissolution, the first oily manifestation of Sulphur, the future Light of Lights. Below, in the circle of Perfection, the Four Elements are converted into the Quintessential Perfection of the Philosopher's Stone.

392 The first and most important step in the alchemical Work is the Dissolution in Water of the *corpus* of the Stone of the Philosophers. Like Pegasus or like Moses, the alchemist strikes with a martial rod the rock which yields the Water of the Wise, which attracts the celestial influx by which it is vivified. This fountain of living Water, the purified — hence naked — Mercury of the Wise, once sublimated by all the subsequent operations, will attain the Ultimate Fixed Perfection.

393 The Sibyls point to the place where the secret Subject of the Wise may be discovered, from which the Philosopher's Stone (which is the Cornucopia, or Horn of Plenty) is elaborated. They point to the earth, since the Subject is a metallic Earth which will be dissolved in the Sea of the Wise with the help of the Secret Fire symbolized by the ruined castle — the dwelling-place of one of its components. The ten Sibyls are the ten elaborations needed to perform the Great Work.

394 Here is the Exalted, Perfect Sun of the Wise, the Almighty Philosopher's Stone, bearer of the ultimate gifts.

395 This planetary series proceeds in a descending order. The Moon, equivalent to the White Rose, is the First Perfection. She reaches for the last Arrow, the last Fixation, before the Final Perfection.

396 Mars is placed in this unusual sequential order because of his abundance of Sulphur. He symbolizes here the Principle of Fixity of Sulphur.

397 Everything in this Work is accomplished through Mercury, which — it must again be stressed — is not vulgar quicksilver but the Principle of Volatility and the Symbol of Sublimation.

398 Jupiter with his Eagle combines both the Fixation of the Volatile (with one foot on the ground) and the Volatilization of the Fixed (with one foot off the ground). He also represents among other things the first light of Dawn, or the Greyness that follows the Blackness of Putrefaction.

399 Venus, in truth, is our Earth or Subject. She is, in a sense, the Antimony of the Wise; born of the castration of Uranus, the goddess arose from the sea into which his genitals had fallen. She is accompanied by Eros, her loving son, emblem of the Secret Fire.

400 Saturn or Chronos is shown emasculated, like his father Uranus. Having been told that one of his children would dethrone him, he ate them at birth. Jupiter, the last, eluded him by substituting a stone. Saturn's action reflects the Night or Blackness of Dissolution, the Raven's Head or *Caput Corvi*: the Crow which is the Crown of the Work, since there can be no Generation without Putrefaction.

Goossen van Vreeswijk
De Roode Leeuw, 1674

De Roode Leeuw, of het Sout der Philosophen; Waer in wonderlijke Bedenkkingen over het Groote Werk, heerlijk bearbeiden der Metalen en Mineralen, Kostelijke Medicynen, suivere Brandewynen uit allerley Vruchten, en vele nutte Konsten de Liefhebberen van de Natuur uit eigen ervarentheit mede gedeelt worden. Door Goossen van Vreeswyk, Berg-meester. Allesins met noodige Kopere Platen verciert. t'Amsterdam, By Pieter Arentsz. Bookverkooper, in de Beurs-straat, in de drie Rapen, 1672.

The Red Lion, or the Salt of the Philosophers; wherein wondrous reflections upon the Great Work, excellent working of metals and minerals, precious medicines, pure spirituous liquors made from all sorts of fruits, and many useful arts are communicated to the lovers of Nature from personal experience. By Goossen van Vreeswijk, master miner. Fully furnished with necessary copperplates. Amsterdam, sold by Pieter Arentsz., bookseller, in Beurs-straat, at the Three Turnips, 1672.

Born in 1626, Goossen van Vreeswijk or Vreeswyk was a master miner with a profound knowledge of natural things. In 1672 he had a laboratory in Amsterdam and could write that 'for more than twenty years, day and night, with great difficulties, through a thousand dangers and great expense, I have examined the animal, vegetable and mineral bodies as well as the salts in Guelders, Holland, France, the East Indies and other countries, and I have made thousands of experiments with regard to the medicines and the lofty Work of the Philosophers'.

In 1663 he was mine director in Guyana; in 1664 he went to Guadeloupe, in 1665 to Canada. In 1666 he was in Quebec and received information about minerals from the Indians. In 1667 and 1668 he had no less than seven furnaces in the town of Nijmegen. In 1670 he was at Aachen, Amsterdam and Limburg. He was director of mines at Liège in 1673, and in Sweden in 1674. He also visited Paris seven times.

He had a vast knowledge of alchemical literature; though his writings are collections of spagyrical recipes, the symbolic illustrations reveal a Hermetick Philosopher of the highest order. These emblems now appear for the first time since the original editions, which are among the rarest of the rare.

DE Roode Leeuw,

OF HET SOUT der PHILOSOPHEN.

Gedrukt voor den Autheur.

406

408

409

411

412

413

414

415

De Roode Leeuw · 243

401 Here is a complete spectrum of the Great Work. The Trees of Sun and Moon are the apparently irreconcilable initial Natures – or twin Principles – which must be conjoined; but they are also the end products: the first Perfection, which is symbolized by the Moon, and the final one, by the Sun. Between the Trees are the Water of Dissolution, the first Mercury ☿ , and the Subject to be dissolved ☿ .

402 Death or Dissolution can be effected only by an agent very similar in nature to the Subject to be dissolved. The required agent, extracted from our Magnesia, assumes the aspect of a metallic Body loaded with metallic Spirits although it is not a metal. This has inspired the Adepts to bestow upon it, among many other names, that of Saturn ♄ .

403 The dissolving action of the First Mercury is represented by the action of ivy upon the Tree. The goal of this operation is the acquisition of Sulphur and its revival by Mercury which dies in the process.

404 The meaning of hermetick emblems must always be sought through natural analogy. Here the student will be wise to study the horticultural operation of layering, in which the plant is 'weaned' in autumn by section of the roots just above the point where they penetrate the ground. This weaning corresponds to the Philosophick Calcination or Separation of the Elements.

405 As previously stated, all hermetick 'laundries are fiery', and all purifications, called Calcinations, take place in, by and with Fire. From our Stone proceeds initially an obscure, stinking Water from which thick, volatile, toxic fumes arise. The Tower in the background is hermetically considered as the attle of the volatile first Dissolvent, otherwise known as common or first Mercury.

406 Here is the first Sulphur or Gold of the Wise in the guise of a green, unripe fruit (a gourd), beneath the Tree of the Art. In the Long or Wet Way, such a result may take 150 days. Yet there can be no further progress until the undaunted Artist, imitating Saturn, retraces his steps and redissolves this green fruit in Mercury.

407 Nourished by Fire, and ever growing in Fixity – therefore impervious to its flames – the Philosophick Sulphur matures toward Perfection. The quality of the fire shown is obtained from the two saline substances which together compose the Secret Fire, a fire burning without flames. The ancient Philosophers considered that the refractory properties of sulphur, its resistance to fire, could only belong to fire or to some spirit of igneous nature. That induced them to designate their Fire by the name of Sulphur (which some Artists believe is because of its appearance), although it bears no resemblance whatsoever to common sulphur. Philosophick Sulphur, god and mainspring of the Great Work, reveals by its action a formative energy comparable to that of the Divine Spirit. In consequence, although precedence in the order of successive acquisitions is retained by Mercury, it is Sulphur, the incomprehensible Soul of Metals, that provides alchemy with its mysterious and somewhat supernatural characteristics. (See Fulcanelli, *D.Ph.T.*, II.156.)

408 The triangle △ , which is subtly drawn within the upper space between thumb and index, indicates that within the grapes is found one of the secrets of the Secret Fire.

409 This emblem underlines the ripening, 'enlivening' action of the celestial dynamism enriching the second saline substance of the Secret Fire and contributing to the ripeness of the golden apples: that is of the Coagulating Principle of Sulphur. Mercury as we see is fixated and stopped in his flight, just as Atalanta was stopped three times in her course by the golden apples thrown by Hippomenes.

410 On the benches of the School of Nature, learning the lessons of analogy, we are taught to consider the conditions and prerequisites of grafting, a minute and delicate operation which besides its material execution requires precise attention to the proper and favourable season. 'The elements to be associated', stresses the *Larousse Agricole*, 'must present certain structural analogies and certain biochemical affinities'. Thus the two initial Natures will complement each other, and their union will produce their offspring, heralded, in the Night of the Work, by the Star of the Wise. The celestial hand pulling on the stalk indicates that there is a knack to this graft which once achieved must no longer be interfered with. Art allows Nature to take its course.

411 Everything, claim the Wise, is found contained within their Mercury. Truly the animator and the motor of the Great Work, Mercury begins, sustains, perfects, and completes it. Hence this monument to its merits.

412 Held aloft by the *putto* and barely visible is the hieroglyph of the Subject of the Wise, the vehicle or support of the Light which it bears hidden within itself. Upon the shining Mercurial Waters, the emblem of Sulphur is clearly visible. The Sulphurous Earth of our Subject is dissolved in its own Mercurial Water (the Sea of the Wise). The Dissolution liberates its hidden virtue – or Sulphur – which floats upon the Waters.

413 Mercury yields its own life to animate and nourish Sulphur, and it is Sulphur that is ultimately exalted as the Elixir of the Wise and multiplied as the Philosopher's Stone.

414 'Make the Earth fly', enjoin the authors; and indeed the Dissolution of our chosen Subject opens the portals of the Garden of the Wise. In rising from the Earth below to the Sky above, the Subject acquires the strength that is strong of all strength.

415 The celestial influx influences the action of the two saline agents which constitute the Secret Fire. The provenance of one is clearly indicated by the cask, which, I can safely assure the reader, is made of oak. 'That Fire', stresses Basil Valentine, 'does not burn and is not burnt.'

Goossen van Vreeswijk
De Groene Leeuw, 1674

De Groene Leeuw, of het Licht der Philosophen; Vertoonende alle Koninklijke Handelingen in het openen en ontsluiten der Metalen, Mineralen, Vegetabilische en Animalische saken, het onderkennen van hare Natuur en Souten, seer dienstig tot vele heelijke Medicynen, tot verscheide schoone Verwen en Tincturen, en meer andere nutte voortreffelijke werken der Konst, uit eigen ondervinding gunstig voorgesteld, Door Goossen van Vreeswyk, Berg-meester. Met vele noodige kopere Platen verciert. t'Amsterdam gedrukt voor den Autheur. Zijn mede te bekomen by Johannes Janssonius van Waesberge, 1674.

The Green Lion, or the Light of the Philosophers; exhibiting all the royal actions in the opening and unlocking of metals, minerals, vegetable and animal things, the knowledge of their nature and salts, highly serviceable for many magnificent medicines, for divers beautiful colours and tinctures, and other useful and excellent works of Art, generously presented from his own experience by Goossen van Vreeswijk, master miner. With many necessary copperplates. Amsterdam, printed for the author. Are to be had of Johan Jansson van Waesberge. 1674.

Barthélemy Pielat praised Goossen van Vreeswijk in French verses appended to *De Groene Leeuw*:

'To the honour of the author of this treatise: Let us all listen to Vreeswik, who comes to us to present the secrets of the true God who governs the world. He will show us that he can, without boasting, extract the treasures of the barren earth. Everything that he does surprises the most learned brains. Alas it must however be that his Experience, of which few people partake, makes fools speak ill of the effects of his noble Science. Has one ever heard of a spirit who can better separate every thing either similar or contrary? Does it not seem that he came from the Heavens? From the Knowledge that he has, celestial or sublunary, let us seek his savour, if we cherish gold. Let us hear him discourse against the Galenic: As long as he shall make me partake of his rich treasure I shall fear neither Tyrant nor Critic. B. PIELAT. Medic. Doctor.'

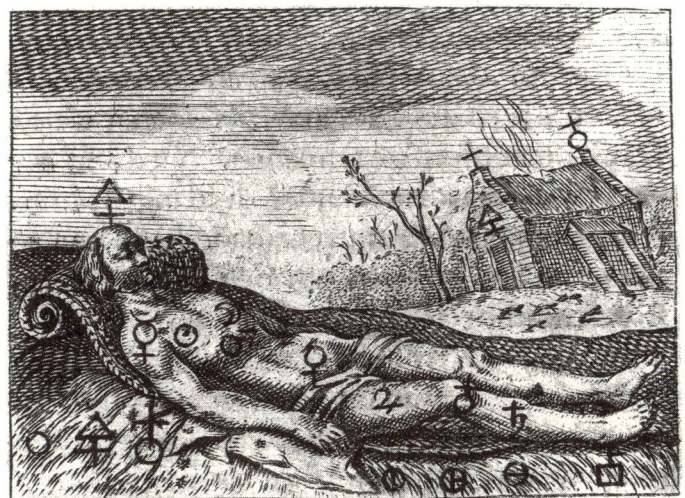
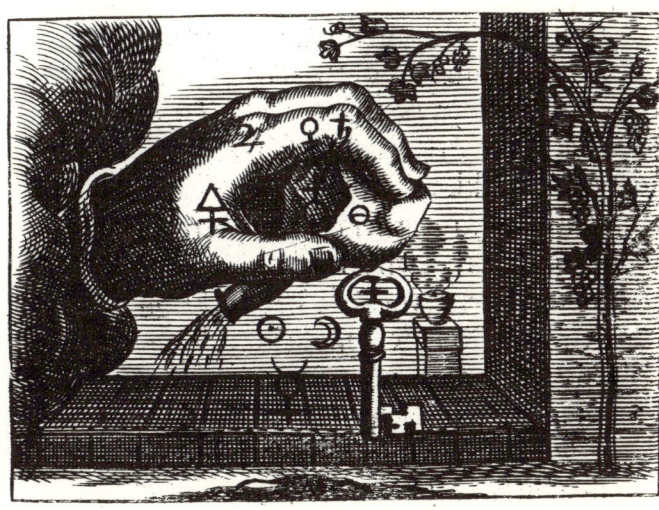

De Groene Leeuw

425

426

427

428

429

430

De Groene Leeuw · 249

431

432

433

416 Eros, the Volatile Principle of the Subject of the Wise, incarnates the early stages of the Work (whence his youth), as well as Volatility (whence his wings). His counterpart is represented as a young man confidently staring at the Sun of Perfection. This is because the Fixation of the Volatile, symbolized by the Caduceus or Staff of Mercury, takes place at a later stage and results in the attainment of Perfection. Having become the vitrified vehicle of the cosmic fluid, the Salt of the Wise acquires a green colour, while its density is considerably increased. It is then called Vitriol or Green Lion.

417 Here lies our Corpse (*Corpus*), which through the action of the Secret Fire will assume all the Colours and transit through the realms of all the Planets. It will dissolve into Mercury, coagulate into Sulphur, beget the Lunar Perfection and then the Solar Perfection of the Philosopher's Stone.

418 A triple Dissolution is the Key to the obtaining of our Pontick Water or Universal Dissolvent. This permanent water, which 'does not wet the hands', is the Philosophick Mercury upon whose surface the mysterious Spirit of Light traces a geometric network of interwoven lines compared to the weave of a basket or to the mesh of a net. This philosophick signature becomes stronger and stronger as the degree of purity increases, but it is obtained only after a long series of difficult purifications. These must never be neglected, as the celestial influx will never dwell permanently in an impure, insufficiently prepared Matter.

419 'To make the Bird fly' is to free the Spirit from its material prison, that it may soar in the alchemical sky and bring back Below the benefits of what is Above. The whole Work, as I have repeatedly stated, is a series of Dissolutions.

420 The Tree of the Art with the Raven (*Nigredo*). At the root of the Tree is ☿, hieroglyph of the Subject of the Wise. An interesting connection is underlined here between the Mars ♂ and the Sun ☉ or Gold of the Wise.

421 Here is a very complex emblem containing virtually all the symbols of the operations of the Great Work. The lady, who is the Incarnation of ✶ Harmony, wields in one hand the arrow of the Secret Fire, which dissolves the Subject into Mercury, and in the other the anchor, emblem of the coagulating Sulphur. In the fountain, Fixed and Volatile are shown in conjunction. The student will be well advised to study all the various correspondences, too numerous to spell out here.

422 The gradual thickening of Mercury into a paste until its final Fixation is a long operation traditionally compared to a sea voyage in bad weather. The Hermetick Sea of the Compost is rough, bubbles burst upon its surface in endless succession, and heavy vapours cloud the atmosphere, darkening the glass of the Vessel. A minute tempest is blowing. Nevertheless Noah's ark sails on (see *De goude Leeuw, 436*) and the Dolphin swims upon the stormy seas. All this goes on until the invisible legendary fish, Remora, stops the ship dead in its tracks. And as the weather clears there appears the island of Delos, which is the beginning of true Fixation.

423 *Ignis et Azoth tibi sufficiunt* – Fire and Azoth are sufficient for thee – claim the Philosophers. The Secret Fire and the celestial dynamism are indeed the means needed to conquer the alchemical citadel. On its pinnacle is ☿, hieroglyph of our raw Subject which dissolves into the darkness of Saturn. On either turret are ☿ and ♃, the dual Principles resulting from the Philosophick Dissolution followed by the Philosophick Coagulation or Fixation, according to the axiom *Solve et Coagula*.

424 The Hermetick Labyrinth symbolizes the material realization of the Great Work. The maze expresses two main difficulties: how to reach its centre and how to get out again. To reach the centre, one must first acquire sure knowledge of the Subject of the Art, and of its preparation, which is accomplished at the central pavilion. The return journey – when the chances of getting lost are greatly increased – signifies the mutation of the prepared Matter with the help of Fire. One sees Fire leading Matter on, guided by Ariadne's thread. The thread is the Possibility of Nature: the fact that like produces like.

425 An unsuspected Light is concealed within the body of the She-Wolf, which, when revealed, runs like a lustrous stream and crystallizes as a green salt. The emblem shows the She-Wolf as the Mother of all the aspects of the Work, and a close kin to the Secret Fire. On her brow shines the future Solar Perfection. The student will notice that the Subject must be carefully shielded from the light.

426 Hieroglyph of the *Materia Prima*, the Lady or Venus of the Wise. Our ☿ Subject, once 'opened' by ♂ Mars, releases toxic fumes, which precede the Snakes or first Mercury. The latter is called the Universal Dissolvent, not as is erroneously thought because it dissolves all bodies, but because it is all-powerful in the microcosmic universe constituted by the Great Work.

427 The essential Dissolution, or Death, which is the reduction of solids into Waters of Darkness, is followed by 'Love's Rescue', which means that with the help of Fire

(notice that the space between the legs of the rescuer forms △ the triangle of Fire) the Artist collects upon the surface of the Bath the precious substance which is the true agent of the Philosopher's Stone. Therefore any Dissolution must be followed by Coagulation until the perfect state of Solar Fixity is reached.

428 From the union of our Matter ♂ with a martial agent is born a son, 'surpassing his parents in vigour'. This son shows a pronounced aversion to his own mother, to whom he must, however, be mated. Eros, emblem of the Secret Fire, shoots a paralysing shaft, described as iron-tipped, which brings the wayward son to better feelings. Dying, he is brought to his mother's bed and remains in close union with her (Dissolution) while she yields her own blood and flesh and dies to revive him. Thus is obtained the Philosophick or Twofold Mercury.

429 After its preparation, the Subject of the Art becomes the Saturn of the Wise, also called the Tortoise or Turtle, because of the precise analogy of the scales of its shell with the enamel-like substance which occurs upon the mercurial surface. Thus prepared, the Tortoise will pursue its slow but irresistible progress toward the Fixed Solar Perfection of the Lion.

430 The Dissolution of the Subject of the Wise yields their Mercury, of which the Dog, traditionally associated with Mercury, is an emblem. The subsequent Putrefaction will bring the Matter through the Night and Death of saturnine Putrefaction toward the first Lunar Perfection (the Duck) and then on to the celestial splendour of the Sun.

431 Here is the Shining Perfection held by the hands of the Absolute. Two major riddles must be solved by the one aspiring to possess it: (1) knowledge of the nature of our Subject ♂ and its preparation; (2) the Secret of Saturn, or the way to dissolve and putrefy. Everything else — and there is a lot more to be said, here and elsewhere — is secondary.

432 Here is shown the possible shape of a 'raw' sample of the *Materia Prima* ♂ and the necessity to dissolve it until there emerges from the Darkness the starry aspect which is neither a fiction nor a mere symbol but an alchemical reality.

433 The twofold power of the first Dissolvent 'sharpens' metals in such a way that, having dissociated them, and partially digested them, in becoming acidified it acquires a caustic virtue and thus a greater power of penetration.

Goossen van Vreeswijk
De Goude Leeuw, 1675

De Goude Leeuw, of den Asijn der Wysen. Waer in ontallyke heerlyke Konsten en nutte Verborgentheden ontdekt worden: als de Anima uit alle Metalen en Mineralen te trekken; vele ongemeene Medicynen, Schilder-gout, Brandewynen uit Koorn sonder viese smaeck, uitstekend Blancketsel, kostelyke Gesteenten, &c. te maken. Alles met eigen handen gewrocht, en met vele kopere Platen aen den dach gegeven. Door Goossen van Vreeswyk, Berg-meester. t'Amsterdam gedrukt voor den Autheur, Zijn mede te bekomen by Johannes Janssonius van Waesberge. 1675.

The Golden Lion, or the Vinegar of the Wise. Wherein countless excellent arts and useful secrets are uncovered: how the Anima is to be extracted from all metals and minerals; many uncommon medicines, painters' gold, spirituous liquors made from grain without an ill taste, excellent whitewash for the skin, precious stones, &c. may be made. All wrought with his own hands, and made public with many copperplates, by Goossen van Vreeswijk, master miner. Amsterdam, printed for the author. Are to be had of Johan Jansson van Waesberge. 1675.

DE GOUDE LEEUW, of den Afijn der Wyfen.

T'AMSTERDAM, Gedrukt voor den Autheur, 1676.

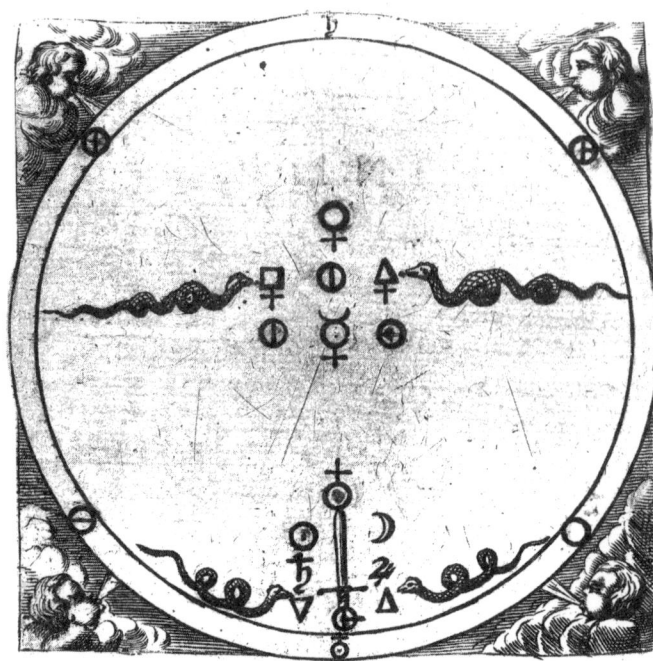

439

440

441

442

443

444

De Goude Leeuw · 255

445

446

448

450

De Goude Leeuw · 257

434 Hercules as a child throttled the snakes sent by Juno to kill him. In alchemical symbolism Hercules is the Artist; the killing of the Snakes is Fixation of the Volatile; and the flight of the Birds is Volatilization. The Four Elements are represented by Dolphin, Dragon, Bird and Salamander. As all the Philosophers maintain, he who can convert Earth into Water, the same Water into Air, the same Air into Fire, and the same Fire into Earth, shall know the entire process of the Philosopher's Stone.

435 Opened by the martial sword, our Subject yields the Vitriol of the Wise. (For design reasons the publisher has here rearranged the images from *De goude Leeuw*. The original order is 435–36, 447, 437, 445, 446, 448–50, 438–44.)

436 Under the action of the external Fire upon the Secret Fire, the whole compost liquefies; this is that 'Sea' agitated by fermentation which ancient authors called the Flood. A film appears on the waters: this is Noah's Ark, the equivalent of the floating island of Delos where Latona takes refuge to give birth to the Hermetick Twins, Diana and Apollo. The end of the saturnine Night is heralded by the colours of the Rainbow, followed by the rule of Jupiter.

437 Tempted by the grapes, the dog will drop what he carries. This analogy shows the action of the dissolving Secret Fire or Tartar of the Wise upon ♂ our Subject. The celestial hand indicates the 'knack' involved, and the necessity to enhance the power of that 'Salt' through the agency of the mysterious celestial dynamism.

438 The Harmony imposed by the saline mediator ✳ is reflected in the harmonious layout of the Gardens of the Art.

439 The Salamander, hieroglyph of the Secret Fire of the Wise, is also the emblem of Sulphur.

440 An allegory of Aquarius, this emblem means that the Calcination of the Wise (as opposed to vulgar calcination) is obtained by means of a humid Fire, or Pontick Water, which reduces the Bodies to their first principles without destroying their seminal qualities, shown here swimming like fishes in the Waters of Dissolution.

441 The amphibious Crocodile is a natural hieroglyph of the Subject of the Wise. Between its gaping jaws creeps its foe the Ichneumon, a rat-like creature which devours its entrails. Thus, Sulphur feeds upon the Subject before absorbing and transforming its watery nature into perfect Fixity.

442 Death rides the Crocodile, prodding it with the arrow of the Secret Fire towards Dissolution and its rule of darkness.

443 The insertion within the Subject of the igneous agent which promotes its evolution has often been hidden under the guise of a combat between an Eagle and a Lion. The volatile Eagle is replaced here by the winged *putto*.

444 'Our whole Secret', writes Philaletha, 'is in our ☿ and in our ☉ ; our ☿ is our way, and without it nothing is done; our ☉ also is not ☉ vulgar, yet in ☉ vulgar is our ☉ , else how could Metals be homegeneal? If then thou know how to illuminate our ☿ as it ought to be, thou mayest for want of our ☉ joyn with Gold vulgar, but yet know that the actuation of the ☿ ought to be different for the one, and for the other, and in a true Regimen of them, in an hundred and fifty dayes, thou shalt have our ☉ , for our ☉ naturally comes out of our ☿ : if then ☉ vulgar be by ☿ divided into its Elements, and afterwards joyned, all the mixture by the help of the fire, will become our ☉ , which then being joyned with that ☿ , which we prepared, and call our Virgin's Milk, by reiterate decoction it will give all the signs which the Philosophers have described in such a fire as they have written of in their Books.'

That fire is the Secret Fire, composed of two saline substances, the external heat being used only to activate the Secret Fire and to repulse the cold. The Snake, as always, is the Mercury of the Wise.

445 Here is the Mercury of the Wise which is the *Materia Prima* and 'the only thing required to accomplish our Work from beginning to end', write many authors who conveniently forget to mention all the preliminaries including the Dissolution ☋ of the twin Principles ☿ and ♂ which precedes its acquisition. In this guise, naked and purified, 'our Mercury' is the root of gold, that is to say, the spirit of gold contained within an oily green substance, easily coagulated, called Vitriol – *vitri oleum*, oil of glass. To confuse the unwary, the Philosophers refer to that very same substance in its crystalline form as a Salt – *Sal Petrae*, the salt of (our) Stone – and call it by every conceivable saline name: *Sal Saturni, Sal Gemmae* etc. Below the large hieroglyph of Vitriol ⊕ , the reader cannot fail to recognize the double-edged sword of the Philosophick or Secret Fire, secret promoter of all transformations.

446 In the first Dissolution, the *Materia Prima* ☋ is dissolved in its own mercurial Waters. Such is the meaning of the hieroglyphs on the Mountain. Philosophick Mercury, thus obtained, is the Universal Dissolvent of the Wise or *Aqua Ardens* ⊛ , which bears and nurtures its own future Fixity, which is Philosophick Sulphur ♁ . The Universal Dissolvent, Mother of the Stone, is also the Moon of the Philosophers. The ancient Alchemists placed this First

Mercury under the protection of Diana, bearing the horns of the Moon.

447 The Secret Fire is the combination of the Tartar of the Wise with their Salt of Harmony. The origin of the Tartar of the Wise is indicated by the grapes. The Dissolution of the Subject by the Secret Fire in the crucible ✛ produces the Snake, the Mercury of the Wise.

448 The Subject of the Wise, naked (that is purified), enters the waters of Dissolution bearing a saturnine disc to show that he will sink into that Blackness which is the key to the whole Work, and without which there can be no Regeneration.

449 Dissolution continues until the whole Subject has disappeared under the black watery rule of Saturn.

450 The rule of Jupiter, which follows the rule of Saturn, is the first sign of Fixity, the grey Dawn which follows the dark Night of Chaos.

Goossen van Vreeswijk
De Goude Son, 1675

Vervolg van 't Cabinet der Mineralen, of De Goude Son der Philosophen. Waer in alle bewerckingen der Metalen en Mineralen, met de gereedschappen daer toe dienende, hare Openingen, Verwen, en Tincturen, nevens verscheide heerlijke Medicynen, en andere seer nutte Konsten, uit eigen ondervinding aen 't licht gegeven. Door Goossen van Vreeswyk, Berg-meester. Met vele noodige kopere Plaaten verciert. t' Amsterdam gedrukt voor den Autheur. Zijn mede te bekomen by Johannes Janssonius van Waesberge, 1675.

Continuation of the Cabinet of Minerals or the Golden Sun of the Philosophers. Wherein all the workings of metals and minerals, with the tools appertaining thereto, their openings, colours and tinctures, together with divers excellent medicines and other highly useful arts, are set forth from his own experience by Goossen van Vreeswijk, master miner. With many necessary copperplates. Amsterdam, printed for the author. Are to be had of Johan Jansson van Waesberge, 1675.

Vervolg van 't
Cabinet der Mineralen,
OF DE GOUDE SON
der
PHILOSOPHEN.

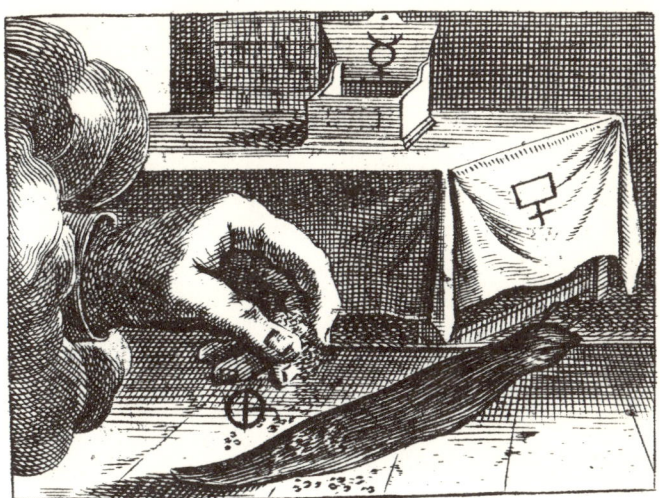

t' Amsterdam gedruckt voor den Autheur:

Zijn mede te bekomen by JOHANNES
JANSSONIUS van WAESBERGE. 167..

De Goude Son · 261

456

457

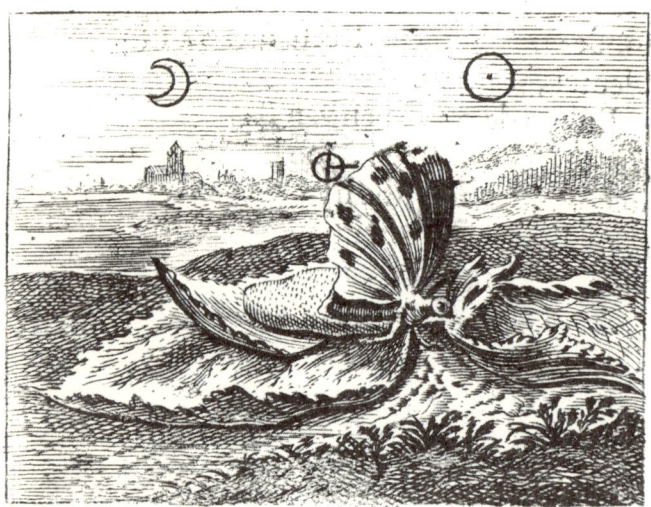

458

459

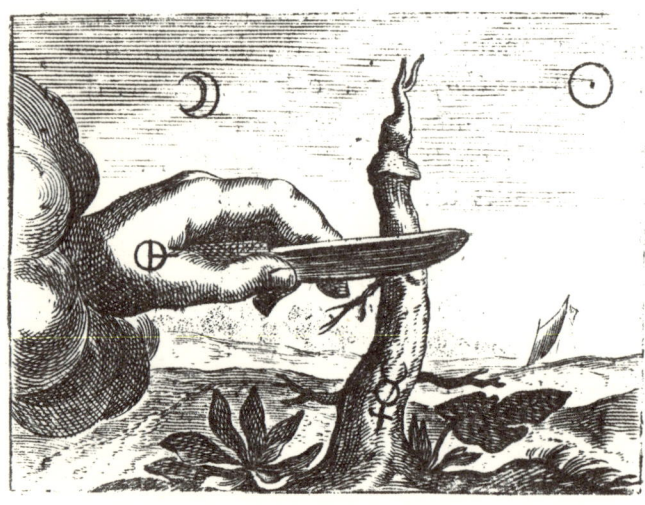

460

461

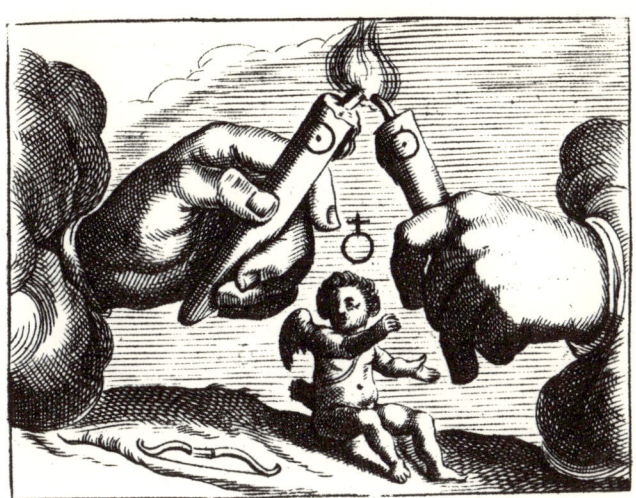

De Goude Son · 263

451 The Vine of the Wise is their Subject. Its Wine is their Dissolvent or Mercury. The Sheep is another emblem of their Subject. The Shepherd is Sulphur, their mysterious Spirit, or principle of Fixity. The carcass of the horse is a reminder that there can be no generation without prior corruption and also of the necessity to 'kill the live to revive the dead'.

452 The Volatile Spirit is fixed like a fly in a spider's web.

453 Dissolution of the Fixed: the Subject is dissolved by the Vitriol of the Wise, just as a slug melts under the action of ordinary salt.

454 The 'knack' of the first preparation or 'Separation' is depicted in a blacksmith's forge. Purified, the first Mercury rises like smoke or vapour from the Darkness resulting from the first conjunction of Mars ♂ with Our Venus ♀ (☿). The flaming hammer and the saline hieroglyph ⊕ upon the anvil emphasize the action of the Secret Fire, mediator and promoter of the Work.

455 The twin Principles of the Work as Adam and Eve (the second born from the first will cause the Fall of both into the Chaos of the Wise.) 'Grow and Multiply' was God's command to his creatures. Each has its proper mate, without which, in every realm of Nature, there can be no generation. The Possibility of Nature (see p. 251) must always be borne in mind.

456 The result of assiduous studies, speculations and theories will be verified by practice. The spiritual dimension of Alchemy can only be attained by using one's hands. *Ora et Labora sic habebis*: 'Pray and Work, thus thou shalt receive.'

457 Experience shows that the energy of the Universal Spirit – *Spiritus Mundi* – has its signature in the sword, and that the sword has its correspondence in the Sun, sole ultimate agent of the successive metamorphoses of our Subject.

458 The separation of the Subtle from the Gross, represented by the separation of the Butterfly from the chrysalis, aptly characterizes the Sublimation of the Wise. The living water – or Vitriol – is the agent of this transformation, which, in our Subject, yields a green oil (*vitri oleum*). The pear-tree butterfly (*Saturnia pyri*), which lays green eggs, is the cabalistic hieroglyph of our green Mercury, agent of Putrefaction and Regeneration.

459 The Ram – with or without horns – is always a hieroglyph of the Subject of the Wise. Its fleece, stamped with the saline hieroglyph of the Secret Fire, promoter of the Work, becomes in due course the Philosopher's Stone.

460 'Grafting has been spoken of as "ennobling", the branch which is transferred being spoken of as the "scion" and the tree to which it is attached as the "stock". The scion becomes as it were parasitic upon the stock, and, by carefully removing all branches which spring from the stock below the point of union, gardeners are enabled to divert to the scion all the energy produced by the roots of the stock. It is only possible to graft a scion onto a stock of a nearly allied species.' (J. Coutts, *Everyday Gardening*, London and Melbourne 1931.) This operation offers precise analogies with the task facing the alchemist, who must graft Spirit upon his chosen Matter, the former absorbing the life of the latter.

461 The initial preparation of our Matter is compared to the preparation of chestnuts, first gathered into the basket, then cut and put into the fire until the shell bursts.

462 The Alchemical Couple are the parents of ☉ Philosophick Gold. Notice the active stance of the Woman as opposed to the initial passivity of the Man.

463 Exalted to the highest degree of Fixed Perfection, the Stone of the Philosophers has become the Philosopher's Stone. The texts stress that the principle of transformation of Earth into Fire resides in Fire, just as that of transmutation into gold is found within gold. For as the horse begets a horse and not a cow, lead will produce lead and not silver, and gold will produce gold and not a tincture. The Philosophers' Gold must be added as a ferment to their Stone at the end of the Work. Indeed, a ferment converts the fermented body into its own nature; without which the desired end could never be reached. Once this is accomplished, the conversion becomes as easy as lighting one candle from another.

464 According to classical fables, the god Mercury made the first lyre from the shell of a tortoise which he found, according to some accounts, on the banks of the Nile, or by a pit, according to others. The tortoise is therefore a hieroglyph of the Subject of the Wise, which once prepared becomes an instrument of great power. Its gift appeased the wrath of Apollo, who in return presented the mighty Caduceus to its inventor. The sign of Vitriol ⊕ on its shell underlines the need to visit the interior of the earth and find the hidden stone: VISITA INTERIORA TERRAE RECTIFICANDOQUE INVENIES OCCULTUM LAPIDEM VERAM MEDICINAM. (Search the interior of the earth and by rectifying thou shalt find the hidden Stone, the true medicine.) The first letters of each word spell VITRIOLUM, a contraction of *vitri oleum*.

465 The Art of Music – or of Harmony – is a classic synonym of Alchemy. Numerous treatises develop this theme. To each note, to each chord, corresponds a degree in the process of the transmutation of the Stone of the Philosophers into the Philosopher's Stone.

466 According to the rules of the Art, what causes the death of one of the Principles brings life to the other. The flame of the life of the first Mercury is extinguished to provide the Sulphur of the dissolved metal with the elements of its Resurrection. Life needing Life must be joined to Life, and thus the live active Sulphur is united to the first-born Mercury (Diana) in order to obtain Philosophick Mercury. That last operation is concealed under the allegory of an incestuous wedding of the brother to his sister – as both are of the same blood and of the same origin.

467 In the elaboration of the Mercury of the Philosophers, called the Salt of our Stone (because it is that Mercury which is the Stone of the Philosophers), nothing may be substituted for the Secret Fire of the Wise hidden under its saline aspect. The power of one of the components of this invisible agent is shown by the bursting of the barrel from which it is obtained.

ALTUS
Mutus liber, 1677

Mutus liber, in quo tamen tota Philosophia hermetica, figuris hieroglyphicis depingitur, ter optimo maximo Deo misericordi consecratus, solisque filiis artis dedicatus, authore cuius nomen est Altus. 2i.ii.82. Neg: 93.82.72. Neg: 82.8i.33. Tued.

The mute book, in which nonetheless all the Hermetick Philosophy is depicted in hieroglyphic figures, thrice consecrated to God the Compassionate, Greatest and Best, and dedicated solely to the Sons of the Art [*or* dedicated to the Sons of the Art of the Sun], by an author whose name is Altus. 21.ii.82. Neg: 93.82.72. Neg: 82. 8i.33. Tued.

The *Mutus liber* — mute because it has no text — was first published at La Rochelle in 1677. This revised edition, published without indication of place or date, probably toward the end of the seventeenth century, is similar if not identical to a version of the same work contained in J.J. Manget's *Bibliotheca chemica curiosa* (Geneva 1702).

A facsimile of the original edition, published by Jean-Jacques Pauvert (Paris 1967), has an introduction and commentaries by my late distinguished friend Eugène Canseliet, without whose help I could not have hoped to penetrate the mysteries of the *Mutus liber*, 'which is mute only in appearance'. My initial intention was to refer the advanced reader to Canseliet's learned work, but the rarity of the latter compels me to attempt to provide fellow seekers with a commentary, distilled from Canseliet's exegesis and my own 'observations'. This does not, indeed cannot, aspire to explain this complex work.

The author of the *Mutus liber* is almost certainly Jacob Sulat or Saulat, whose name appears in the *Privilège du Roy* published with the original edition, which grants him exclusive rights: *Nostre bien amé Jacob Saulat, Sieur des Marez, Nous a fait remontrer qu'il luy est tombé entre les mains un Livre de la haute Chimie d'Hermès, intitulé: Mutus Liber* . . . ('Our well-beloved Jacob Saulat, Sieur des Marez, has represented to us that there has fallen into his hands a book of the exalted Chymistry of Hermes, entitled *Mutus Liber* . . . '). Canseliet has pointed out that the scrolls proceeding simultaneously from the mouths of the kneeling Alchemical Couple on the last plate of the work, which read OCULATUS ABIS ('Thou departest seeing'), are an anagram of IACOBUS SULAT. The subject of the title-page, Jacob's Dream, tends to confirm the name. However, the name does not provide an identifiable personage. The title of Sieur des Marez, which can be interpreted either as Lord of the Tides (*marées*) or Lord of the Swamps (*marais*), is suitably ambiguous — although the former, applied to celestial tides, has some relevance. Another anagram of ALTUS is SALUT, which can be read either as a greeting or as 'salvation', which is more appropriate; ALTUS of course means 'high'.

As I have elsewhere stated, the names of alchemical authors are especially interesting when they draw attention to hidden particularities of the Secret Art. And it is precisely the intercourse between sky and earth which transports alchemy onto an altogether higher plane than that of vulgar chemistry.

469

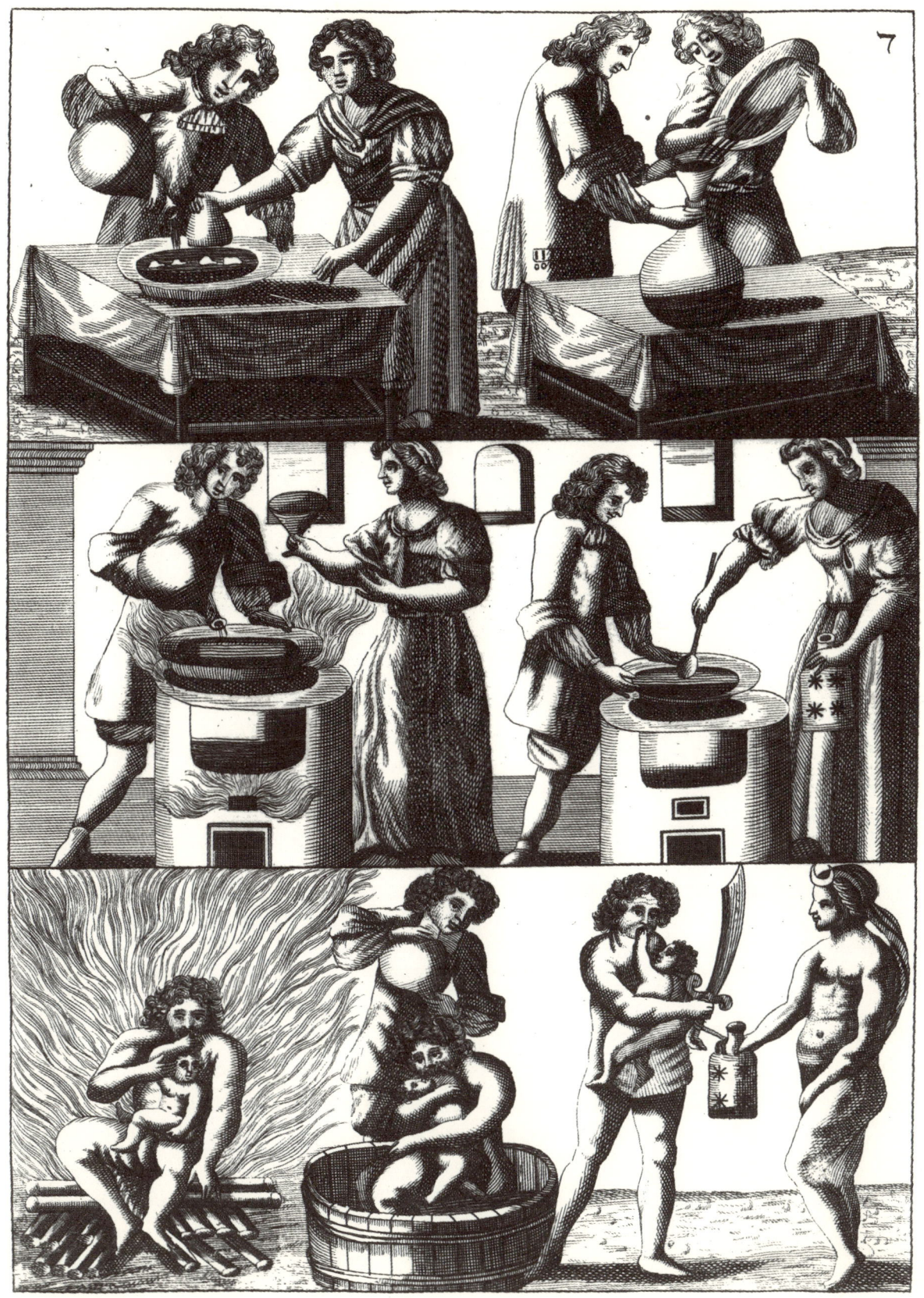

476

Mutus liber · 275

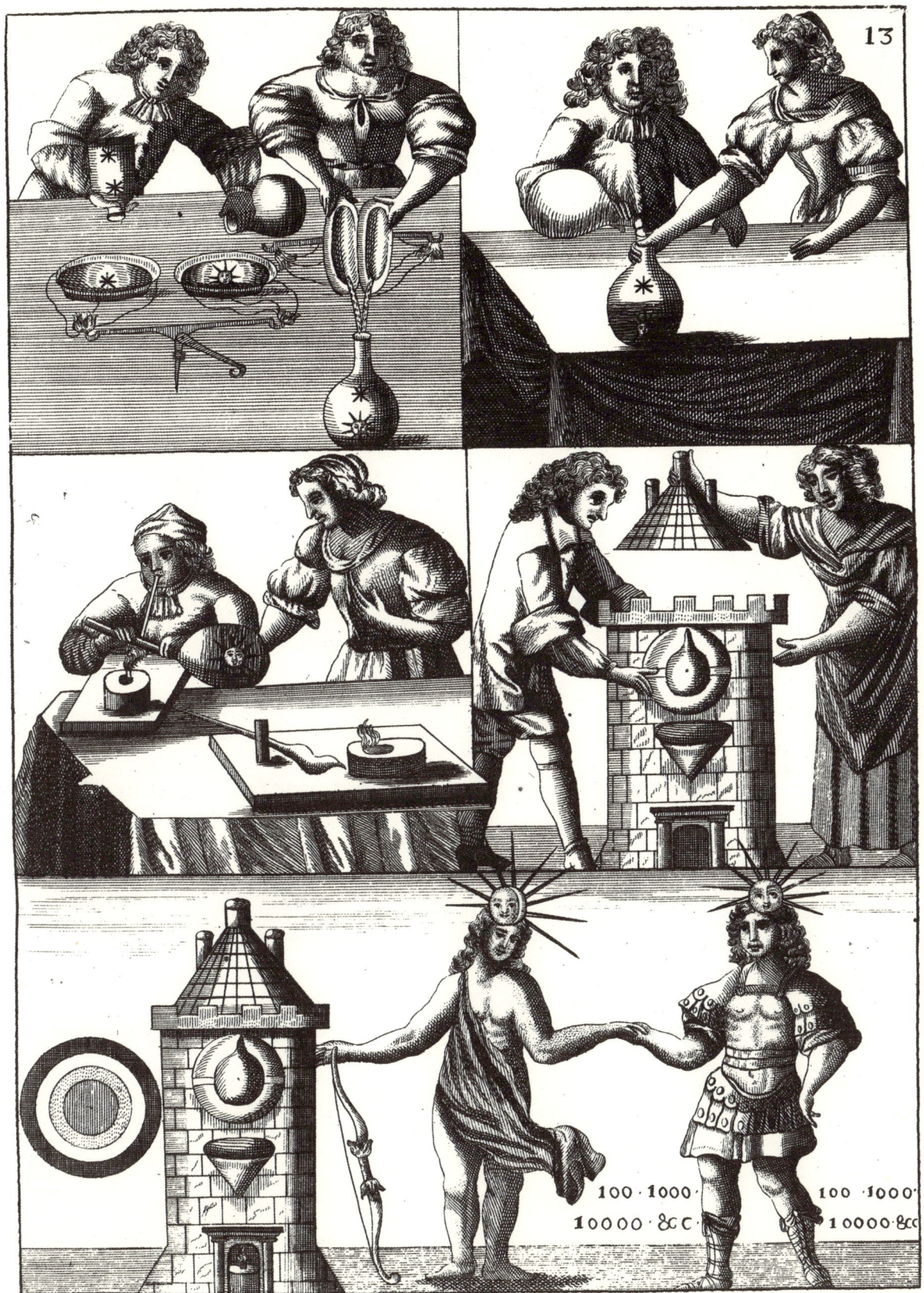

468 The mysterious numbers and letters which are found on the title-page must be read backwards: Thus, 21.ii.82 Neg = Gen. 28.11–12: 'and he [Jacob] lighted upon a certain place and tarried there all night, because the sun was set; and he took the stones of that place, and put them for his pillows, and lay down in that place to sleep. And he dreamed, and behold a ladder set up on the earth, and the top of it reached to heaven: and behold the angels of God ascending and descending on it.'

The reader is earnestly advised to read and meditate the rest of the same chapter. Gen 28.18–19, for instance, reads: 'And Jacob rose up early in the morning, and took the stone that he had put for his pillows, and set it up for a pillar, and poured oil upon the top of it. And he called the name of that place Beth-el: but the name of that city was called Luz at the first.'

The rose branches neatly tied with a knot form an X, which is the Greek letter *chi*, symbolizing, according to Fulcanelli, the Hidden Light, while the sharp tips of each branch evoke the double power of the Secret Fire. In the original edition of the work the landscape is arid, while in the present one the waters flow past the dreamer. I feel that this was done on purpose to insist upon the imperious necessity of dissolving the dark Stone which is the secret Subject of the Wise.

The Angels upon the ladders are of course the Volatile element, while Jacob and the rocks are the Fixed. But ladder and trumpets also evoke two ancient alchemical treatises, the *Scala philosophorum* (Ladder of the Philosophers) and *Clangor buccinae* (Sound of the Trumpet), published in the *Ars aurifera quam chemica vocant*, Basle 1593. Jacob and his rocky pillow are the *Materia Prima* in need of a strong electromagnetic shock to awaken its potential.

The second inscription, 93.82.72 Neg = Gen. 27.28,39, refers to the dew of heaven, with which the *Mutus liber* is much concerned. Gen. 27.28: 'Therefore God give thee of the dew of heaven and the fatness of the earth and plenty of corn and wine.' Gen. 27.39: 'And Isaac his father answered and said unto him, Behold thy dwelling shall be the fatness of the earth, and of the dew of heaven from above.'

The last reference is 82.3i.33 Tued = Deut. 33.13,28. The 3 in 13 is clearly legible in the original version, while in the present one it has erroneously been closed into an 8. 'And of Joseph he [Moses] said, Blessed of the Lord be his land, for the precious things of heaven, for the dew, and for the deep that coucheth beneath. Israel then shall dwell in safety alone: the fountain of Jacob shall be upon a land of corn and wine; also his heaven shall drop down dew.'

Alchemical Dew is the Vitriol of the Wise and the Philosophers' Green Lion. From the collection of morning dew, the Artist obtains one of the saline substances used in the composition of the Secret Fire.

Canseliet believed that the Moon had erroneously been reversed, as it is shown waning whereas it should be waxing. I feel that this was done deliberately, and that he who deciphered the biblical references would use the same device with respect to the Moon; for the beginning of these operations must always correspond with the New Moon. The ten stars correspond to the ten Eagles or Sublimations. The reader will have noticed already the division of darkness and light and should reflect upon the device POST TENEBRAS LUX: 'After darkness, light.' Indeed, the best definition of alchemy is concealed in these words on every level.

469 Neptune, armed with the trident of the triple Dissolution, heralds the birth of Diana and Apollo, future parents of the Philosopher's Stone, on the island of Delos, which upon the Dolphin's back is the first sign of Coagulation and Fixity. Thus arises Light, separated from Darkness and underlined by the Sun and the Angels. This result is achieved only after much tedious and repetitive work and concentrated attention sustained by prayer.

Several plates could precede this one, which in turn ought to precede the eighth.

470 In this figure the main devices leading to the Solar Realization are shown in their multiple interactions.

At the centre of the wheel Neptune (the first Dissolvent) darts his iron trident into the Earth, that is into the Subject that must be dissolved between the opposite Principles. The Dissolution is always followed by Coagulation, which is why Neptune holds on with his other hand to his mercurial consort who has captured the Dolphin, that is the first pure Principle of Fixity. The union of the latter with his mercurial Mother is symbolized by the Mermaid. The Ram and the Bull refer to the astrological spring signs of Aries and Taurus, a time when such operations should be performed; they are also used to denote the fixed earthly sphere. The ten flying Birds correspond to the ten Sublimations, the Peacock to the stage known as the Peacock's Tail, Jupiter upon the Eagle to the Greyness preceding the Albification, symbolized by the Moon, which in turn precedes the Solar Perfection. Read another way, Jupiter is the Fixation of the Volatile and the Volatilization of the Fixed; the Sun is the external heat; the Moon and the clouds are the celestial influences which are the agents of transformation.

471 The celestial dynamism abundant during some unclouded spring nights galvanizes our chosen Subject, whose hieroglyph is seen on the church spire. In the foreground is shown the method by which dew is gathered.

472 Poured into a distilling apparatus, the abundant collection of dew yields one of the principles of Lunatick Vulcan (the Secret Fire). Below centre is the number 40, which signifies the slow digestion of our Subject during forty days and nights. A moderate degree of heat and a great deal of patience are essential.

473 Here the Flower of Fixity is obtained, separated, and presented to its 'father' the martial Sun-god. The personages, manipulations and instruments shown in the *Mutus liber* correspond symbolically to actual operations, but one must not naively believe that the alchemical *modus operandi* is minutely described, as might appear to be the case.

474 The seventh figure shows the preparation of both saline substances composing the Secret Fire.

475 The Son of the Sun and the Moon, here borne by Angels, is the Philosophick Mercury. Of the ten Birds symbolizing the careful repetitions of the same operation leading to purity, two on either side of the Vessel bear the spagyrical signs of the twin saline substances composing the Secret Fire.

476 The ninth plate is not in the correct sequence; it ought to follow the fourth. It shows that the dew collected in the fourth plate should be enriched by the cosmic influx of the spring and the rays of the Sun reflected by the Moon. The scene below shows the future destination of this yet-to-be-prepared substance.

477 Again the reader must be warned never to interpret the scenes for what they appear to be. This plate insists upon the correct proportions between the saline agent or Mercury and the floral spirit of Sulphur sealed within the Philosophick Egg. The Hermetick Seal is (in the Dry Way) effected by the Salt composing the crystalline shell of the Philosophick Egg, which is placed within the Furnace or Athanor.

Indeed, the secret Vessel is not the container but the content itself, which at fusion point assumes the aspect of liquefied glass and holds captive the spirit of Sulphur, which, feeding upon increasing heat, grows ever stronger.

478 At first glance this figure appears to be identical to the eighth one. But a number of important modifications have occurred. The ground under Mercury's feet has been levelled, two rays of the Sun penetrate his foot, and three of the Snakes on the Caduceus have sunk their fangs into his arm. The Sun darts his rays with increasing vigour, indicating the enhanced degree of Fire, and the flying Birds have considerably shortened tails. There appears, in addition to the spagyrical sign of Sulphur or Tartar (borne by the Bird below the Vessel on the left), the sign of Sublimation ♎ which resembles the scales of Libra. The lamp in the Athanor or Philosophick Furnace is now lit, and the curtains have disappeared.

The Mercury of the Wise is now the Mirror of Nature, in which are reflected its secret truths.

479 Again, the twelfth plate seems identical to the ninth. But upon closer inspection the church, bearing on its spire the hieroglyph of the Subject of the Wise, is closer to us, while numerous trees have grown and new buildings have appeared on either side. The Bull shows greater activity and excitement, while the 'liquor' exposed in the six shallow dishes shimmers, loaded with dynamic virtue.

480 Once more, there are many similarities between this thirteenth plate and the tenth one. However, the presence of the Sun in the scales and the Vessels, replacing the Flower, shows the attainment of Fixed Sulphur, the Gold of the Wise whose coagulative virtue, excited by the flames of the external Fire, elevates Mercury to its highest degree of Fixity.

The union of Apollo and Diana symbolizes the Multiplication. According to the texts, each time the Stone is redissolved in its Mercury it augments its power tenfold: 10; 100; 1,000; 10,000; 100,000; etc. Fulcanelli warns, however, that the risk of losing everything should temper the megalomaniac thirst for unlimited Multiplication. Each degree of augmentation requires one-eighth of the time of the preceding one; and, since the fourth reiteration takes no more than two hours, one may appreciate the danger of pushing things too far!

481 'Three Fires are used in the Great Work,' writes Artephius, 'without which one labours in vain.' The first and noblest is the Natural Fire which is the spirit of life hidden in Matter; the second is the Secret Fire or Lunatick Vulcan composed by the alchemists from two saline substances, and the third is the external, Elemental Fire produced by combustion, which excites and animates the preceding ones. To those fires correspond the three Furnaces.

The roman numerals correspond to six successive colours, or the six-pointed Star of our Subject, to two principles, and to ten reiterations or Sublimations. The two women and the child indicate the ultimate phase, ironically described as Child's Play (*Ludus puerorum*) and Women's Work (*Opus mulierum*). Diligence in this Work should be directed toward preventing heat failure. Instruments required at the very beginning of the Work, mortar and pestle, are mixed with ones which also occupy a symbolical function such as the scales. Within the vessel on the left is achieved Luna or the White Stone, and on the right the final Solar Perfection. Three days are necessary to achieve the former, and three days more for the latter, claims the notation.

If we follow the right index finger of the man pointing at the puzzling instrument above him, we may read that the first step towards Philosophick Mercury is a Dissolution (*solve*). The second, indicated by the woman's two fingers, is a Coagulation (*coagula*).

Ora Lege Lege Relege labora et Invenies. In silence, we are urged: 'Pray, read, read, re-read, work, and thou shalt find.'

482 Crowned with laurels, borne up by Angels, the Absolute Quintessence bearing the twin Roses (the White with seven leaves, the Red with nine), the victorious Adept is spiritualized, that is to say carried beyond the ken of mortality onto the plane of Pure Vision: *Oculatus abis*, or *Oculatus ab is*. His counterpart Hercules finds in death much-needed rest. This single emblem expresses many alchemical axioms, from 'Kill the live to quicken the dead', to the capital verses added at the end of the *Fontaine des amoureux de science*:

> *Si fixum solvas, faciasque volare solutum,*
> *Et volucrem figas, faciet te vivere tutum;*

which could be translated:

> *If the Fixed thou dissolvest, and the Dissolved makest fly,*
> *And the winged stillest, it will surely make thee live.*

Barent Coenders van Helpen
Escalier des sages, 1689

Escalier des Sages, ou la Philosophie des Anciens avec des Belles Figures. Par un amateur de la Vérité qui a pour l'anagramme de son nom EN DEBES PULCHRA FERUNDO SCIRE A Groningue, chez Charles Pieman, Imprimeur et Libraire à la Rue dor, An. 1689.

Stairway of the Wise, or the Philosophy of the Ancients with fine figures. By an admirer of the truth who has as the anagram of his name EN DEBES PULCHRA FERUNDO SCIRE Groningen, published by Charles Pieman, Printer and Bookseller, 1689.

Barent Coenders van Helpen, a Flemish gentleman, thus published anonymously the first two editions of his only known work. The second edition, which appeared at Paris the same year, was according to Duveen retouched by F.M.P. Colonne. Called *Introduction à la Philosophie des Anciens*, it was reviewed and praised in the *Journal des Sçavans* (Monday 21 March 1690). The third edition appeared at Cologne in 1693 bearing the author's name for the first time: *Escalier des sages. Thresor de la philosophie des Anciens où l'on conduit le Lecteur par degrez à la connoissance de tous les Metaux et Mineraux et de la manière de les travailler et de s'en servir pour arriver enfin à la perfection du Grand Oeuvre. En forme de dialogues et enrichis de très belles tailles douces. Mis en lumière Par Barent Coenders van Helpen Gentil-homme. A Cologne chez Claude le Jeune, 1693.* Stairway of the Wise. Thesaurus of the philosophy of the ancients in which the reader is led by degrees to the knowledge of all metals and minerals, and of the manner of working and using them in order to attain at last the perfection of the Great Work. In the form of dialogues and enriched with very fine engravings. Brought to light by Barent Coenders van Helpen, Gentleman. Cologne, published by Claude le Jeune, 1693.

Despite the different title pages, the third edition is virtually identical with the first.

483

286 · BARENT COENDERS VAN HELPEN

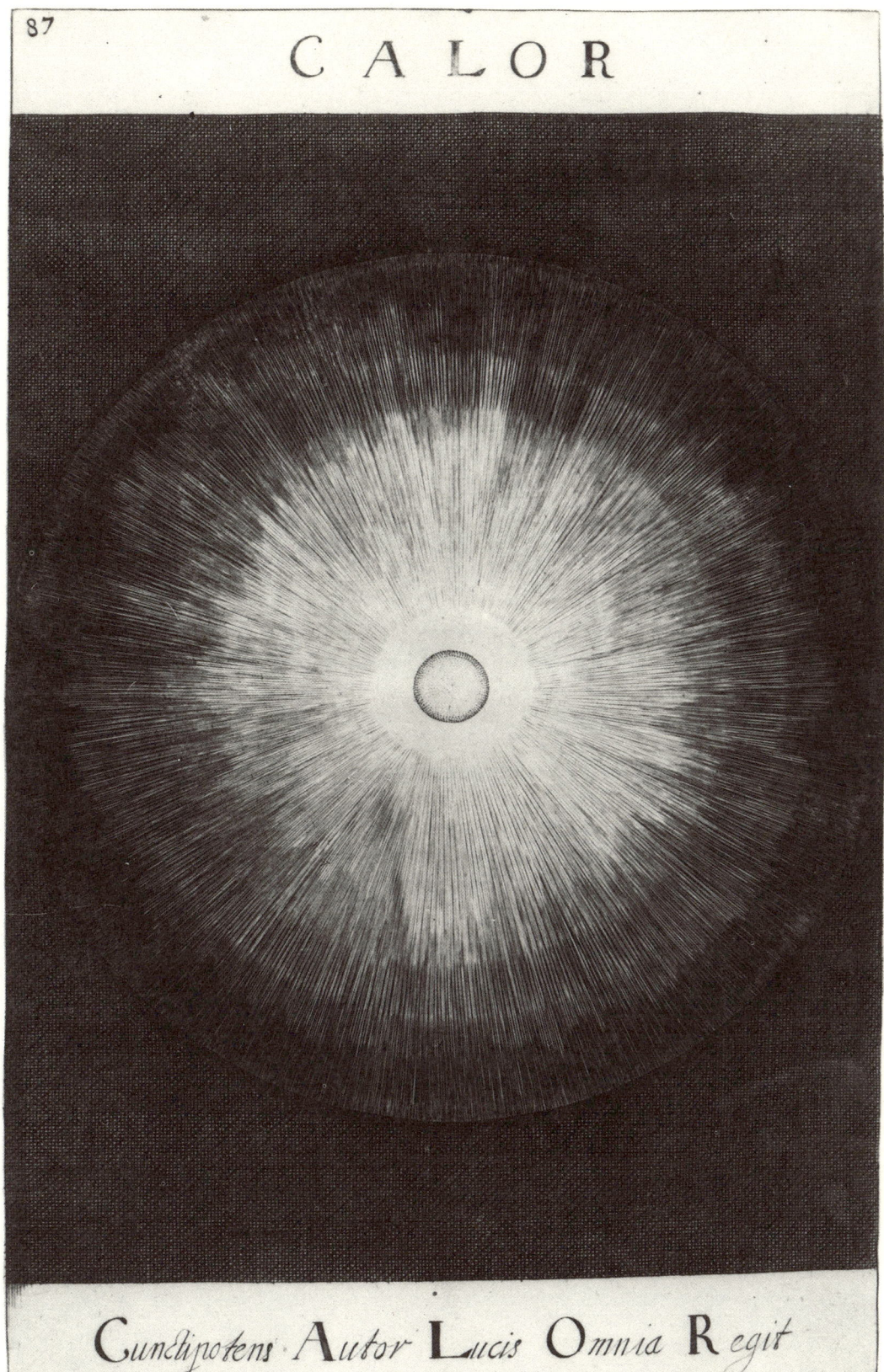

IGNIS.

Iucunde Generat Natura Ignea Solis.

TERRA

Trium Elementorum Receptaculum Recondo Aurifodinam

Escalier des sages · 295

483 In his preface, the author briefly explains his choice of title, suggesting a progression towards the goal of Philosophy: 'Therefore I thought the title of Stairway of the Wise would not be inapt to this Philosophy, and that I would do well to make it appear in the manner of a dialogue between François and Vrederic, the first being the one who will base his argument upon Theory, and the other upon Practice and upon Experience.'

The Stairway of the Wise leads to the Philosopher's goal, which is the Divine Splendour, the Sublime Quintessence (five-pointed crown) of God Himself. The Deity's right hand indicates the numbers 1 (the *Materia Prima*), 2 (the complementary opposing Principles), 3 (Body, Soul and Spirit) and 4 (the Elements), which add up to 10 (the return to Divine Unity). The mythological gods and goddesses, easily identifiable by their attributes, are each in turn the protagonists of the stages of the Great Work.

484 ALCHIMIA. Acronym: 'The Laborious Art Converting the Igneous Humidity of Metals to Mercury.' The Adept points to Mercury conferring with Jupiter, Pluto and Neptune. These four are the Philosophick Elements: Neptune, Water; Pluto, Earth (the mineral ores); Jupiter, Air (and Heavenly Fire); Mercury the Quintessence, the winged messenger, assuming the many forms of all the Elements.

485 CHAOS. Acronym: 'Heat, Moisture, Cold, Hidden Dryness.' According to the Orphic Doctrines (whose paternity was traditionally attributed to Orpheus), Chronos (Time) was the first principle whence Chaos and Aether proceeded. Chaos, surrounded by Night, formed the envelope under which cosmic Matter was slowly organized by the creative action of Aether. Matter, at length, assumed the shape of a gigantic Egg whose shell was Night. At the core of that Egg the first being, Phanes (Light), was born. It is Phanes, the Alpha and Omega of Alchemy, who created the Heavens and the Earth through his union with Night.

486 CALOR. Acronym: 'The Almighty Author of Light Rules All.' According to the most ancient traditions of Alchemy, its central mystery is one of Love, the Omnipotent King of the World. The prepared Matter of the Wise attracts the Love of Heaven, as the magnet draws iron towards itself; but the celestial dynamism can be tapped only at the proper season, if favourable meteorological conditions prevail. The alchemist is in a position analogous to that of the farmer, dependent on the proper season and weather conditions to reap a rich harvest.

487 AMOR. Acronym: 'Author of the World, Almighty King.' Robert Fludd writes: 'This Immaculate Nymph desires assiduously the presence, society and assistance of her Deiform spouse that she may lead her Work to still greater perfection. . . . Thus this most fair sister, immaculate dove and friend, speaks to her beloved from the depths of her desire: "Stay me with flowers, comfort me with apples, for I am sick with love" [Song of Solomon, 2.5]. Therefore the Philosopher in his sacred sermon also says "Out of the light a Word was made and descended on Nature, warming her" [Hermes, *Poimandres* 1.5]. Similarly the Spirit of the Lord, which is the igneous love having the virtue of the Father and the Word, was borne over the waters and gave them it fiery vigour. So this burning Love, a flashing Spirit of Wisdom, is that true supercelestial desire, projecting its igneous seeds into the matrix of the universal waters . . . that is, into the womb of Physis, whose chosen daughter is the immaculate Psyche and bride of the bridegroom.' *Tractatus theologophilosophicus . . .*, Oppenheim, J.T. de Bry, 1617, pp. 35–36, as translated by Joscelyn Godwin in *Robert Fludd*, 1979.

488 IGNIS. Acronym: 'The Fiery Nature of the Sun Engenders Joyfully.' Fire is the Heat of Life which must, in the Work, be neither excessive nor deficient, lest all be lost.

489 IGNIS PHILOSOPHORUM. Acronym: 'In Gehenna is the Fire of Our Science.' *Ignis Philosophorum*, The Fire of the Philosophers, is found in Gehenna: which is to say in places of refuse. Knowledge of this 'great mystery of the Art' was essential to Jason in his conquest of the Golden Fleece. Limojon de Saint-Didier, while refusing to reveal its secret, nevertheless provides valuable clues to its identity: 'The Secret Fire of the Wise is a fire that the Artist prepares, according to the Art, or that he may have prepared for him by those with a perfect knowledge of Chemistry; this fire is not actually hot: but is an igneous spirit introduced within a Subject of the same nature as the Stone, which, once moderately excited by the outer fire, calcinates it, dissolves it, sublimes it and resolves it in dry water according to the words of Cosmopolita.' (*Le Triomphe Hermetique*.)

490 AER. Acronym: 'I the Gold-making Queen.' Jupiter, assuming the shape of a rain of gold, seduced Danaë locked in a tower. In alchemical symbolism this fable emphasizes the magnetic attraction exerted by the Matter of the Philosophers, confined within the Athanor (the tower), upon the volatile parts charged with celestial influences.

491 AQUA. Acronym: 'Which Bears the White Gold.' The Water of the Philosophers is their Mercury. From Darkness, between Pluto and Neptune, steps Jupiter as the Swan, the Whiteness obtained by the washing of Latona by her Water. The Whiteness heralds the advent of the Sun, whose horses are already in sight.

492 TERRA. Acronym: 'I Conceal the Gold-bearing Refuge of Three Elements.' Earth, says Hermes, is the Mother of the Elements; from Earth they proceed and to Earth they return. The Stone of the Philosophers is an Earth, which is why they claim that it is found everywhere – what kind of Earth it is, the seeker must discover. The Philosopher's Stone is that very Earth brought to the highest Perfection.

493 SULPHUR. Acronym: 'By Separating the Venom the Philosopher Gently Revives the Homogeneous Viscosity.' From an oil released by the Putrefaction of Matter, Sulphur, principle of Fixity, is obtained. But the presence of Pluto (in the background) implies the necessity for the hero to cross the Stygian Waters again before the conquest of the Philosopher's Stone is complete.

494 MERCURIUS. Acronym: 'I Create the Universal and Royal Red Medicine in the Womb, for the Sun.' The slaying of Argus by Mercury, acting on Jupiter's behalf, is the subject of the present emblem. The object of Jupiter's lust, Io, had been transformed into a cow by Juno and was guarded by the many-eyed Argus. Mercury, on Jupiter's orders, played his flute so skilfully that Argus fell asleep; Mercury slew him and stole Io. Knowledge of alchemy (which is the Art of Music) allows the Volatile (Mercury) to dissolve (kill) the Fixed (Argus). The death of the latter symbolizes the Blackness; his countless eyes were then set on the Peacock's Tail (Juno's bird); which is another stage in the Putrefaction. Io, the White Cow, is the Whiteness, or First Perfection.

495 SAL. Acronym: 'Alone I Work Higher Things.' The problem of Salt, catalyst and mediator of the Great Work, is unlikely to be easily solved. However, Jupiter shows one of the components of this twofold Matter, while Neptune shows another; and Pluto, reaching for it with one hand and holding a key in the other, indicates that knowledge of the saline substance is essential for the key operation of Putrefaction, which opens the door to Pluto's infernal kingdom.

Alexandre Toussaint de Limojon de Saint-Didier

Le Triomphe Hermetique, 1689

Le Triomphe Hermetique, ou La Pierre Philosophale victorieuse. Traitté plus complet et plus intelligible, qu'il y en ait eu jusques ici, touchant le Magistère Hermetique. A Amsterdam, chez Henry Wetstein, 1689.

The Hermetick Triumph, or The Philosopher's Stone Victorious. The most complete and most intelligible treatise that there has ever been concerning the Hermetick Magistery. Amsterdam, Henry Wetstein, 1689.

Limojon de Saint-Didier was born around 1630 at Avignon of a noble family belonging to the Dauphiné. He was squire to Jean-Antoine de Mesme, Count d'Avaux, whose confidence and esteem he gained, and was entrusted with many important matters. In 1678 he accompanied Avaux to the Congress of Nijmegen, an account of which he published at Paris in 1680. He was with his patron in Holland when the latter was ambassador there in 1684 and also accompanied him on an embassy to James VII and II in Ireland in 1689. He was a Knight of Mount Carmel, and of St Lazarus of Jerusalem. Allegedly, Limojon de Saint-Didier perished on his way back from Ireland to France.

His hermetick writings are among the very best of the best and are highly recommended. *Le Triomphe Hermetique* contains three tracts, each having a separate half-title page: (1) *L'Ancienne Guerre des chevaliers, ou entretien de la Pierre des philosophes avec l'or et le mercure composé originalement en Allemagne;* (2) *Entretien d'Eudoxe et de Pyrophile sur L'Ancienne Guerre des Chevaliers;* (3) *Lettre aux Vrays Disciples d'Hermès contenant six principales clefs de la Philosophie secrète.* This is signed *Dives Sicut Ardens S****, i.e. Sanctus Desiderius, or Saint-Didier.

Subsequent editions were published in Amsterdam in 1699 and 1710; an English edition appeared in 1723 and a German edition in 1765.

Baro Urbigerus
Aphorismi Urbigerani, 1690

Aphorismi Urbigerani, or certain rules, clearly demonstrating the three infallible ways of preparing the Grand Elixir or Circulatum Majus of the Philosophers, discovering the Secret of Secrets, and detecting the errors of vulgar chymists in their operations: contained in one hundred and one aphorisms: To which are added, the three ways of preparing the vegetable elixir or Circulatum monas: All deduced from never-erring experience by Baro Urbigerus, a servant of God, in the Kingdom of Nature. Experto crede. London, printed for Henry Faithorne, at the Rose in St Paul's Church-yard, 1690.

Nothing certain can be found about the author who calls himself Baro Urbiger or Urbigerus. In his dedication to Duke Frederick of Saxe-Gotha the author explains why his aphorisms came to be published at London. 'Being at present in England, tho' we are no Native of this Kingdom, we think it necessary to set forth these Aphorisms on the English Tongue, not in the least doubting, that the Knowing, minding only the Sense, will easily pardon any Impropriety, they may find in our Expressions: and when Providence shall carry us into any other Country, we, having attain'd to some competent Knowledge of most European Languages, shall again take care to publish them in the Speech of the Place where we shall be.' A German edition appeared the following year: *Aphorismi urbigerani oder gewisse Reguln . . . verteutschet, und publicirt zu Erffurdt, von selbigem Authore. Verlegts, Johann Caspar Birckner, 1691.*

CHRISTOPHER LOVE MORLEY and THEODORUS MUYKENS
Collectanea chymica, 1693

Collectanea chymica Leidensia, Maëtsiana, Margravina, Le Mortiana. Olim trium in Academia Lugduno-Batava Facultatis Chymicae quâ publicé, quâ privatim, professorum, viventium, atque docentium, qui isthaec discipulis suis, ex omni Europa illo confluentibus, illis annis, non solum ostenderunt, verum etiam suis verbis dictarunt. Ante hac collecta, digesta, edita, à Christophoro Love Morley M.D. Anglo. Nunc autem plurimis novis elegantioribus & accuratioribus experimentis instructa & aucta meliorem in ordinem reducta, ubivis correcta, a superfluis processibus mundata per Theodorum Muykens, Med. Doct. Amstelod. Opus nulli non Physico-medico Chymico & Pharmacopaeo necessarium & perutile. Lugduni Batavorum, Sumptib. Corneli Boutesteyn & Frederici Haaring, 1693.

Leyden Chymical Collections of Maëts, Margraff and Le Mort, three former professors at the Faculty of Chymistry in the University of Leyden, who in their lifetimes taught these things, and indeed dictated them in their own words, to students who flocked to hear them from all over Europe. Previously collected, digested, and edited by Christopher Love Morley, M.D., an Englishman. Now drawn up and augmented with several new and more elegant and accurate experiments, put in better order, and in places corrected and purged of superfluous processes, by Theodorus Muykens, M.D., of Amsterdam. A work that is necessary, and of the utmost utility, to every Physician, Chymist and Pharmacist. Leyden, printed for Cornelius Boutesteyn and Frederik Haaring, 1693.

The English physician Christopher Love Morley was born *c.* 1646; he was a medical student at Leyden in 1676 and graduated M.D. in 1679. According to his preface in the 1684 edition of the *Collectanea chymica*, he had travelled extensively before coming to Holland and had already practised medicine. He took extensive lecture notes which give an interesting picture of the state of medical education at Leyden at the time. The *Collectanea* is extracted from these notebooks. It consists of a large number of chemical and pharmaceutical recipes taken from the lectures of three professors of chemistry at Leyden, Maëts, Margraff, and le Mort. The original edition appeared at Leyden in 1684 but did not contain the engraved frontispiece.

Theodorus Muykens, born at Amsterdam in 1665, studied medicine at Leyden where he graduated in 1691. In 1693 he re-edited and enlarged Morley's book. The work subsequently appeared in German (Jena, 1696) and once more in Latin (Antwerp, 1702).

Joseph Mulder, who engraved this remarkable plate, was an engraver and draughtsman born at Amsterdam in 1660. A pupil of Hendrick Bogaert, he married in 1689. He appears to have died in 1735.

De cavernis metallorum occultus est, qui Lapis est venerabilis. HERMES.

496 *Le Triomphe Hermetique.* 'In the caverns of metals is hidden that Stone which is venerable.' (Hermes.) The Stone of the Philosophers, the metallic Earth, when identified, is extracted from the mine, purified and dissolved. The first Mercury is obtained, then the second or Philosophick Mercury symbolized by the entwined Snakes; next in order comes Sulphur, which is then elaborated into the Perfection of the Phoenix and crowned by the Triple Crown. Notice that on top of the topmost crown is the hieroglyph of the Stone of the Philosophers; this also corresponds to the spring season of Aries, Taurus and Gemini, when the celestial influx can be received by 'our Matter'. Then only will the Sky wed the Earth.

497 *Aphorismi urbigerani.* 'Virtue united is stronger.' (*Virtus unita fortior*.) The virtue inherent in the Seed produces the miracle of the Tree. As the acorn becomes the oak, so does the Stone of the Philosophers grow into the Philosopher's Stone. *Nil sine vobis*, 'Naught without you,' says the mercurial Snake with the martial tail, to his opposite number the winged Dragon with the saturnine tail. *Per Nos omnia*, 'Through us, everything,' answers the latter who, being the symbol of the *Materia Prima*, contains its future potentialities.

'I am a captive of thy beauty,' whispers Apollo to his sister Diana, indicating his incestuous designs (and the initial domination of the female in their tryst). 'I will vanquish thee yet further,' answers Diana, pointing to the rising Waters of Dissolution. The hieroglyph, which is in the place of an arrow on her bow, is the symbol of Gaea, the Earth, which indicates the kind of earth that must be dissolved in their fiery embrace. On the other side of the Tree, as the waters recede, the Rebis-Hermaphrodite emerges, and his/her lunar face addresses its *alter ego* (the Sun): 'Thy Regeneration is in my power.' The other face gratefully exclaims: 'By thee [living water] I shall live.'

498 *Collectanea chymica.* 'The Mercury of the Philosophers', Fulcanelli tell us, 'is nicknamed *chamaileōn* — Chameleon or Crawling Lion [*lion rampant*], because he successively dons all the colours of the spectrum.' Here it is also an emblem of Fixity, as opposed to the volatile Eagle which is its counterpart. The hair of Lady Alchimia is Fire. Her eyes are Sun and Moon, the twin Principles – Mercury and Sulphur – of the Work. Her breath is Air and the influx carried in the shape of rays by Light. The three Stars on her forehead are the three Works, and the milk flowing from her generous breasts is *Lac Virginis*, the Virgin's Milk which nourishes the Stone in accordance with the hermetick axiom from the Emerald Table which states '*Nutrix eius terra est*' (see Emblema II of *Atalanta fugiens, 31*). The wings on her feet identify her positively as the mercurial Volatile Principle, which the Eagle on her arm confirms. The King on her left is Sulphur, her spouse and fixed counterpart. The Philosopher on the right points to the combat of the Fixed and Volatile Principles within the Vessel.

Jacob Böhme
Theosophische Wercken, 1682

Des Gottseeligen Hoch-Erleuchteten Jacob Böhmens Teutonici Philosophi Alle Theosophische Wercken. Darinnen alle tieffe Geheimnisse GOttes der ewigen and zeitlichen Natur und Creatur, samt dem wahren Grunde Christlicher Religion und der Gottseeligkeit, nach dem Apostolischen Gezeugnüss offenbahret werden. Theils aus des Authoris eigenen Originalen, Theils aus den ersten und nachgesehenen besten Copyen auffs fleissigste corrigiret. Und In Beyfügung etlicher Clavium so vorhin noch nie gedruckt, nebenst einem zweyfachen Register. Den Liebhabern Göttlicher und Natürlicher Weissheit zum besten an Tag Gegeben. Zu Amsterdam, Gedruckt im Jahre Christi, 1682.

The Blessed and Illuminated Jacob Böhme, Teutonic Philosopher: Complete Theosophical Works, wherein all profound secrets of God, of eternal and temporal Nature and Creature together with the true ground of Christian religion and beatitude are expounded according to Apostolic testimony. Diligently corrected, in part from the author's originals, in part from the first, and revised, best copies. And subjoined thereto, sundry keys which have never before been printed, together with a double index. Published for the sake of the lovers of divine and natural wisdom. Amsterdam, printed in the year of our Lord 1682.

This pictorial appendix to our hermetick theme is composed of the frontispieces to Jacob Böhme's theosophical works, published by his disciple Gichtel in 1682. These rare images, in which the symbolism of alchemy is used for purely mystical purposes, are of abiding interest. Böhme borrowed from Paracelsus the means to express his own beatific vision in alchemical terms, and his works had tremendous influence.

Jacob Böhme, Boehme, Böhmen or Behmen (1575–1624) was born at Alt-Seidenberg in Upper Lusatia. He became apprenticed to a shoemaker in 1589 and was himself a working shoemaker until 1612, when as the result of a sudden illumination he wrote *Aurora, oder die Morgenröte im Aufgang.* Denounced by the local pastor as heretical, the manuscript was seized by the town council, who ordered Böhme to refrain from such writing. He did nothing of the kind and continued to write. *Aurora* studies God in Himself, while the study of God's manifestations in the structure of the world, and of Man, is pursued in *Die drei Principien göttlichen Wesens, Vom dreifagen Leben der Menschen, Von der Menschwerdung Christi,* and *Von der Geburt und Bezeichnung aller Wesen.*

His work culminated in his exposition of the life of God in the soul of man: *Von der Genadenwahl, Mysterium magnum, Von Christi Testamenten.* Böhme's last published work was *Der Weeg zu Christo* (1624). To Böhme, God is both immanent and transcendent: the

'Creation' is the manifestation of forms dwelling in the latent formlessness of eternal Divine Nature. The play of contrasts, *Solve et Coagula*, Light and Darkness, is the mainspring of life. Evil is the dark or wrathful aspect of God. But the world in three stages serves the purpose of demonstrating first decline and fall, then balance, and ultimately the triumph of Love equivalent to the triumph of the Light.

Gichtel, who published Böhme's works in the present edition, described his own transfiguration of his subtle body in a process unconnected with traditional alchemy. Yet he claimed he was presented several times with the Philosopher's Stone and declined the offer on the grounds that this 'stone' only allowed access to the solar stage of psycho-spiritual ascension, which he claimed he had already superseded!

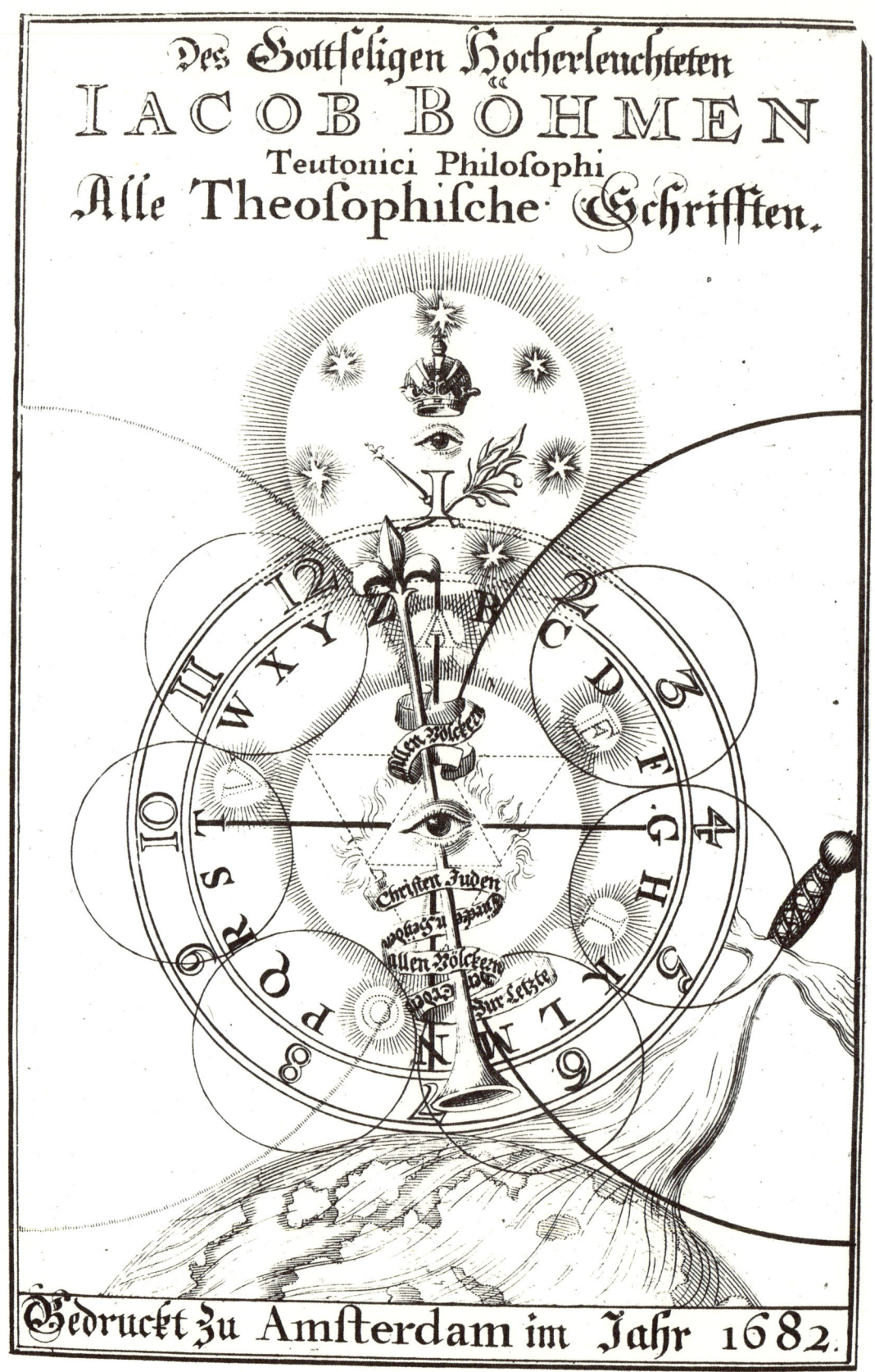

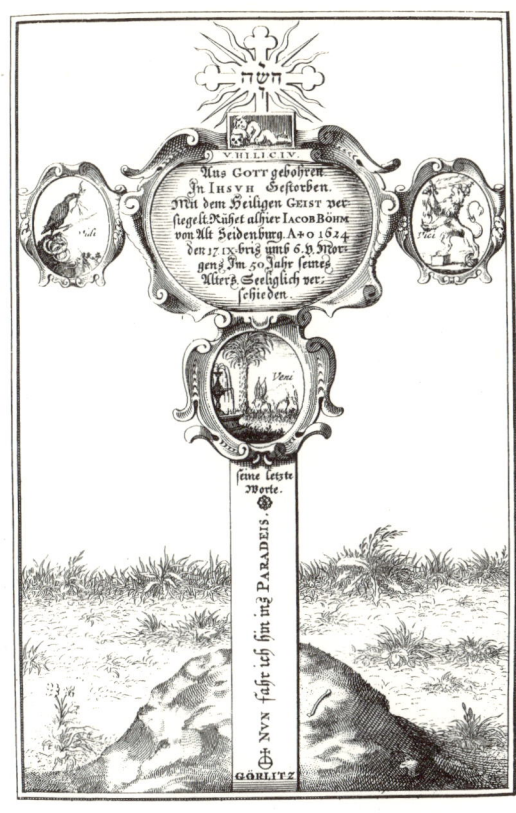

500

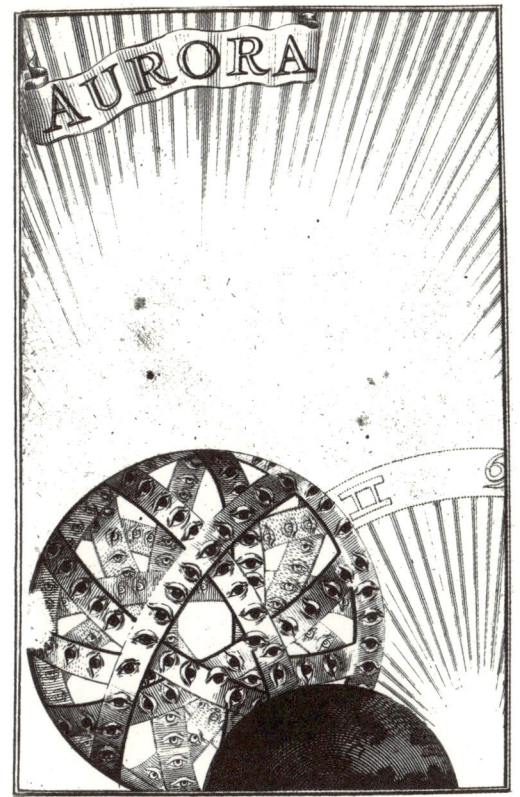

501

502

503

Theosophische Wercken · 311

504

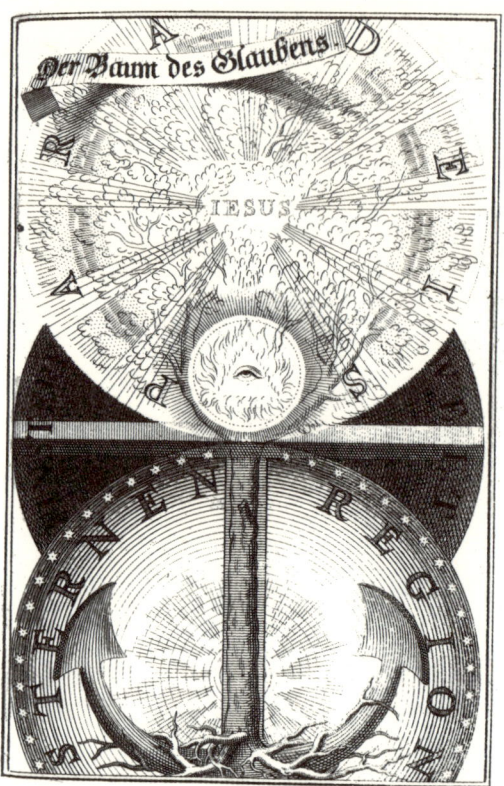

505

507

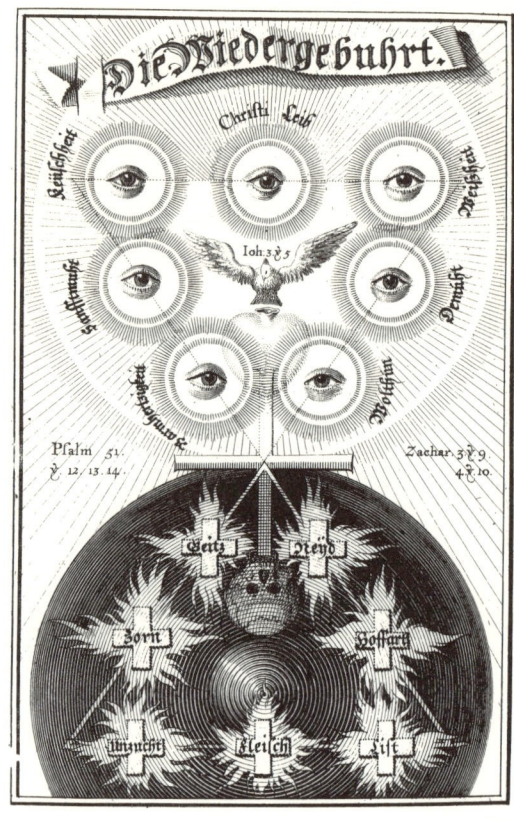

512

513

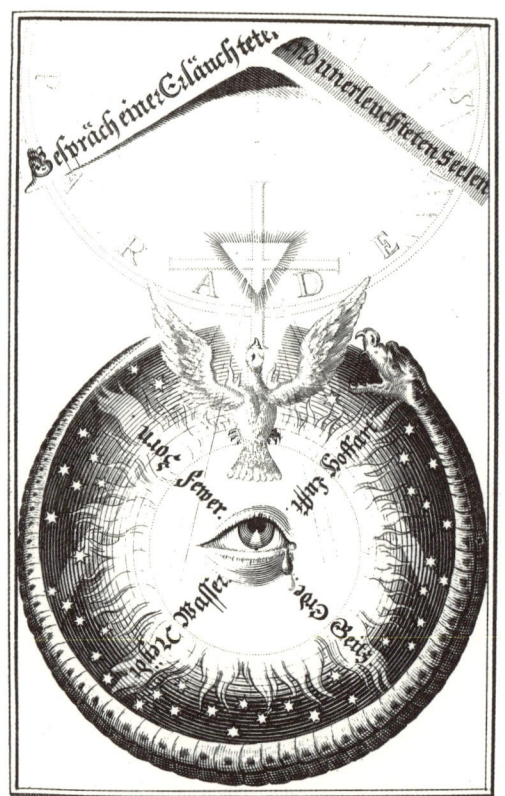

514

515

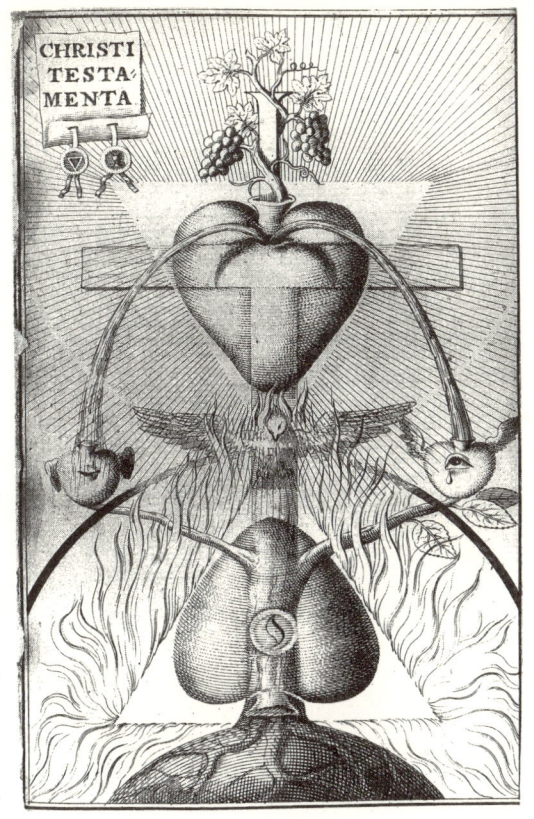

516

517

518

Theosophische Wercken · 315

MYSTERIUM MAGNUM
Messias
Moses.

FEVR
Himmlische Tinctur
Mayestät
DREY
יהוה

520

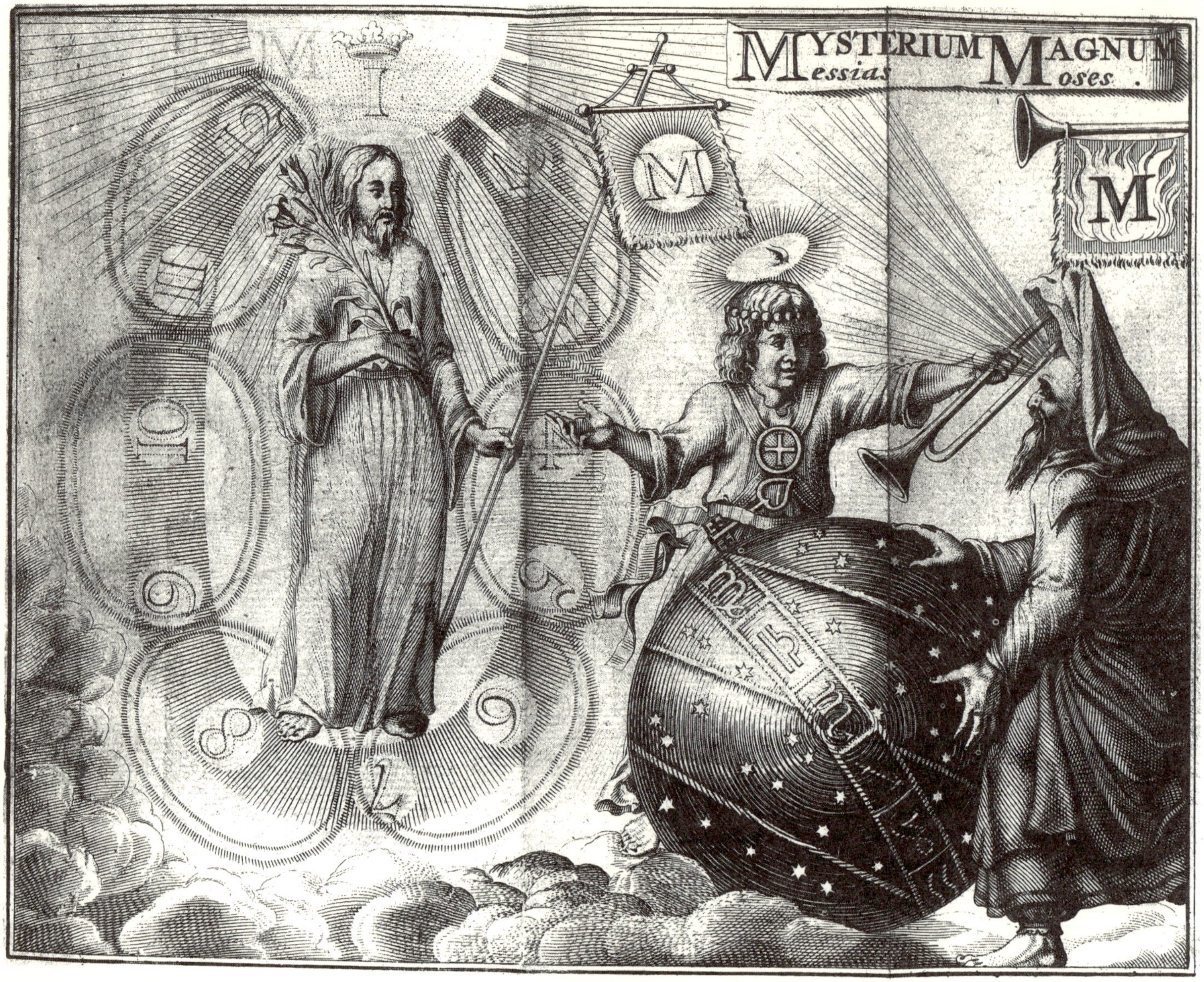

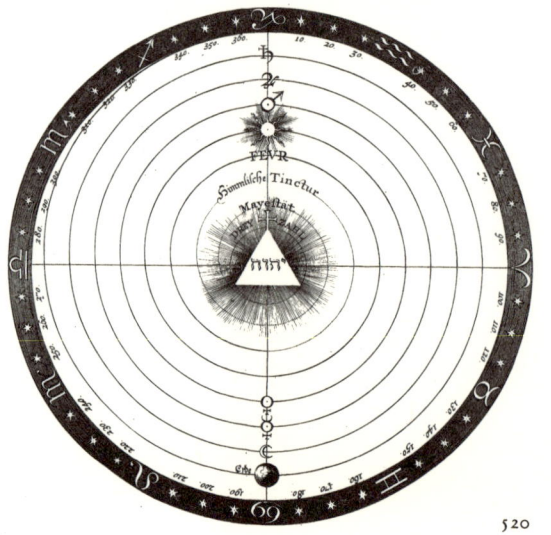

499 Frontispiece to the *Theosophische Wercken*. Like all the plates in this edition, this has a brief gloss of its own and a list of references to the text which need to be looked up before it can be rightly interpreted. (Thus, the fact that the figure I, God or Adam, has slipped from the topmost position on our clock faces is a type of the Fall. . . .)

500 'Born of God. Died in IHSVH. Sealed with the holy Ghost. Here lies Jacob Böhm of Alt Seidenburg. Who died blessedly on 17 September 1624 about 6 in the morning in the 50th year of his age. His last words: Now I depart into Paradise.' (From the prefatory *Life* by Abraham von Frankenberg.)

501 'Dawn.' (Frontispiece of *Morgenröte im Aufgang*. . . .)

502 'Signature of things.' (Frontispiece of *De signatura rerum* . . .: 'How all things arise from one Mystery.')

503 'Threefold life.' (Frontispiece of *Dreyfaches Leben*. . . .)

504 'Forty questions of the Soul.' (Frontispiece of *Viertzig Fragen von der Seelen Urstand . . . und Eigenschaft . . .*, in which Böhme is interviewed by Dr Balthasar Walter.)

505 'The Tree of Faith, Paradise, Dark World, Astral region.' (From *Von der Menschwerdung Jesu Christi*. . . .)

506 'Of the Passion and Death of Jesus Christ.' (From *Von der Menschwerdung Jesu Christi*. . . .)

507 'Six points.' (Frontispiece of *Von sechs Punkten hohe und tieffe Gründung*. . . .)

508 'Apologetics.' (Frontispiece of *Apologia, betreffend die Vollkommenheit des Menschen*. . . .)

509 'Epistles.' (Frontispiece of *Theosophische Send-Briefe*; the messenger pigeons represent God, Nature and Art.)

510 'The Way to Christ.' (Frontispiece of *Der Weeg zu Christo*. . . .)

511 'Tranquillity.' (Or Moderation; frontispiece to book 4 of *Der Weeg zu Christo*. . . .)

512 'Rebirth. Christ's body. Compassion, gentleness, chastity, beneficence, humility, wisdom. Avarice, envy, anger, pride, lust, the flesh, treachery.' (Frontispiece to book 5 of *Der Weeg zu Christo*. . . .)

513 'The life which transcends sense, and divine contemplation.' (Frontispiece to book 6 of *Der Weeg zu Christo*. . . .)

514 'Conversation between an enlightened and an unenlightened soul.' (Frontispiece to book 8 of *Der Weeg zu Christo*. . . .)

515 'Of divine revelation.' (Frontispiece to the fragmentary *Betrachtung göttlicher Offenbarung*. . . .)

516 'Christ's testaments.' (Frontispiece to *Von Christi Testamenten*. . . .)

517 'Election of Grace. From a single power – penance, forgiveness; obstinacy, wickedness – from a single juice. Come hither to the Throne of Grace. Go hence to the Throne of Fire.' (Frontispiece of *Von der Genaden-Wahl*. . . .)

518 No text. (From *Mysterium magnum*. . . .)

519 'The great mystery. Messiah. Moses.' (Frontispiece to *Mysterium magnum* . . .; 'Opposites must coexist.')

520 'Fire, Celestial Tincture, Majesty, Triplicity, Tetragrammaton, Earth.' (From *Dreyfaches Leben*. . . .)

SELECT BIBLIOGRAPHY

Baltrusaitis, Jurgis. *La Quête d'Isis*. Paris 1967.

Bénézit, E. *Dictionnaire des peintres, sculpteurs, dessinateurs et graveurs*, Paris 1976.

Bryan. *Dictionary of Painters and Engravers*, 5 vols. London 1905.

Canseliet, Eugène. *Alchimie, Etudes diverses de symbolisme hermétique et de pratique philosophale*. Paris 1964.

———. *L'Alchimie et son Livre Muet (Mutus Liber)*. Paris 1967.

———. *L'Alchimie expliquée sur ses textes classiques*. Paris 1972.

———. *Deux Logis Alchimiques*, new ed. Paris 1979.

Duveen, Denis I. *Bibliotheca alchemica et chemica*. London 1949.

Ferguson, John. *Bibliotheca chemica*, 2 vols. Glasgow 1906.

Fulcanelli. *Le Mystère des Cathédrales*. Paris 1926.

———. *Les Demeures philosophales*, 2 vols. Paris 1930. (There have been numerous re-editions of Fulcanelli's capital works.)

Godwin, Joscelyn. *Robert Fludd: Hermetic Philosopher and Surveyor of Two Worlds*. London 1979.

Hind, Arthur M. *A History of Engraving and Etching*. London 1927.

Holmyard, E.J. *Alchemy*. London 1957.

Iversen, E. *The Myth of Egypt and its Hieroglyphs in European Tradition*, Copenhagen 1961.

Jensen, Hans. *Sign, Symbol and Script. An account of man's effort to write* (transl. George Unwin, third edition). London 1970.

Josten, C.H., ed. *Elias Ashmole, 1617–1692* (with biographical introduction), 5 vols. Oxford 1966.

Monod-Herzen, G.E. *L'Alchimie méditerranéenne*. Paris 1962.

Needham, Joseph. *Science and Civilization in China*, vol. 5. Cambridge 1974.

Obrist, Barbara. *Les Débuts de l'imagerie alchimique (XIVe–XVe siècles)*. Paris 1982.

Panofsky, Erwin. *Albrecht Dürer*. Princeton 1943.

Pope, Maurice. *The Story of Decipherment: From Egyptian hieroglyphic to Linear B*. London 1975.

Praz, Mario. *Studies in Seventeenth-Century Imagery*, second edn. Rome 1964 and Part II Rome 1974.

Pritchard, Alan. *Alchemy, A Bibliography of English Language Writings*. London 1980.

Ranque, Georges. *La Pierre Philosophale*. Paris 1972.

Seligmann, Kurt. *Magic, Supernaturalism and Religion*. New York 1948.

Tervarent, Guy de. *Attributs symboles dans l'art profane 1450–1600 – Dictionnaire d'un langage perdu*. Geneva 1958.

Thorndike, Lynn. *A History of Magic and Experimental Science*, 8 vols (vol. 7–8, The Seventeenth Century). New York 1923–1958.

Van Lennep, J. *Art et alchimie*. Brussels 1971.

Wittkower, Rudolf. *Allegory and the Migration of Symbols*. London 1977.

Yates, Frances A. *Giordano Bruno and the Hermetic Tradition*. London 1964.

———. *The Rosicrucian Enlightenment*. London 1972.

FORMATS AND DIMENSIONS

Dimensions of images are given in cm. Slight variations within sequences have been disregarded (tp = title-page).

Beroalde, *Le Tableau*, quarto: 25 × 15.5. *Voyages*, octavo: 15.1 × 8.5.

Khunrath, *Amphitheatrum*, folio: 24 × 15.5; 21.5 × 14.5; circles diameter 22.5; large engravings 27.8 × 32.2.

Libavius, *Alchimia*, folio: 24 × 17 (page).

Michelspacher, *Cabala*, quarto: all 31 × 25.

Maier, *Arcana*, quarto: 16.5 × 12. *Lusus*, quarto: 18.5 × 15 (page). *Examen*, quarto: 20 × 15 (page). *Jocus*, quarto: 11.6 × 6.8. *Atalanta*, quarto: tp 17.7 × 13.4; rest 10 wide. *Symbola*, quarto: tp 17.2 × 13.5; portrait 10.6 × 9.5; rest 7.7 × 10. *Tripus*, quarto: tp vignettes 9.5 × 9.8, 9 × 8; Keys (1–7) 6.8 × 9.5, (8–9) 6.5 × 6.5, (10) 7.3 × 9.2, (11–12) 6.8 × 9.5. *Viatorium*, quarto: tp 15.5 × 12; rest 9.5 × 7.5.

Mylius, *Opus medico-chymicum*, quarto: 19 × 14.5 (page); foldouts 117 19.5 × 28.5, 118 27 × 27, 119, 120 27 × 33.

Antidotarium, quarto: 18 × 14 (page).

Croll, *Basilica*, quarto: 22 × 17 (page).

Maier, *Septimana*, quarto: tp 17 × 13; 1st image app. 30 wide; rest 7.7 × 10.

Mylius, *Philosophia*, quarto: tp 7.3 wide; rest 6 × 7.3 except Tree 9.1 × 9.1.

Musaeum hermeticum, quarto: tp 17.5 × 13.5; rest 10.5 wide.

Lambsprinck, *De lapide*, quarto: tp 17.6 × 10.6; arms 8.5 × 7.1; rest 10.5 × 10.5.

Mylius, *Anatomia*, quarto: tp 17.5 × 14; dedication 16.8 × 13; rest 14.5 × 10.

Planis Campy, *L'Hydre*, octavo: 15 × 9.8. *L'Ouverture*, octavo: tp & portrait 15.2 × 9.9.

Ashmole, *Theatrum*, quarto: all 14.5 × 11 except Last Judgment 15.2 × 12.

Monte-Snyders, *Metamorphosis*, octavo: 15.5 × 9.5 (page).

Becher, *Oedipus*, duodecimo: 11.5 × 6.3.

Kerckring, *Currus*, duodecimo: 11.7 × 7.

Monte-Snyders(?), *Chymica vannus*, quarto: all 13 wide.

Van Vreeswijk, *Roode Leeuw, Groene Leeuw, Goude Son, Goude Leeuw*, all octavo: all 7 wide.

Altus, *Mutus liber*, folio: all 26.5 × 18.

Van Helpen, *Escalier*, folio: all 29 × 18.3.

Saint-Didier, *Triomphe*, duodecimo: 17.2 × 13.

Morley & Muykens, *Collectanea*, quarto: 14.5 × 9.6.

Urbigerus, *Aphorismi*, octavo: 13.9 × 8.1.

Böhme, *Theosophische Wercken*, octavo: tp 18 × 14.5; rest 9 wide.

INDEX

ARMATH, 151
emarus, 151
[J]far the Alexandrian, 150
[A]gidius, 153
[Ag]athocles, 132
[Al]anus, 152
[Al]bertus Magnus (St Albert the Great), 16–17, 114, 115, 151
[Al]bugazal, 151
[Al]ciati, Andrea, 13, 21
[Al]dus Manutius, 10, 11, 20, 42
[Al]exander, 154
[Al]exander of Aegae, 22
[Al]phidius, 100
[Altus], 266–84
[Am]man, Jost, 45
[An]axagoras, 150
[An]dreae, Johann Valentin, 62
[An]droicus, Bishop, 153
[An]thony, Francis, 61
[An]ton, Wilhelm, 29
[Ap]ollonius of Tyana, 150
[Ap]ostolicus, Dominicus, 153
[Ap]ostolicus, Hugo, 153
[Ar]anus, 154
[Ar]da, 154
[Ar]entszoon, Pieter, 240
[Ar]isleus, 155, 207
[Ar]istophanes, 22
[Ar]istotle, 51, 154
[Ar]nold, Philosopher, 152
[Ar]nold of Villa Nova, 114, 115, 152
[Ar]sianus, 151
[Ar]tephius, 151, 221
[As]hmole, Elias, 19, 42, 214–21
[Au]brey, John, 21
[Au]gurellus, John Aurelius, 153
[A]vicenna, Avicen, 103, 114, 132, 151, 197
[A]zinabam, 151

[B]ACASTER, 102
[Ba]con, Roger, 114, 115, 125, 153
[Ba]lten, Pieter, 52
[Bar]naud, Nicolaus, 197
[Ba]ur von Eyseneck, Johann Martin, 207
[Ba]vran, 154
[Ba]yer, Albert, 154
[Be]cher, Johann Joachim, 222
[Be]linus, 151
[Be]rnard, Count of Treviso, 151

Birckner, Johann Caspar, 300
Böhme, Jacob, 308–17
Bogaert, Hendrick, 301
Boissard, Jean-Jacques, 14
Bosco, Valerandus de, 152
Boutesteyn, Cornelius, 301
Bracesco, Giovanni, 16
Bry, Johann Israel de, 14, 15
Bry, Johann Theodor de, 14, 15, 21, 22, 68, 127
Bry, Maria Magdalena de, 21
Bry, Theodor de, 14, 21, 22, 60, 62
Bry, Thomas de, 61
Buondelmonti, Cristoforo, 9, 20

CALID, KING OF EGYPT, 150
Calid the Jew, 150
Campen, Jan Diricks van, 29, 30
Canseliet, Eugène, 266, 283
Chaeremon of Alexandria, 16, 22
Chevalier, Pierre, 25
Christian I, Prince of Anhalt-Bernberg, 59, 62, 127, 157
Christian II, Elector of Saxony, 116
Christian William, Margrave of Brandenburg, 161
Christopher of Paris, 152
Chrysippus, John, 153
Clauder, Gabriel, 226
Clement IV, Pope, 115
Cleopatra, Queen of Egypt, 150
Coenders van Helpen, Barent, 285–300
Colonna, Fra Francesco, 11, 20
Cremer, John, 125
Croll, Oswald, 127, 155, 157–60
Custos, Dominicus, 52
Custos, Raphael, 52

DA BOLOGNA, FRANCESCO, 20
Daniel, Philosopher, 152
Dante, 151
Dastin, John, 153
Datin, 151
Dee, Arthur, 214
Dee, John, 42
Democritus, 114, 132, 150
Diocletian, 20
Diodorus Siculus, 114
Dominicus, Bishop, 153
Doort, Paullus van de, 29, 30, 42
Dürer, Albrecht, 10
Dufresnoy, Langlet, 29, 222
Dumbeleius, 154

Durandus, 153
Duveen, Denis, 228

EFFERARIUS, 153
Elbo, 151
Elizabeth, Queen of Bohemia, 61
Empedocles, 16
Ernst, Count of Holstein, Schaumburg and Sternberg, 105
Espagnet, Jean d', 97, 214
Euthica, 150
Euthices, 151

FAITHORNE, HENRY, 300
Ferdinand I, Emperor, 115
Ferdinand II, Emperor, 127, 157
Fernley, John, Ambiensis, 152
Ficino, Marsilio, 9
Flamel, Nicolas, 18, 103, 152, 185
Fludd, Robert, 14, 22, 62, 299
Franken, David, 52
Frederick, Duke of Saxe-Gotha, 300
Frederick, Duke of Württemberg, 116
Frederick, Prince of Norway, 105
Frederick V, Elector Palatine, King of Bohemia, 22, 59–60, 62
Frederick Henry, Prince of Nassau, 133
Frisius, Andreas, 226
Fulcanelli, 43, 125, 282

GALEN, 51, 156
Galienus, 151
Galler, Hieronymus, 60, 68, 127
Galud, King of Babylon, 151
Garcia, Cardinal, 153
Gaulthier, Léonard, 25
Geber, 151
Gellius, Aulus, 132
Gichtel, J. 308, 309
Giehlow, Karl, 10
Gigil, 151
Gilbert, Cardinal, 153
Goebel, Severin, 59
Gorrozel, Gilles, 13
Gratianus, 152
Gravia, Bernard de, 154
Greverus, Jodocus, 98, 152
Grosseteste, Robert, Bishop of Lincoln, 115
Guainerius, Antonius, 117
Guden, Johann Moritz, 117
Guillemot, Matthieu, 25

HAARING, FREDERIK, 301
Hakluyt, Richard, 21
Hamilton, William, 116
Hamuel, 151
Hasolle, James see Ashmole, Elias
Helisardes, 151
Helpen, see Coenders
Helvetius, Johannes Fridericus, 185
Henri III, King of France, 25
Henri IV, King of France, 25
Henry III, King of England, 115
Heraclitus, 150
Hercules, Philosopher, 151
Hermes Trismegistus (Hermes the Egyptian), 8, 42, 51, 114, 150, 158
Herodotus, 8
Hesiod, 22
Hippocrates, 51, 213
Hiram (Hyram), Prince of Tyre, 161
Hirschberger, Joachim, 61
Hoffmann, Nicholas, 61
Holland, Isaac, the Elder, 152
Holland, Isaac, the Younger, 152
Homer, 16
Horace, 60
Horapollo (Horus Apollo), 9–11, 12, 16, 20
Hortulanus, 153
Hummius, Antonius, 105

ISAAC, PHILOSOPHER, 152
Iversen, E. 8

JACOB, PAUL, 117
James VI & I, King of Great Britain, 61
James VII & II, King of Great Britain, 301
Jansson van Waesberge, Johan, 224, 228, 246, 253, 260
Jennis, Lucas, 15, 22, 60, 62, 105, 117, 133, 156, 161, 167, 185, 197, 198
John XXII, Pope, 115
John of Aquino, 153
John of Austria, 152
John of Padua, 152
Justinian, Emperor, 20

KELLER, GEORG, 45
Kelley, Edward, 153
Kerckring, Theodorus, 226
Kerver, Jacques, 12

319

Khalid ibn Jazid ibn Mu'awijah, Prince, 114
Khunrath, Heinrich, 29–43
Kopffius, Petrus, 45
Kuhdorfer, Heinrich, 51, 198

La Perrière, Guillaume de, 13
Lacinius, John, 153
Ladislaus II, King of Hungary, 115
Lambsprinck, 197
Landolfo, Count of Aquino, 115
Lant, Thomas, 21
Lazarellus, Ludovic, 153
Le Jeune, Claude, 285
Le Mort, Jacob, 301
Le Moyne, Jacques, 21
Leibniz, Gottfried Wilhelm von, 226
Lemnius, Levinus, 224
Leopold I, Emperor, 222
Leucippus, 114
Libavius, Andreas, 45–51
Limojon, see Saint-Didier
Louis II, King of France, 115
Louis XIII, King of France, 25, 208, 213
Louis XIV, King of France, 213
Lull, Raymond, 98, 102, 114, 153

Madathanus, Henricus, 185
Maëts, C.L. de 301
Mahomet, 151
Maier, Johann, 59
Maier, Michael, 14, 17, 18, 20, 59–132, 161–6, 167, 185
Malchamech, 154
Malus, 151
Manget, J.J., 266
Margraff, Christian, 301
Marie de Médicis, Queen of France, 25
Marlianus, Aloysius, 153
Mary the Jewess, 114, 150
Massara, Philosopher of, 151
Matheus, Jean, 208
Matthias, Emperor, 157
Maurice of Nassau, Landgrave of Hesse, 59, 62, 105, 133, 161
Maximilian I, Emperor, 10
Medera, 150
Medici, Cosimo de', 9

Mehung, Johannes (John) de, 152, 166, 185
Melchior Cibinensis (Nicholas Melchior Szebeni), 115, 154
Merian, Caspar, 22
Merian, Matthäus, 14, 15, 21–2, 97, 133, 150, 158, 186
Merian, Matthäus the Younger, 22
Mesme, Jean-Antoine de, Count d'Avaux, 301
Meyer, Dietrich, 21
Michelspacher, Steffan, 52–8
Mitigo, 151
Montanor, Guido de, 152
Monte-Snyders, Joannes de, 224, 228–39
Morienus, 98, 114, 151
Morley, Christopher Love, 301
Mosanus, Jacob, 61
Mulder, Joseph, 301
Musa, 150
Muykens, Theodorus, 301
Mylius, Georg, 133
Mylius, Johann Christoph, 133
Mylius, Johann Daniel, 133–56, 167–82, 198–207

Needham, Joseph, 19
Nero, Emperor, 16, 22
Newton, Isaac, 224
Norton, Thomas, 60, 117, 125, 153, 214, 221

Ovid, 16, 208

Palingenius, Marcellus, 153
Palthenius, Hartmann, 161
Panofsky, Erwin, 10
Pantheus, Augustine, 153
Paracelsus, Philippus Theophrastus, 152, 213
Pauvert, Jean-Jacques, 266
Pernety, Antoine Joseph, 17–18, 103
Peter, Monk and Philosopher, 153
Peter of Villa Nova, 152
Petrus Bonus, 16, 152
Petrus Peregrinus, 115
Philaletha, Aeyrenaeus, 19, 183, 258
Philip of Ravilasco, 152
Philippos, 9

Photius, 20
Pielat, Barthélemy, 246
Pirckheimer, Willibald, 10
Planis Campy, David de, 208–13
Plato, 151
Plotinus, 9
Pontanus, John, 152, 221
Psellus, Michael, 151

Rachaidibi, 154
Raleigh, Sir Walter, 21
Rasis (Rhasis), 151
Raymond of Marseilles, 152
Reinhart, Christoph, 68
Remmelin, Johann, 52
Rhodianus, 154
Richard, Philosopher, 153
Ripa, Cesare, 13
Ripley, George, 153
Robertus Castrensis, 114
Rosinus, 151
Ruccius, M. Andr., 42
Rudolph II, Emperor, 29, 42, 59, 116, 157
Rumpf, Christian, 61
Rupescissa, John de, 153
Russell, Richard, 226

S., Erasmus Wolfart, 29
Sacro Bosco, John de 152
Sadeler, Aegidius, 157
Sadeler, Jan, 157
Sadeler, Raphael, 157
Saint-Didier, Alexandre Toussaint de Limojon de, 301
Sande, Hermann van de, 185, 222
Sande, Johann Maximilian van de, 185
Saurius, Joannes, 45
Schwan, Balthasar, 166, 167
Scotus, 153
Scotus, John Duns, 154
Scotus, Michael, 154
Sendivogius, Michael, 116, 185
Seneca, 151
Senior, 151
Serapio, 154
Seton, Alexander, 116
Sheba, Queen of, 161
Sigismund III Vasa, King of Poland, 116

Solomon, King, 161
Spinola, Ambrogio di, 15
Spinoza, Baruch, 226
Stabius, 10
Stephen, Philosopher and Chymist, 152
Steyner, Heinrich, 13
Stolcius, Daniel, 116, 167
Sulat, Jacob, 266

Tampach, Gottfried, 157
Thaphuntia, 150
Theobanus, John, 153
Therapus, Janus Lacinius, 22
Tholden, Johann, 117
Thomas Aquinas, St, 114, 115
Thorndike, Lynn, 30
Tzetzes, John, 16, 22

Uffenbach, Philipp, 45
Urbigerus, Baro, 300

Vadis, Aegidius de, 153
Valentine, Basil, 18, 99, 117, 12, 132, 133, 151, 167, 180, 226
Valeriano, Piero, 13
Vaughan, Robert, 214
Verville, François Beroalde de, 1 21, 25–8
Vincent of Beauvais, 152
Virgil, 16
Vredeman de Vries, Hans, 30
Vreeswijk, Goossen van, 228–6

Walter, Balthasar, 317
Wessel, Wilhelm, 62
Weyerstraeten, Elizeus, 224
White, John, 21
Whitney, Geoffrey, 13
William of Paris, 152
Wittkower, Rudolf, 10
Wood, Anthony à, 214

Yates, Frances A., 62, 127
Yezid, 151

Zacharias, Dionysius, 152
Zalento, Peter de, 152
Zamolxis, 150
Zeiller, Martin, 22
Zozimos of Panapolis, 114